DIVERSITY, CONFLICT, AND LEADERSHIP

VOLUME 15 • 2011

DIVERSITY, CONFLICT, AND LEADERSHIP

Editor: M. AFZALUR RAHIM

VOLUME 15 • 2011

CURRENT TOPICS IN MANAGEMENT

Routledge
Taylor & Francis Group
LONDON AND NEW YORK

First published 2011 by Transaction Publishers

Published 2017 by Routledge
2 Park Square, Milton Park, Abingdon, Oxon OX14 4RN
711 Third Avenue, New York, NY 10017, USA

First issued in paperback 2017

Routledge is an imprint of the Taylor & Francis Group, an informa business

Copyright © 2011 by Taylor & Francis.

All rights reserved. No part of this book may be reprinted or reproduced or utilised in any form or by any electronic, mechanical, or other means, now known or hereafter invented, including photocopying and recording, or in any information storage or retrieval system, without permission in writing from the publishers.

Notice:
Product or corporate names may be trademarks or registered trademarks, and are used only for identification and explanation without intent to infringe.

ISSN: 1529-2088

ISBN 13: 978-1-138-50927-6 (pbk)
ISBN 13: 978-1-4128-4266-2 (hbk)

Contents

PREFACE

As *Current Topics in Management* moves further along in its second decade—this is Vol. 15 and with the processes for Vol. 16 already underway. *Current Topics* is now included in Cabell's list of journals and it is being treated as a scholarly annual journal. *Current Topics* presents basic research on the theory and practice of management and administration. It includes both invited contributions and revised versions of papers presented at the annual International Conference on Advances in Management. *Current Topics in Management* exemplifies ICAM's comparative orientation, in its broad scope of management and administration perspectives, in its diverse locations of research as well as its application, and in its comparisons of findings, methodologies, and operational definitions. The culture of ICAM features universality, collegiality, and broad involvement. Volumes 1 through 15 have rested on such cultural features and so will volumes 16 and beyond. We follow the APA guidelines for reviewing and preparing papers for publication. As usual, all the papers in Vol. 15 were double-blind reviewed and I acknowledge the contributions of the following reviewers:

1. Feruccio Bilich, University of Aveiro, Portugal
2. Dieter Bögenhold, Free University of Bolzano, Italy
3. Phyllis A. Duncan, Our Lady of the Lake University
4. Mike Henry, Grant MacEwan College
5. Astrid Kersten, La Roche College
6. Ahmed Amin Mohamed, German University in Cairo
7. Clement Psenicka, Youngstown State University
8. Don Schley, Colorado Technical University

M. Afzalur Rahim
November 30, 2010

PREFACE

Current Topics in Management, **Vol. 15, 2011, pp. 1-9**

MANAGING DIVERSE SITUATIONS IN ORGANIZATIONS

M. Afzalur Rahim

Current Topics in Management is a scholarly annual journal started about sixteen years ago; we are now in 2010 completing the fifteenth volume; and the challenge is now continuous improvement in quality of the content of each succeeding volume. How does this volume attempt to meet our resolve to do better as we move deeper into the series? Overall, Volume 15 contains 11 contributions divided into four sections, which are identified below and also constitute the basic structure of this introduction. The editor attempts to frame the volume with Chapter 1. The other chapters were the survivors of competitive reviews of submissions to the 17th annual International Conference on Advances in Management held at Atlanta, Georgia during July 2010. All competitive and invited papers were evaluated through a double-blind review process. During this review process, each paper was revised two to three times to improve quality.

To accommodate to the desiderate of linkage, the articles below also are sorted into four major sections: (1) Managing Conflict and Justice, (2) Leadership, Social Capital, and Personality, (3) Entrepreneurship and Small Business, and (4) Ethics, Learning, and Change. A brief review of each article is provided to help orient the readers.

Part I: Managing Conflict and Justice

This first section contains three contributions—two empirical studies on organizational conflict and its effects and a theoretical work that deals with the application of organizational justice theory to the domain of consumer behavior.

The Moderating Role of Social Attitudes in the Relationship between Diversity and Conflict by Nailah Ayub and Karen A. Jehn

In this study, Nailah and Jehn explore attitudes of group members to explain whether diversity will have positive or negative consequences on group processes and outcomes. A set of studies investigates propositions that members with diverse national or racioethnic backgrounds, especially if they have strong nationalistic attitudes, are likely to experience more conflict than nationally or racioethnically homogenous groups (and/or if members do not hold strong nationalistic views). Other moderators of conflict and outcomes that the authors examine using multiple methods (field, scenario, and lab studies) include social distances, national stereotypes, similarity preferences, and perceived respect. Study 1 showed that nationalistic derogation had a moderating effect on the national diversity–conflict relationship such that there was greater relationship as well as task conflict in nationally diverse groups when members reported nationalistic derogation. Study 2 showed that national diversity interacted with social distance such that high national diversity increased task conflict and reduced relationship conflict. National diversity also interacted with negative national stereotypes to give higher task conflict and decreased process conflict. The social distance and national stereotypes to outcomes relationship was fully or partially mediated by conflict types. Finally, study 3 showed that efficiency of racioethnically diverse workgroups decreased in the presence of similarity preference while perceived respect increased efficiency of such groups. Similar to the finding in the first study the researchers found that task conflict was high despite high similarity preference. Respect increased task conflict and helped reduce relationship and process conflicts. Analyses also showed that conflicts mediate the relationship between racioethnic diversity and efficiency.

Moderating Effects of Geographic Dispersion and Team Tenure on the Task–Affective Conflict Relationship by Patricia J. Holahan, Ann C. Mooney, and Laura Finnerty Paul

This study investigates the impact of geographic dispersion and team tenure on the link between task and affective conflict. This link is crucial because when teams experience task conflict, research suggests that team members have a tendency to react by making negative attributions about other team members, which in turn triggers affective conflict that is harmful to team performance. An understanding of how geographic dispersion and team tenure influence the task conflict–affective conflict link is important because so many teams today are geographically dispersed.

Using data from 94 project teams, Holahan, Mooney, and Paul find support for their hypothesis that geographically dispersed teams are more likely to trigger affective conflict when they engage in task conflict. The rationale

for this hypothesis is based largely on theory suggesting that geographically dispersed teams are likely to rely on technology-mediated communication. Technology-mediated communication provides less social and contextual information which may lead to a higher incidence of negative attributions and encourage more uninhibited behavior and harsher language than face-to-face communication.

They also explore the impact of team tenure as a moderator of the impact of geographic dispersion on the task conflict–affective conflict link. Theory suggests that as co-located teams work together, they develop behavioral norms and a shared identity which helps them keep conflict task-oriented. As expected, team tenure decreased the strong positive correlation between task and affective conflict in co-located teams. However, team tenure had no effect on the task–affective conflict link in geographically distributed teams. Thus, it appears that keeping conflict task-oriented is problematic for geographically distributed teams and this problem persists over time even as teams gain more experience working together. In short, compared to co-located teams, geographically dispersed teams seem to experience more affective conflict that festers longer and resists resolution.

Fairness and Consumer Behavior: A WWJD (What Would Justice Do?) Analysis by Kelly Schwind Wilson, Donald E. Conlon, and Joel Koopman

In this theoretical work Wilson, Conlon, and Koopman apply organizational justice theory to the domain of consumer behavior. First, a descriptive model of the interaction process between customers and service providers is presented. Next, the authors use the fourfold model of organizational justice (distributive-procedural-interpersonal-informational) and demonstrate how it has been applied to the various stages of this customer-service provider model.

By doing so, the authors highlight that in some areas, a great deal of attention has been paid to issues of fairness (for example, in service recovery situations, where a customer has paid for a product or service and perceives the item did not perform to expectations), whereas in others, very little attention has been paid to issues of fairness. The authors close by noting practical implications for managers (i.e., interventions they can make at each stage of the interaction process model) as well as research suggestions for scholars studying justice in customer service settings.

Part II: Leadership, Social Capital, and Personality

This section contains three empirical studies relating to the leadership language used by Senators Hillary Clinton and Barak Obama during the last national election, building social capital through leader–member exchange, and

the relationship between personality and financial performance of professional fund managers.

Obama vs. Clinton: A Study Exploring the Impact of Leadership Language by Diana Hargrove, Phyllis A. Duncan, Mark T. Green, Charles Salter, and John M. Trayhan

This study investigated why Obama could win the Democratic Party's nomination as their candidate for the presidency over Clinton? Hargrove, Duncan, Green, Salter, and Trayhan performed a content analysis to determine if the leadership language communicated by Senators Hillary Rodham Clinton and Barack Hussein Obama was congruent with the media portrayal of their leadership style. The leadership language themes identified were limited to transformational leadership, transactional leadership, and passive leadership. Additional themes identified were issues frequently addressed in the speeches and included economy, health care, and foreign policy.

The words of a politician during a campaign can tell us a great deal about that person, including the leadership style we might expect him or her to utilize once in office. Today voters become acquainted with political candidates through a multitude of communication mediums including: (a) campaign speeches, (b) network and cable television news and talk shows, (c) candidate web sites, (d) nonpartisan and independent web sites, (e) email, (f) blogs, (g) political ads, (h) newspapers, (i) magazines, (j) radio, and (k) political polls. The volume and complexity of the political communications make it difficult for the voter to comprehend, process, and utilize the information for deciding which candidate to support. Too often decisions are made ballots cast without regard for the type of leadership that will be provided in the future. Since leadership language is magnified during elections, the 2008 United States Presidential election campaign speeches presented opportunities for analysis of leadership style based on the language used.

The results indicated Hillary Clinton used more transformational language than Barack Obama. However, Barack Obama used more passive language than Hillary Clinton. For Hillary Clinton, transformational leadership language was positively correlated with campaign month, while transactional language was negatively correlated with campaign month. Overall, the difference in mean frequency percentages of foreign policy issues language by campaign month was significant.

Social Capital Via Leader–Member Exchanges: An Avenue to Human Capital? by E. Edward Stark and Francis L. Jeffries

This study discusses the concept of "strategic human resource management" that has received increasing attention from practitioners and academics alike.

This perspective advocates that human resource management is a potential source of sustained competitive advantage when firms create value in a way that is rare and difficult for competitors to emulate. Thus, management is confronted with ensuring that employees combine their knowledge, skills, and work related behavior in a synergistic, integrative manner to create human capital, but realization of human capital at the firm level is not likely to occur until management recognizes the pivotal role of social capital.

Within organizational settings, social capital is a resource that is derived from the relationships among individuals and results from expectations of actors that have formed as a result of being part of social structures. Central to these relationships are ongoing exchanges such as described in Leader–Member Exchange theory. These exchanges generate norms of reciprocity along with other components of a close relationship such as trust, respect, and mutual obligation, all of which represent various manifestations of social capital.

For the manager, the results of this study suggests that leveraging the human resources of a firm through pursuit of high quality LMX that generates high levels of social capital has the potential to contribute to creation of greater amounts of human capital. For the scholar, the results of the study support much of what has been hypothesized about the relationship between generation of social capital and human capital. Differing levels of perceived LMX and inherent social capital are associated with the variance common to an employee's intent to stay with an employer and a positive disposition toward the employment relationship. Stark and Jeffries assert that this variance represents a form of human capital that can be organized to achieve levels of rarity, inimitability, and non-substitutability, thus endowing a firm strategic with advantages over competitors.

Relationship between the Big-Five Personality and the Financial Performance of Fund Managers by Selin Camgoz, Mehmet Baha Karan, and Azize Ergeneli

Researchers in the field of behavioral finance argued that individuals' thoughts, perceptions, and fears are displayed in their behavioral actions and judgments and, financially speaking, in their investment choices regarding their risk preferences. This study by Camgoz, Karen, and Ergeneli addressed which personality traits and some demographics (gender, marital status, and age) would distinguish successful versus unsuccessful financial performance of professional fund managers. The authors measured the personality traits of fund managers by the Big-Five and observed their investment outcomes in the real market. The 44-item Big-Five Inventory (BFI) was served as the research instrument to assess the personality typologies of professional fund managers. The financial performance of fund managers was estimated with Sharpe indexes, which were calculated upon a total of 113 observations of weekly

returns of equity mutual funds for two consecutive years. Logistic regression analysis suggested that extraversion and conscientiousness were found to be associated with high financial performance. Moreover, the study revealed that younger participants exhibited better financial performance. The findings of this study provided support for the relevance of the five-factor model in predicting job performance. Therefore, it might be reasonable to include the Big-Five in personnel selection batteries for the "personality–job fit" purposes.

Part III: Issues in Entrepreneurship and Small Business

This section contains an essay on revising Phelan's model on entrepreneurship and a case study on a small business organization.

Modifying Phelan's Model: A Conceptual Framework Linking Entrepreneurs to International New Venture Competitiveness by Florinel-Frank Cotae

A long-standing view in the literature has been that international new ventures (INV) are affected by liabilities such as smallness, newness, and foreignness. In focusing on finding a model that would define, identify, and explain the factors affecting the link between entrepreneurs, networks, international new ventures and internationalization related liabilities Cotae suggests that at the center of a dialogue the individual must be considered as the cornerstone of such a link. One model that stands out—advanced by Phelan, Dalgic, and Sethi (2006)—allows for just such an origination point for a dialogue as it is based upon an entrepreneur's traits of social astuteness and competence that are expected to offer relief from the above referenced detriments. Cotae argues in this chaper that Phelan et al. model, while important as a contribution, is not sufficient in mitigating the globalization related challenges. Through the medium of extant research and studies, the model is analyzed as part of three fragments. First, the model is compared with findings from internationalization—reflecting economic condition as key—embeddedness—the only one found to reflect some of the model's conceptual framework—and tacit theories—reflecting entrepreneurial uniqueness in recognizing and pursuing opportunities key as for securing INVs competitive advantage. Second, external factors such as behavior, legal environment and goal commitment are applied to INV competitiveness. The third segment points out to geographic differences, as further considerations that refute some of model's claim, suggesting that INVs come to existence due to small domestic markets and strong immigrant communities, and place into the foreground the concepts of national attitudes and entrepreneurial maturity. The concluding fragment presents a modified theoretical framework for addressing the factors affecting INV success and competitiveness. The author concludes that the implications for manag-

ers are two pronged: one related to increased awareness and understanding of the external factors affecting international market entry and second related to acquiring the ability to model INV according to general framework capable to mitigate cost related consideration.

BSL Printing Company: A Case Study by Joseph P. Lakatos, Donald R. Soucy, and Stephen J. Bukowy

This is a case study of BSL Printing Company. In its early years, the company managed to stay afloat with the support of its largest customer, Advent Textile, which operates in the same county as BSL. Over the years, the families of the CEO's of both companies became very close friends. By 2008, BSL's sales reached nearly $18 million. As part of its sales strategy, BSL offered its preferred customers significant quantity discounts. However, in recent years, with a slowdown in the economy, these customers were ordering just enough to receive discounts while only taking a small fraction of the amount while BSL stored the rest. Therefore, while BSL's customers were getting the benefit of the discounts, BSL was not getting the benefit of faster cash flow and was paying suppliers for raw materials to prepare the orders. Meanwhile, Advent's cash flow was deteriorating significantly, eventually forcing Advent to file for Chapter 11 bankruptcy. As part of its reorganization under Chapter 11, Advent sought the help of BSL. Advent requested an extension on the payables it owed BSL and continued discounts on current year's orders of cartons. However, offering such assistance could put BSL in financial difficulty. BSL's CEO must demonstrate strong leadership skills in developing and implementing a strategic plan that will balance the associated benefits and risks of stakeholders. In the analysis of this case study, prominent theories relating to leadership styles and ethics are applied. Readers will come to find that the application of these theories go hand in hand when analyzing business problems, leading to better decisions.

Part IV: Ethics, Learning, and Change

This section contains three contributions: a theoretical chapter that conceptualizes the self as an expanding web of external and internal conversations, a theoretical chapter that deals with entry mode choices of multinational enterprises, and an empirical study that deals with administration of state governments.

Ethics, Rhetoric, and the Self as an Expanding Web of Conversations by Can M. Alpaslan, Sandy E. Green, and Ian I. Mitroff

This chapter challenges the conventional view of the self as a unitary entity. Drawing on a discursive understanding of the self, Alpaslan, Green, and

Mitroff conceptualize the self as an expanding web of external and internal conversations. They argue that the self, and the self's interests and morality, are at least partially constructed and shaped by the language and rhetoric of external conversations to which the self is exposed during its developmental process. This view of the self as an expanding web of conversations resonates with the ideas of William James, Charles Peirce, and Robert Solomon: a moral philosophy cannot be finalized prior to experience, the only moral goal is the constant expansion of the self, and the guarantor of moral conduct is good judgment, respectively.

Conceptualizing the self as constructed and shaped by conversations, and conceptualizing organizations as a set of managerial conversations allow us to use rhetorical theory to study and operationalize the effects of managerial conversations on the self's moral reasoning and ethical/unethical decision making. Scholars may use the rich array of analytical frameworks rhetorical theory offers to study the self as an expanding web of conversations. These frameworks include but are not limited to persuasive appeals such as pathos/logos/ethos, virtues of style such as clarity/propriety, oratorical styles such as judicial/deliberative/epideictic, and tropes such as metaphor/irony. The authors believe that an awareness of the effects of rhetoric and conversations on moral reasoning enables managers and organizations to manage ethical conduct better, and educators to teach ethics in a more effective way. They invite scholars to uncover the role of rhetoric and language in shaping the self and constructing the interests the self seeks.

Flexibility, Learning, and Control: Entry Mode Choice under Uncertainty by Mujtaba Ahsan and Martina Musteen

Ahsan and Musteen have developed a new categorization of entry modes: (1) flexible entry modes characterized by a minimum investment and high reversibility, (2) collaborative entry modes distinguished by a high potential for experiential learning and development of capabilities, and (3) control modes defined as modes that allow multinational enterprises (MNEs) to internalize most activities in the foreign market and get the most direct access to local market and resources. They present propositions related to entry mode choices under uncertainty in a three-dimensional framework which incorporates uncertainty, MNEs' previous experience, and the role of the local context conceptualized as market attractiveness. It is argued that previous experience provides MNEs with insights that can help them cope with endogenous uncertainties in new markets and, as a result, enables them to enter foreign markets via higher control modes. The authors suggest that the relationship between exogenous and endogenous uncertainty and the preference for flexibility and collaborative modes of entry can weaken or strengthen, respectively, depending on the attractiveness of the local market or its unique resources.

The contribution of this work to literature is three-fold. First, it highlights the notion that MNEs can dispel endogenous uncertainty through learning while they have no control over exogenous uncertainty. Second, the work builds theory relevant to entry mode research by offering a parsimonious view on the role of uncertainty in the entry mode choice. Third, by acknowledging that various types of uncertainty have a systematically different influence on the entry mode decision and can contribute to valuable, proprietary learning, this review provides a more complete explanation of the entry mode choice and also offers normative recommendations to managers of MNEs.

The Politics-Administration Continuum in American State Governments: Administrative Accountability as a Positive-Sum Pattern by Cheryl Miller and Deil S. Wright

This study suggests that the mingling of policy and administration and the issue of administrative accountability are prominent management concerns of both theoretical and empirical interest. One of the paramount empirical issues is the extent to which this intersection occurs because of the aggrandizing tendencies of bureaucracy. What are the patterns of actual influence from various sources (or actors) on the public administrator? And, which sources/actors does the administrator prefer to exercise influence? This study addresses these central questions by examining the views of state agency heads on the extent of actual and preferred influence exercised by various actors on bureaucratic initiatives. Using data from the 1984, 1994, and 2004 American State Administrators Project (ASAP) surveys, Miller and Wright assessed the perceptions of state agency heads of the actual and preferred levels of influence exerted on major policy decisions by numerous persons and groups. Results show a consistent positive-sum pattern over three decades. State agency heads prefer a higher level of influence by numerous institutional and extra-agency actors. Of the eight policy actors whose influence is probed, only for state legislators and state courts do administrators attribute too much influence. Yes, state administrators prescribe greater influence for themselves, their agencies, and the governor, among other policy actors. But greater self/agency influence is not associated with preferred decreases in the influence of other actors. The findings of this study that administrators look both inward and outward for policy guidance in a positive-sum pluralistic pattern suggest that multiple sources and mechanisms of administrative accountability might work better than is the conventional wisdom.

Cumulatively, these contributions and others to follow in subsequent years seek an integration of theory, research, and practice which reflects in shorthand the essential goal of *Current Topics in Management* and, more broadly, to the expanding usefulness of the International Conference on Advances in Management.

PART I

MANAGING CONFLICT AND JUSTICE

Current Topics in Management, **Vol. 15, 2011, pp. 13-40**

THE MODERATING ROLE OF SOCIAL ATTITUDES IN THE RELATIONSHIP BETWEEN DIVERSITY AND CONFLICT

Nailah Ayub and Karen A. Jehn

Both diversity and conflict are defined in terms of differences. Diversity is differences in visible (Hicks-Clarke & Illes, 2000) or less visible characteristics (Thatcher & Jehn, 1998; Williams & O'Reilly, 1998) that are used by group members to differentiate themselves from one another. Conflict is often defined in terms of differences in ideas and opinions, which give rise to tension among the group members (De Dreu, Harinck, & van Vianen, 1999). While conflict is generally considered to have negative consequences (e.g., De Dreu & Weingart, 2003), research on diversity has struggled to find the 'value-in-diversity.' Williams and O'Reilly (1998) reviewed diversity research over 40 years and observed that research remains inconclusive as to whether diversity has positive or negative effects (also Milliken & Martins, 1996). They, however, concluded that the consequences of diversity depend upon type of diversity and other factors that moderate or mediate the effects of diversity (van Knippenberg & Schippers, 2007). Although research has shown that diversity itself can be beneficial (e.g., Jehn, Northcraft, & Neale, 1999; McLeoad, Lobel, & Cox, 1996; Watson, Kumar, & Michaelson, 1993) or bad (O'Reilly, Caldwell, & Barnett, 1989; Mannix & Neale, 2005), the effects of diversity are noticeably associated with other factors that make it good or bad. Proponents of value-in-diversity endorse diversity through factors such as promoting beliefs or positive attitudes towards diversity (Homan, van Knippenberg, van Kleef, & De Dreu, 2007). Individual attitudes can possibly be one of the significant indicators of whether diversity will have positive or negative effects. In this chapter, we describe our research that aimed at studying how certain individual attitudes

create tension among members of a workgroup characterized by specific type(s) of diversity. For empirical investigations, we selected national and racioethnic diversity and examined the moderating role of social attitudes of nationalism, national stereotypes, and social distance.

Through a series of studies, we contribute to the diversity, multinational workgroups, and conflict literature by examining social attitudes (nationalism, social distance, and national stereotypes) that influence relationships and behavior at workplaces. Our main contributions of this research were to determine influences of national diversity on workgroup processes (e.g., conflicts) and performance (e.g., efficiency); to determine the moderating role of social attitudes in the diversity to conflicts relationship; to explore the positive role of diversity in terms of numerical composition of workgroups; and to verify the generalization of theories and propositions across samples. Whereas diversity research often explores its negative aspects, we examined positive potentials of diversity and explored the positive elements of group culture in terms of perceived respect.

Nationalism in Workgroups

Depending on its characteristics and context, one diversity type can have a larger impact than others (Tsui, Egan, & O'Reilly, 1992). Nationality is observed to be an important demographic characteristic of group members (Ayub & Jehn, 2006; Earley & Mosakowski, 2000) indicating that national diversity will be impactful when present in a group. A nationally diverse workgroup is composed of members with different national backgrounds (Dahlin, Weingart, & Hinds, 2005). When a group includes members with diverse nationalities (i.e., nationally diverse), members tend to seek those who are from their own nationality group. This signifies the importance of national diversity in multinational setup where national similarity or differences are more salient beyond ethnicity or culture. We focused specifically on national diversity as an important diversity type in multinational workgroups. We began with proposing a multi-level theoretical framework to examine the moderating effect of nationalism on the relationship between national diversity and conflict (for details see Ayub & Jehn, 2006). We then proceeded with an empirical study to verify this model (Ayub & Jehn, 2010a).

Brief et al., (2005) noticed the significance of attitudes from the communities that are introduced to workgroups through the workgroup members. These social attitudes are yet to be substantially explored by organizational studies on diversity and conflict. As discussed above, we were interested in studying social attitudes in nationally diverse groups. We propose that members from different nationalities in nationally diverse groups will likely hold attitudes related to their national background that would guide their behavior within the group. Every social group safeguards its existence by inculcating certain

attitudes in its members in defense of the group's ideology and existence. This nationalism will be activated in relevant contexts, such as nationally diverse workgroups, for interpersonal behavior within these groups. Since nationalism is a negative attitude by definition, intragroup communication and exchange may be stressful when members exhibit or perceive nationalism and thus, we predict will experience conflict.

National Diversity and Conflict

Before establishing the moderating effect of nationalism, we first develop the direct relationship between national diversity and types of conflict. Jehn (1997; Jehn & Mannix, 2001) identified three types of conflict. Relationship conflict is defined as interpersonal incompatibilities among group members that are not directly related to the tasks that individuals and groups have to do. Task conflict is disagreements about the content of the tasks, such as differences in viewpoints, ideas, and opinions. Thirdly, process conflict is arguments about handling and distribution of responsibilities or resources or coordinating an agenda. We propose that national diversity will lead to relationship conflict due to decreased relationship quality (Brief et al., 2005), decreased group integration (O'Reilly, Caldwell, & Barnett, 1989; Triandis, 1994), and increased categorization processes (Bayazit & Mannix, 2003). National diversity is thus related to relationship conflict which may negatively affect the group. On the other hand, national diversity could be helpful in task accomplishment if it acts as informational diversity (Jehn, 1997) by combining the experience and expertise of members who belong to different national backgrounds and social networks. National diversity, in this sense, can be beneficial to the group through its association with task conflict (Jehn et al., 1999).

In addition to relationship and task conflicts, national diversity is proposed to be positively related to process conflict as well (Ayub & Jehn, 2006). Process conflict may arise due to (self) exclusion from procedural decision making and misunderstandings due to stereotypical biases as well as misunderstandings due to communication issues. Dissimilarity among nationally diverse members will decrease workgroup involvement as some members may be excluded from information and opportunity networks (Mor-Barak, Cherin, & Berkman, 1998). Perception of such biased behavior will cause some members to withdraw from the group (Turner, Hogg, Oakes, Reicher, & Wetherell, 1987) and thus contribute less to the task performance (Kirchmeyer, 1993; Kirchmeyer & Cohen, 1992). This will negatively effect communication among group members as well (Zenger & Lawrence, 1989). We, therefore, propose that when members perceive national diversity in their workgroup they will likely experience more process conflict than the members of a workgroup perceiving low national diversity.

Nationalism as a Moderator

After establishing the direct relationships between national diversity and conflict types, we introduce nationalism as the moderator. We propose that the presence of members with nationalistic attitudes (e.g., ingroup favoritism and outgroup rejection) in nationally diverse workgroups will strengthen the positive relationship between national diversity and relationship and task conflicts and will weaken the national diversity to task conflict relationship. Relationship conflict can be exaggerated due to differences in attitudes (such as nationalism) of group members (cf. Earley & Mosakowski, 2000). Group members may avoid each other due to their nationalistic attitudes or perception of these attitudes. This will also disrupt information sharing (Armstrong & Cole, 1995; Milliken & Martins, 1996). That is, we propose that nationalism will moderate the positive relationship between national diversity and task conflict such that any task conflict due to national diversity will be decreased in the presence of nationalism. Nationalistic attitudes may also disturb the group processes such as communication (Cramton & Hinds, 2005) regarding how to accomplish group tasks. Roles and resource allocations may be biased in favor of the ingroup or against the outgroup members that could incite fighting and cheating (Dennen, 1987). Nationalism may lead to blaming group members for unfair distribution and behavior or hold them responsible for failure at working towards task accomplishments (Brewer, 2000). Accordingly, we propose that the positive relationship between national diversity and process conflict will be strengthened in the presence of nationalistic group members.

Study 1: Nationalism as a Moderator of National Diversity to Conflict Relationship. After developing the basic model, we designed an empirical study to test our theoretical model (for details see Ayub & Jehn, 2010a). We distinguished two forms of nationalism: national ingroup preference for one's own nationality and derogation of other nationalities. We selected a Pakistani sample for this study. Even though Pakistanis make a significant part of diversity in workgroups around the world (Ogbonna & Harris, 2006) there is barely any study that focuses on them. Knowledge of such national groups has become important especially after the remarkable events such as September 11 attack on the New York twin towers. The incident has made nationality a salient characteristic and has also influenced attitudes of people towards certain nationalities. We hypothesized that outgroup derogation was a stronger moderator of the relationship between national diversity and conflict compared to national preference. We argued that nationalistic outgroup derogation had a rather negative intent that was more likely a stimulant of negative reaction from the perceiver. National preference, on the other hand, was a favoring behavior which would not directly target anyone with harmful intent.

We adapted two Zellmer-Bruhn et al. (2008) items to measure perceived national diversity of group members. One item was a 7-point Likert item about how much respondents considered their workgroup was diverse with refer-

ence to nationality. The second item asked about approximate percentage of nationalities that were present in the workgroup different from respondents' own nationality. The percentage scores were converted to match 7-point scale. The items gave a mean value of 1.51 (*SD* = 1.01) and an alpha coefficient of .76. Jehn's (1995) scales were used to measure task and relationship conflict. We used 4 items for task conflict (e.g., "How much conflict of ideas is there among the members of this workgroup?") and 5 items for relationship conflict (e.g., "How much do members differ about personal issues?") with 7-point Likert scale ranging from 1 (Never) to 7 (A Lot). Principal component analysis with oblique rotation validated the scales for Pakistani sample. The Cronbach alpha coefficients for task and relationship conflict were .86 and .90, respectively. To measure nationalism, we included items from Dekker et al.'s (2003) nationalism scale (e.g., "I feel I am a member of one Pakistani family"; "Pakistan is the best country to live in"; "In general, I like Pakistanis better.") and Pettigrew and Meertens' (1995) blatant rejection subscale (e.g., "Other nationalities have jobs that Pakistanis should have only because of their nationalities"; "Pakistanis can never be comfortable with other nationalities even if they are close friends") with 7-point Likert scales (1= strongly disagree, 7 = strongly agree). The reliability coefficients for national preference and nationalistic outgroup derogation were .91 and .78 respectively. We initially controlled for age and gender for their possible effects on the perception of conflict (Jehn, 1995; Jehn et al., 1999; Pelled, 1996) but found no significant differences in results due to these variables.

We retained survey data from 131 information technology professionals working in 29 workgroups, out of the 160 surveys distributed, in organizations located in Islamabad, Pakistan. We discarded 29 surveys due to erroneous or incomplete responses. National diversity in this sample of workgroups was around 30% diverse members in groups with an average group size of 7.73 members (*SD* = 3.45). This gave a representative sample for national diversity within Pakistani multinational workplaces. The diverse groups generally included one or two non-Pakistani members. The sample included 23 (17.6%) women. The mean age of the participants was 28.94 (*SD* = 6.62) with the age range of 28 to 63 years.

We tested the hypotheses with the help of regression analyses after computing descriptive statistics (see Table 1). National diversity had a main effect on perceptions of task conflict, thus verifying our hypothesis that national diversity is positively related to task conflict (see Table 2). We could not find support for our hypothesis regarding the positive relationship between national diversity and relationship conflict. However, nationalistic derogation had a moderating effect on the relationship between national diversity and relationship conflict such that there was more relationship conflict in nationally diverse groups with members reporting nationalistic derogation. In addition, nationalistic derogation strengthened the positive relationship between national diversity and task conflict. We also found nationalistic derogation to be a significant moderator compared to national preference.

Table 1
Means, Standard Deviations, and Intercorrelations of Seven Variables

Variables	*M*	*SD*	1	2	3	4	5	6
1. Age	28.97	6.64	–					
2. Gender	1.18	.38	–.25**	–				
3. National diversity	1.51	1.01	–.06	–.04	–			
4. National preference	5.20	1.32	–.12	.15	–.03	–		
5. Nationalistic derogation	3.10	1.21	–.26**	.17	.31**	.31**	–	
6. Relationship conflict	2.75	1.28	–.24**	.12	.13	–.09	.30**	–
7. Task conflict	3.59	1.19	–.29**	.07	.21*	.07	.24**	.62**

Note: $N = 131$
* $p < .05$. ** $p < .01$.

Table 2
Regression Analysis for the Moderation Effect of Nationalism

	Dependent Variable									
	Task Conflict					Relationship Conflict				
Predictors	β	*F*	R^2	ΔF	ΔR^2	β	*F*	R^2	ΔF	ΔR^2
Step 1: Main effects										
National diversity (ND)	.16					.03				
Ingroup preference (IP)	–.02					–.22*				
Outgroup derogation (OD)	.22*	3.68*	.09	3.68	.09	.36**	6.04**	.14	6.04**	.14
Step 2: Two-way interactions										
ND × IP	–.15					–.13				
ND × OD	.21	2.52*	.11	.81	.01	.34*	5.33**	.20	3.79*	.06

Note: $N = 131$
* $p < .05$. ** $p < .01$.

Workgroup Diversity and Social Attitudes: Social Distances and National Stereotypes

Our first study gave some interesting results where we observed that nationalistic derogation, that has a very negative connotation, could also give positive results such as heightened task conflict in nationally diverse groups. A closer look at the sample suggested that national diversity could be a prized feature

in certain workgroups. Workgroups in Pakistan seldom include non-Pakistani members and thus it is likely that national diversity is a cherished distinction. Also of importance is the national diversity composition, that is, what national groups make up national diversity in a workgroup.

To further explore social attitudes in workgroups, we studied social distance among group members. If members have nationalistic attitudes, they are likely to have differential attitudes towards other nationalities. In that one may not exhibit similar nationalistic derogation towards other nationalities. Thus a member may be nationalistic and have strong reservations against some nationality while another nationality may be quite acceptable for interaction. Such contact preferences are studied as social distances. Social distance is a negative attitude that determines social relations marking the willingness or acceptability to interact (Bogardus, 1967; Chan & Goto, 2003). It evokes negative feelings that motivates the avoidance of outgroups (Hagendoorn & Kleinpenning, 1991). To understand the results of our first study, we explored the notion that a workgroup may have nationalistic members but without their negative effects when there are small social distances among the group members.

Another variable that could illustrate our results for nationalistic derogation is national stereotypes. We selected two attitudinal variables for a somewhat detailed depiction of social attitudes and beliefs. Whereas social distances are based on social differences, stereotypes are based on particular traits. Stereotypes are the *beliefs* and *expectations* about the characteristics of members of a social category (Hamilton & Sherman, 1994). These stereotypes could be positive or negative and a person may be seen as acceptable or objectionable depending on how his/her national group is stereotyped. Relevant stereotypes are brought forth to guide our interaction (Greenwald & Banaji, 1995) depending upon the context. We propose that stereotypes related to work are referred to for our interpersonal behavior within workgroups. Thereby, persons may be stereotyped positively despite large social distance based on nationalities.

From our first study, we noticed that nationalism can have a negative effect in diverse groups. However, diversity itself may also be advantageous to the group as a result of cross-national expertise and information (value-in-diversity hypothesis, Cox & Blake, 1991). Also, more choices of interaction indicate increased chance of finding more similar members for interaction and thus reduce anxiety in interacting with dissimilar others or the outgroups.

Social Distance and National Stereotypes in Nationally Diverse Workgroups

Social context can change the form and content of social categories (Kinket & Verkuyten, 1999; Rijswijk & Ellemers, 2002). Thus social judgments and perceptions such as stereotypes and social distances may be modified within a context or frame of reference (Haslam et al., 1992; Hopkins, Regan, & Abell,

1997). That is, a national group can be stereotyped more negatively in the presence of a positively stereotyped national group and a member can be placed at a larger social distance in the presence of a least distant member. This suggests that national diversity will positively moderate the social distance and national stereotypes to conflicts relationship. That is, the presence of more nationalities in workgroups will reduce the negative effects of social distance and national stereotypes. We, therefore, hypothesized that national diversity will moderate the social distance and national stereotypes to conflicts relationship such that the presence of national diversity will weaken the hypothesized relationships between social distance and national stereotypes and types of conflicts.

Study 2: Social Attitudes and Conflict in Nationally Diverse Workgroups. We designed a scenario study to examine how differences in attitudes and beliefs (i.e., social distances and national stereotypes) and national diversity (number of nationalities) affect the conflict experience of workgroup members. We included three outgroup countries that were selected in view of the history and geography of the sample's national group with these countries. Pretests for both samples confirmed our presumptions of social distances and stereotyping of the sample group regarding the selected nationalities. We collected data from Pakistan and the Netherlands where the participants were provided with a workgroup situation including one outgroup category (low national diversity) or 3 outgroup categories (high national diversity). The Pakistani sample was given the scenario with British, Indian, and/or Chinese nationalities and the Dutch sample was given the scenario with British, German, and/or Moroccan nationalities. The scenario description included instructions on a marketing task (making an advertisement) with a group that included members of nationalities different from that of the participant. The participants were then required to complete a survey questionnaire about group processes and performance with reference to the given group context. The data comprised of 267 participants with the mean age of 25.34 years and included 94 females. The two samples included 147 participants from Pakistan and 117 from the Netherlands. The mean age of Pakistani participants was 28.65 years with 26 females and the mean age of the Dutch sample was 21.78 years.

We used the Bogardus Distance scale (1933) to measure social distances towards each of the three given nationalities. The items with a 7-point Likert scale asked how objectionable or acceptable it is to have a given nationality as, for example, a co-worker, a neighbor, or a business partner. The principal component analysis gave one social distance component that explained 57.99% of the variance in the Pakistani sample and 66.08% of variance in the Dutch sample. The Cronbach reliability coefficient was .85 and .91 for the Pakistani and the Dutch sample respectively. Work-related national stereotypes were measured by a list of ten adjectives (e.g., 'reliable', 'hard-working', and 'honest') adapted from Johnson, Terry, and Louis (2005) and Verkuyten and Hagendoorn (2002) scales. Respondents rated the given nationalities on these adjectives

with the help of a 7-point Likert scale. Principal component analysis gave a single stereotype component with 54.05% variance explained in the Pakistani sample and 52.87% variance explained in the Dutch sample. The reliability coefficients were .90 for both Pakistani and the Dutch sample.

Conflict types were measured with Jehn scales (1995) as in study 1. We also included 4 items for process conflict (e.g., Do you expect the members would disagree about the process of how to get the work done?) from Jehn and Mannix (2001). Alpha reliability coefficients for task, relationship, and process conflicts were .82, .86, and .89 respectively for the Pakistani sample and .89, .76, and .89 for the Dutch sample. General performance was measured with four items adapted from Gibson, Zellmer-Bruhn, and Schwab's (2003) measure of team effectiveness (the group will adequately complete assigned duties, perform the expected tasks, fulfill responsibilities as specified, and meet formal performance requirements). Principal component analysis gave a single component with 79.36% and 93.25% variance for the two samples. The Cronbach coefficients for the two samples were .91 and .98. We also used a money distribution item as an indicator of members' behavior towards given group members. Another outcome measure was about the intent to work with the choice of given group members in the future.

We used a number of statistics to test our hypotheses, starting first with descriptives as shown in Table 3. We ran MANOVA using Roy's largest root multivariate test statistic to test the overall significance of the model (see for detailed results, Ayub & Jehn, 2010b). The analyses supported our assumptions that social distance and national stereotypes are directly related to conflict and outcomes and that national diversity moderates the given relationships (see Table 4). We then followed with univariate analyses of covariance (ANCOVAs) to test the mediating effects of conflict types on the interaction of national diversity with social distance and national negative stereotypes (see Table 5). National diversity interacted with social distance such that high national diversity increased task conflict, even more so when social distances were low. National diversity interacted with social distance to give reduced relationship conflict.

National diversity also interacted with negative national stereotypes to give higher task conflict and decreased process conflict. The results sufficiently supported our hypothesis that national diversity moderates the relationship of social distance and national stereotypes with conflict. We observed through ANCOVAs that both social distance and national stereotypes are related to outcomes as well. National diversity positively moderated the relationship between social distance and perceived performance and intent to work. Also, national diversity positively moderated the relationship between national stereotypes and intent to work. Further ANCOVAs showed that the social distance and national stereotypes to outcomes relationship was fully or partially mediated by conflict types.

Table 3
Means, Standard Deviations, and Intercorrelations of Twelve Variables

	M	SD	1	2	3	4	5	6	7	8	9	10	11
1. Age	25.34	6.34											
2. Gender	1.36	.48	−.42**										
3. Nationality	1.46	.50	−.54**	.48**									
4. National diversity	1.54	.50	.03	−.08	**−.11***								
5. Social distance	3.36	1.21	.02	.02	−.01	**−.11***							
6. Negative Stereotypes	3.29	1.04	−.08	.07	**.11***	−.09	**.56****						
7. Task conflict	4.27	1.00	−.18**	.09	**.33****	.05	−.03	.01					
8. Relationship conflict	3.62	1.23	−.08	.09	**.19****	−.09	**.11***	.05	**.48****				
9. Process conflict	3.86	1.10	−.15**	.11*	**.19****	−.06	**.17****	.06	**.51****	**.55****			
10. Performance	4.78	1.52	.22**	−.13*	**−.24****	**−.18****	**−.16****	**−.22****	−.08	−.05	**−.14***		
11. Intent to work	4.85	1.54	.04	.07	−.06	**−.16****	**−.15****	**−.23****	−.04	.01	**−.15****	**.58****	
12. Money distribution	31.52	9.27	−.06	−.03	−.03	**.12***	**−.22****	**−.24****	.06	−.07	−.02	.05	−.01

Note: $N = 375$
* $p < .05$. ** $p < .01$.

Table 4
Analysis for Moderation Effects

	Moderator: Social distance	*Moderator: Negative national stereotypes*
Source	*F*	*F*
DV = *Task conflict*		
Nationality	6.56*	24.74*
National diversity (ND)	1.07	5.81**
Social distance (SD)	1.11	1.58*
ND × SD	1.44*	2.00**
DV = *Relationship conflict*		
Nationality	1.95	2.98
ND	4.15*	.17
SD	1.29	1.18
ND × SD	1.48*	.85
DV = *Process conflict*		
Nationality	.01	7.34*
ND	.48	2.37
SD	1.61*	1.48
ND × SD	1.19	1.62*
DV = *Performance*		
Nationality	5.71*	11.18**
ND	16.21**	5.80*
SD	1.80*	1.16
ND × SD	2.33**	.83
DV = *Money distribution*		
Nationality	.03	.64
ND	1.29	2.89
SD	.80	2.73**
ND × SD	.80	.91
DV = *Intent to work*		
Nationality	2.28	.70
ND	16.33**	.48
SD	1.53*	1.12
ND × SD	1.80**	1.40

$^{*}p \leq .05$. $^{**}p < .01$.

Table 5
Analysis of Covariance for Mediated effects of Conflict Types on Interaction of National Diversity with Social Distance and National Stereotypes: Dependent Variables are Performance, Money Distribution, and Intent to Work

Source	Moderator: Social distance *F*	Moderator: Negative national stereotypes *F*
DV= Performance		
Nationality	8.74**	133.89**
Task conflict	.67	12.64**
Relationship conflict	5.07*	.33
Process conflict	.03	.02
National diversity (ND)	14.95**	2.56
Social distance (SD)	1.82**	6.07*
ND × SD	2.52**	1.01
DV = Money Distribution		
Nationality	.07	.07
Task conflict	.99	4.94*
Relationship conflict	.38	7.74*
Process conflict	.03	0
ND	.84	1.56
SD	.73	2.81**
ND × SD	.79	.82
DV = Intent to work		
Nationality	2.62	.35
Task conflict	4.02*	.35
Relationship conflict	3.92*	2.42
Process conflict	.09	4.73*
ND	14.37**	.54
SD	1.39*	1.12
ND × SD	1.85**	1.29

* $p \leq .05$. ** $p < .01$.

The results of this study signify the importance of studying diversity in view of its distinct aspects. Also of importance is to acknowledge the social aspects that affect the group members and thus directly or indirectly affect the group processes and outcomes. Although social attitudes and beliefs may not be completely eliminated, these social attitudes and beliefs may be modified by introducing and managing national diversity. By presenting interesting results

that are discussed for future investigations as well, this study contributes to diversity and conflict management research.

Interpersonal Attitudes: Similarity Preferences and Respect

Even though open and direct racial animosity, such as implied by nationalism is not normally exhibited in the workplace, stereotypes and beliefs continue to stimulate an implicit tension among racially and ethnically different workers (Barreto & Ellemers, 2009; Townsend & Scott, 2001). From the very beginning of this research project, we realized the sensitivity and difficulty of collecting data on variables such as nationalism. We, therefore, included the less subtle variables of social distance and national stereotypes as negative aspects of nationalism. However, we also aimed at exploring ingroup favoritism that may not have very hostile connotation or negative intentions as that of outgroup derogation. For that reason, we proposed that ingroup favoritism will not have a negative effect as strong as outgroup derogation when we initially explored nationalism in nationally diverse workgroups. We found supportive results for our hypotheses but we remained curious about the effects of ingroup favoritism. Therefore, we proceeded to explore similarity preferences and how these affect the group processes and outcomes. We were also interested in racioethnic diversity as a more specified diversity type. Racioethnicity is defined as the combination of biological and cultural differences (Cox, 2004; Roberson & Block, 2001).

There is inadequate research about the influence of racioethnic diversity on group processes (Bowers, Pharmer, & Salas, 2000; Lawrence, 1997; Pelled, 1996; Pitts, 2005) even though Cox (2004) has noted that it is incorrect to study race apart from ethnicity. Almost every country includes subgroups that can, and prefer to, be distinguished in view of race and ethnicity. Identifying someone as Asian is vague and very general to many Asians. Asians differ in several aspects such as socially, culturally, and traditionally. Asians could be Chinese, Indians, Japanese, or Russians. Even in the West, the whites could be British White or Caucasian White and the "coloured" could be Afro-American, Surinamese, or Hispanics, among others.

Racioethnic diversity also offers a group situation where social categorization is likely to occur. Social categorization in turn would result in ingroup–outgroup biased interactions and communication. We focused on ingroup preference in terms of ingroup similarity preference. Similarity preferences can be defined as values that guide member's attraction to other members in the group (Reade, 2001). These values are usually based on certain similarity characteristics, such as racioethnicity. Similarity preference represents the attitude of choices for contact where stronger similarity preference suggests highly reserved choice for contact. We study similarity preference in racioethnic diversity since racioethnic diversity and similarity preference both share the characteristic of racioethnic differences. Dissimilarities among group members negatively affect

the group (Milliken & Martins, 1996; Pelled, 1996; Tsui, Egan, & O'Reilly, 1992) whereas similarity in values and demographics facilitate effective work environments (Jehn et al., 1999).

We noted in our first study that diversity was positively related to task conflict despite nationalistic outgroup derogation. Although we offered some speculations (Ayub & Jehn, 2010a) about national diversity being an exceptional opportunity in our sample and the minority influence and competition within such workgroups, we did not have empirical data to explain the results that contradicted our hypothesized role of nationalistic derogation. Thereby, we remained interested in exploring the attitudinal variables that could describe relationships such as the relationship between diversity and task conflict. Therefore, we believed that respect within the group culture despite negative attitudes among group members, could be one reason for positive group processes. Respect has been conceptualized as a feeling of recognition and equality (Lalljee, Laham, & Tam, 2007). Similarity preference, on the contrary, appears to be a state of inequality as people have preferred choices of contact. Therefore, we have an interesting model to study with similarity preference as a negative social attitude and respect as a positive aspect of interpersonal interaction.

We have speculated that restricted contact (as in similarity preference) implies misunderstanding and lack of adequate communication and is positively related to conflicts in workgroups. It is, however, possible that the group norms value diversity (cf. Jehn et al., 1999) and members respect each other despite their differences. The contact anxiety that may be present due to these differences may be compensated by similarity preferences while respecting the individual members as a valuable part of the group. This respect then may compensate for the grievances or issues that arise as a result of similarity preference and thus reduce conflict. That is, we expect that similarity preference will intensify conflict in racioethnic diversity whereas respect will reduce conflict in such workgroups. We, therefore, examine the moderating roles of similarity preference and respect in the relationship between racioethnic diversity and conflict.

Racioethnic Diversity and Efficient Performance

Diversity can be a source of wise perspectives and expertise for higher quality decisions, greater creativity, and innovative ideas in workgroups (Ancona & Caldwell, 1992; Bantel & Jackson, 1989, De Dreu & West, 2001). On the contrary, diversity is often found to negatively affect performance (Harrison, Price, & Bell, 1998; Wiersema & Bantel, 1992). Additionally, there are studies that could not find a relationship between diversity and performance (Kilduff, Angelmar, & Mehra, 2000; Kochan et al., 2003). To explore the relationship between diversity, conflict, and performance, we chose to study how racioethnic diversity is related to conflict and efficient performance with the moderating effects of attitudes and norms.

Diversity may affect performance negatively because of miscommunication and conflict (Wagner, Pfeffer, & O'Reilly, 1984; Watson et al., 1993) but could also have a positive effect under conditions like perceived respect (Kochan et al., 2003). Similarity preference is likely to result in conflict and reduced efficiency due to little contact and communication. We hypothesize that racioethnic diversity will be negatively related to efficiency in the presence of similarity preference. We also hypothesize, however, that racioethnic diversity will be positively related to efficiency when the group members perceive respect. A study of positive and negative moderators simultaneously will help us understand how diversity could positively (or negatively) relate to types of conflict despite certain moderators (as in study 1).

Study 3: Social Attitudes and Respect as Moderators of the Relationship between Diversity and Conflict. To test our model hypotheses, we conducted a field survey with collected cross-cultural data from 3 samples. The data included 541 professionals from 3 industries: information technology, finance corporation, and HR services. The workgroups size ranged to 13 members with a mean group size of 6.64. Most of the participants belonged to the age group of 25–34 years with 243 (43.2%) women. The 3 samples comprised of 137 participants from Pakistan and the two samples from the Netherlands comprised of 105 from one industry and 299 from the other industry. As representative of the workgroups of sample location, the participants in Pakistani sample included Punjabi, Pathan, and Kashmiri ethnicities in majority with few Sindhis, Potoharis, and Balochis. These participants further identified themselves to belong to one of the racial categories within these ethnicities. For example, the Punjabis were Araain, Rajput, or Gujjer while Pathans were Achakzai, Yusufzai, or Aurakzai. The Dutch samples included British, Indian, Chinese, Moroccan, and Germans with few Australians, Brazilians, Italians, Pakistani, and Turkish. These participants identified themselves as White, European, White British, White Latin, Caucasian, Antillean, Asian, Surinamese, Black, and Afro-Dutch.

The participants completed survey questionnaires about a number of group processes and performance for their workgroups. Participants' perception of racioethnic diversity was measured by asking how much the respondents thought their workgroup was diverse with reference to race, ethnicity, and culture (e.g., How diverse is your workgroup in ethnicity?). The items gave an alpha reliability coefficient of .79. We used Reade (2001) and Dekker, Malova, and Haagendoorn (2003) preference subscales to measure similarity preference ("prefer colleagues with shared national background" and "In general, I prefer to have people of my own national background as my work colleagues"). Cronbach alpha coefficient for the preference items was .82. We used two items about perception of respect (Do the group members have a high opinion of one another? Do members in your workgroup respect each other?). The Cronbach reliability coefficient for the respect items was .77. To measure conflicts, we

used Jehn's (1997; Jehn & Mannix, 2001) scales as in study 1 and 2. Cronbach alpha coefficients for task, relationship, and process conflicts were .85, .81, and .86 respectively. We collected supervisor ratings of efficient performance as an objective measure of performance. We also used survey self-report items to measure perceived efficiency of the workgroup members. Gibson, Zellmer-Bruhn, and Schwab's (2003) items were used to measure group efficiency (e.g., This group is effective at getting things done quickly; This group is effective at getting things done in time). The Cronbach alpha coefficients for the three efficiency items were .86. Initially, we controlled for age and gender (Pelled, 1996; Randel, 2002; Segall, Dasen, Berry, & Poortinga, 1990). We also controlled for nationality, industry, group identity, and group size. The effects of our modeled variables remained significant despite controlling for these variables.

Table 6 shows the descriptive statistics for study 3. Regression analyses showed that similarity preference significantly moderated the racioethnic diversity to efficiency relationship such that group efficiency decreased in the presence of reported similarity preference (see Table 7). Interestingly, supervisors rated the groups with higher efficiency for group that reported high similarity preferences among members. This indicated the difference between perceptions of those directly experiencing the group dynamics compared to those who view the group from outside the group. The relationship between racioethnic diversity and perceived group efficiency was positively moderated by perceived respect such that efficiency of racioethnically diverse groups improved in the presence of perceived respect. The results supported our hypotheses for the moderating role of similarity preference and respect in the racioethnic diversity to conflict and efficiency relationship.

Task and process conflicts were high when racioethnic diversity as well as similarity preference was high. Process conflict in racioethnically diverse

Table 6
Descriptive Statistics and Intercorrelations of Eight Variables for Study 3

	M	*SD*	1	2	3	4	5	6	7
1. Racioethnic diversity	3.40	1.77							
2. Similarity preference	2.82	1.69	**–.17****						
3. Respect	5.95	.98	**–.17****	.00					
4. Task conflict	3.34	1.18	**.17****	.03	**–.21****				
5. Relationship conflict	2.29	1.15	**.24****	.07	**–.37****	.52**			
6. Process conflict	2.90	1.23	**.15****	.03	**–.30****	.61**	.57**		
7. Perceived group efficiency	5.36	1.04	–.05	**.19****	**.40****	**–.30****	**–.29****	**–.41****	
8. Supervisor rating	5.13	1.32	.04	.00	–.03	**.10***	**.19****	**.17****	–.055

* $p < .05$. ** $p < .01$.

Table 7
Regression Analysis for the Moderation Effect of Similarity Preference and Respect

	β Efficiency	β Supervisor rating	β TC	β RC	β PC
Racioethnic diversity (RD)	.08	–.00	.16**	.22**	.16**
Cultural preference (CP)	.22**	.01	.06	.11*	.06
Respect (R)	.44**	–.01	–.15**	–.31**	–.26**
R^2	.232	.00	.054	.168	.103
F	37.34**	.02	6.63**	23.77**	13.52**
RD × CP	–.12**	.18**	.12*	.04	.10*
RD × R	–.13**	–.02	–.20**	.16**	.19**
R^2	.259	.029	.101	.192	.144
ΔR^2	.027	.029	.047	.023	.041
F	35.71**	1.86	7.75**	16.61**	11.79**
ΔF	6.70**	4.61*	8.98**	5.05**	8.35**

* $p < .05$. ** $p < .01$.

workgroups was increased in the presence of similarity preference. Similar to our finding in the first study we found again that task conflict was high despite high similarity preference. Respect significantly moderated the relationship between racioethnic diversity and the three conflict types. Respect increased task conflict and helped reduce relationship and process conflicts in racioethnically diverse groups. Hence, respect can be considered as a reason for helping members to pursue tasks as a group despite similarity contact preferences. This shows that when respect is a group norm, issues such as similarity preference that negatively influence group processes, may not be a concern (cf. Jehn & Mannix, 2001).

In addition to the diversity to conflict and efficiency relationships, we also explored the mediating role of conflict in the moderated relationship between racioethnic diversity and efficiency. We computed a series of regression steps for a mediated moderation model (Langfred, 2004). To continue with the mediation analyses, we established the relationship between conflict and efficiency. All three conflict types were significantly related to efficiency. Again, results differed for group members' efficiency reporting from that of supervisors ratings. Conflict negatively related to group members' own perceived efficiency but positively related to the supervisors' ratings of group's performance. Further analyses supported our hypothesis that conflict mediates the relationship between racioethnic diversity and efficiency both for subjective perceptions of efficiency and supervisors' ratings (see Table 8). Conflict partially mediated

Table 8
Regression Analysis for the Mediated Moderation Effect of Cultural Preference

	Efficiency			Supervisor Rating		
	β	B	β	β	β	β
Mediators						
Task conflict	−.31**			.17**		
Relationship conflict		−.28**			.20**	
Process conflict			−.38**			.19**
R^2	.095	.081	.144	.029	.040	.037
F	36.14**	31.03**	59.31**	8.75**	12.45**	11.37**
Interaction Effects						
RD × CP	−.12*	−.11*	−.11*	.17**	.17**	.17**
RD × R	.02	−.01	−.01	−.03	−.04	−.03
R^2	.110	.092	.156	.060	.070	.067
ΔR^2	.016	.011	.011	.031	.030	.031
F	14.23**	11.84**	21.51**	6.24**	7.43**	7.14**
ΔF	3.06*	2.15	2.38	4.87**	4.77**	4.87**

* $p < .05$. ** $p < .01$.

the relationship in the presence of similarity preference while conflict fully mediated the relationship in the presence of perceived respect.

General Discussion

As diversity increases in workgroups, management seeks measures to constitute and manage an effective workforce from diverse members. Whereas diversity has been promoted for reasons of equal opportunities and expected enhanced effectiveness of workgroups, diversity research could not offer very promising findings. Diversity has often been shown to have negative effects on group processes and outcomes with some positive observations under specific circumstances and organizational contexts (Carroll & Harrison, 1998; Jehn & Bezrukova, 2004; Shaw & Barrett-Power, 1998). Since diversity is inevitable in workgroups, research strives to understand and thus find means of using diversity to its advantages.

In this series of studies, we examined how to make use of heterogeneous workforce, such as nationally diverse workgroups and manage its negative effects. Our main contributions and goals of this research were to determine influences of national diversity on workgroup processes (e.g., conflicts) and performance (e.g., efficiency); to determine if social attitudes moderate the relationship between diversity and conflicts; to explore the positive role of

diversity in terms of numerical composition of workgroups; and to verify the generalization of theories and propositions across samples. We contribute to the literature on diversity, conflict, and multinational workgroups by examining the importance of social attitudes and feelings (such as nationalism, social distance, and national stereotypes) that influence the relationships and behavior at workplaces. Whereas diversity research has often explored its negative aspects, we explored positive potential of diversity in terms of numerical composition and positive elements of group culture in terms of perceived respect.

We collected data from multinational organizations and university students with the help of field surveys and scenario studies. We collected data from South Asian and European samples for diverse samples. We noted that such cross-cultural data will not only help explore diversity in socially different workgroup settings but also offer findings that can be generalized across cultures and countries. The first study focused on the perceptions of diversity and intragroup conflict of individual members and their nationalistic attitudes towards their own country and against other countries. We established a basic model introducing nationalism in organizational research and empirically tested the model where we distinguished two aspects of nationalism. We hope this will lead to future research on diversity and conflict with a focus on nationalistic or social attitudes.

Nationality has generally been viewed as demographic diversity and described as social category diversity (e.g., Bayazit & Mannix, 2003; Hinds & Bailey, 2003) with negative consequences on group processes and outcomes. If diversity is viewed or managed appropriately as knowledge diversity in the form of a collection of skills and expertness, diversity such as national diversity can have positive consequences. If nationally diverse groups are managed to encourage a focus on variety of capacities instead of national differences, the efficiency of the groups will improve.

We noticed that research lacks in describing the role of attitudes (social distance) and attributes (stereotypes) in workgroup processes and outcomes such as conflict and performance. Thus far, this is the first study to consider work-related stereotypes and social distances, and their relationship to group processes and outcomes in Pakistan or the South-Asian countries. We studied the potential positive role of diversity in improving performance and found that diversity moderates the negative effects of social distance and national stereotypes on conflict and outcomes. The findings support the value-in-diversity (cf. Jehn et al., 1999) proposition by showing that diversity can be beneficial by moderating the negative effects of variables such as social attitudes and beliefs in workgroups.

Implications for Management

In view of our results, management should realize that national diversity is quite complex and requires awareness and understanding of attitudes and beliefs

of members of various nationalities. Attitudes such as nationalism can be a source of conflicts in nationally diverse workgroups as much as any interaction among members from diverse nationalities. Nationalism is a sensitive issue in the present world due to economic, political, and religious conflicts that should be carefully tackled by management to avoid conflicts among group members. Open communication and clearly defined tasks and responsibilities can reduce misunderstandings and conflict. Managers as well as group members need to learn about diversity, accept it and reflect upon their attitudes toward those who are different, and develop skills for responsive experiences (Manning, 2000). Chances of cross-cultural learning can help members' integration as well as improve performance through coordinated variety of expertise and ideas.

In addition to nationalistic attitudes, managers must be aware of social backgrounds and social differences among the group members and the social distances and stereotypes that come with these social differences and perceptions. We observed in study 3 that supervisors rated the group performance differently from that of the group members. This indicated the differences in perception of those directly involved in group processes and experiences and those who view it from outside and are perhaps uninformed of the true dynamics. Managers should be informed of their as well as group members' social attitudes and perceptions.

Management should form or manage groups in view of nationality faultlines and subgroups prospects so as to avoid negative effects of nationalism, social distances, and national stereotypes. Task interdependence may also facilitate cooperation and interaction and thus should be promoted in view of task type. Members of a highly interdependent group have to resolve their differences so that their progress, which depends on joint efforts, can be achieved. This interdependence could then bring members close as they accept other members as part of the group and respect their contributions. Respect, in turn, will further help in reducing conflict and improve performance. Managers could promote group norms like respect that facilitate positive group processes and outcomes so that the negative influence of similarity preferences can be ameliorated.

In study 3, we noted that similarity preference was lower in diverse groups, but perceived respect was also lower in diverse workgroups. Both the observations have important implications for diversity and conflict management. Grouping members from diverse nationalities can be confusing and stressful for establishing relationships, which reduces perceived respect and likely increase subgrouping due to ingroup preferences, and thus the members experience more conflict. A group with satisfactory performance may be experiencing issues that could ultimately burn out the group members hurting the group integrity and affect performance.

When possible or required, formal re-categorization should be carried out to avoid subgroup segregations and facilitate mutual cooperation and coordination (Kramer & Brewer, 1984; Polzer, Stewart, & Simmons, 1999). For effective re-

categorization, managers should conduct an introductory orientation to clarify the purpose of bringing together a job-focused diverse group. Once groups are selected for certain tasks, management should facilitate positive inclusion and respect. Some of the strategies could be announcing individual performance in terms of team work and cooperation, information sharing, citizenship behavior and such group-focused achievements, reward the best group instead of individuals, and allocate incentives as well as formal structures for cooperation and collaboration. Keeping the focus on the task and task related interaction, relationships could then change at interpersonal and attitudinal levels as well through these strategies. This will ascertain a group with low conflicts and higher performance. Managers should thus provide a safe environment (social and organizational) in view of social attitudes and beliefs to sustain diversity in the workplace.

Limitations and Suggestions for Future Research

Although the sample was representative of workgroups in Pakistan, that is national diversity was very low in workgroups, it also served as a limitation of our study. Due to few nationally diverse workgroups, we could get only a conservative test of our model for national diversity. We, therefore, included a study with racioethnic diversity—a diversity type highly present in workgroups in Pakistan. However, we also remain interested in studying attitudes of Pakistanis (and attitudes of other nationalities towards Pakistanis) and group dynamics outside Pakistan. Such cross-national observations would be an interesting addition to future observations and knowledge as well as offer a verification of our findings.

When studying differences among members such as national differences, distance hierarchy and nationality faultlines (Lau & Murnighan, 1998) should be considered along with social distances from every nationality other than one's own. Depending on the nationalities present in a group and the social distances among those nationalities, national diversity will be more of a problem if subgroups form along nationality faultlines. Subgroup formation endorses certain group attitudes and beliefs and national subgroups may encourage nationalistic attitudes among the subgroup members. Status distances (Phillips & Thomas-Hunt, 2007) and power distances (Hofstede, 1983) may be more significant than social distances for some nationalities and national diversity composition. It seems that status and power distances may even alter social distances such that those held in high prestige or at high status distance could improve group outcomes. Acceptance of one's higher status depends on the positive perception of that distance such as when someone belongs to a social group that has proven to be deserving of high esteem.

In addition to perceived social, status, and power distances, it is important to know how these distances can be altered. Although these distances are

established based on previous direct or indirect learning and experiences, one significant factor that reinforces these distances is assuming other's attitudes and beliefs. One's perceptions are influenced by (mis)perceptions of the other and vice versa (Kenny, 1994). That is, assumptions regarding how another person sees me will affect how I see him. These metaperceptions are perhaps as important for management as are one's own perceptions. Furthermore, individuals within groups have distinctive attitudes and beliefs. To understand group processes based on individual variables, we can consider asymmetry of attitudes and perceptions of group members (Jehn, Greer, Rispens, Barreto, & Rink, 2006; Rispens, Jehn, & Thatcher, 2005). Asymmetry is calculated differences among group members and how these differences influence group processes and outcomes (Jehn & Chatman, 2000). We also observed that respect negatively moderates the positive relationship between diversity and conflict whereas ingroup preferences intensify conflict in diverse workgroups. Future research could also consider if respect can modify nationalistic attitudes such that if group members respect each other, it is probable that they will not favor the ingroup or discriminate the outgroup members, especially if they recognize the contributions of their group members. Research can also explore if respect reduces social distances.

We included efficiency as one of our main outcome variables and hypothesized that group members' attitudes and beliefs (social distance and national stereotypes) affect efficiency, especially through conflict where all types of conflict (task, relationship, and process conflicts) are expected to influence efficiency. It was not surprising that task conflict was also positively related to efficiency. Task conflict can be beneficial to groups in terms of task-specific outcomes such as creativity, innovation, and decision making (e.g., McLeod, Lobel, & Cox, 1996). These outcomes may be valuable to workgroups but are time consuming and thus reduced efficiency. Research should consider task-specific outcomes such as creativity, outcome quality, and decision quality so that we can use task conflict to the possible advantage of workgroups.

Conclusion

In this chapter, we were mainly interested in explaining the relationship between diversity and performance through the moderating effects of social attitudes and beliefs. We began with a basic model and followed it with empirical studies including field surveys in organizations and scenario studies. Starting with nationalistic attitudes, we proposed that nationalism has a negative moderating role in that group members experience more relationship and process conflicts and less task conflict when members of a nationally diverse workgroup hold nationalistic attitudes towards other members within their group. The first empirical study distinguished two elements of nationalism, namely, national preference and nationalistic outgroup derogation. Nationalistic

outgroup derogation was the stronger moderator which increased relationship conflict and task conflict. In our second study, attitudinal variables of social distance and national stereotypes were studied. Social distance and national stereotypes were positively related to conflicts. We also found that diversity could also serve as a moderator of negatively affecting social attitudes and beliefs. The third study further explored the moderating role of social attitude of similarity preference and also perceived respect that could help a group experience positive conflict and perform efficiently. Similarity preference acted as a negative moderator whereas respect positively moderated the relationship between diversity and conflict and performance. In this chapter, we presented empirical studies of the role of social attitudes within workgroup settings and offer practical implications for management as well as suggestions for future research in diversity and conflict management.

References

Ancona, D. G., & Caldwell, D. F. (1992). Demography and design: Predictors of new product team performance. *Organization Science, 5*, 321–341.

Armstrong, D. J., & Cole, P. (1995). Managing distances and differences in geographically distributed work groups. In S. E. Jackson & M. N. Rudderman (Eds.), *Diversity in work teams: Research paradigms for a changing workplace* (pp. 187–216). Washington, DC: American Psychological Association.

Ayub, N., & Jehn, K. A. (2010a). The Moderating influence of nationalism on the relationship between national diversity and conflict. *Negotiation and Conflict Management Research, 3*, 249–275.

Ayub, N., & Jehn, K. A. (2010b). *National diversity and conflict: The role of social attitudes and beliefs*. Unpublished doctoral dissertation, Leiden University, the Netherlands.

Ayub, N., & Jehn, K. A (2006). National diversity and conflict in multinational workgroups: A theoretical model of the moderating effect of nationalism. *International Journal of Conflict Management, 17*, 181–202.

Bantel, K., & Jackson, S. E. (1989).Top management and innovation in banking: Does the composition of the top team make a difference? *Strategic Management Journal, 10*, 107–124.

Barreto, M., & Ellemers, N. (2009).Multiple identities and the paradox of social inclusion. In F. Butera & J. M. Levine (Eds.), *Coping with minority status: Responses to exclusion and inclusion* (pp. 269–292). Cambridge, UK: Cambridge University Press.

Bayazit, M., & Mannix, E. A. (2003), Should I stay or should I go? Predicting team members' intent to remain in the team. *Small Group Research, 34*, 290–321.

Bogardus, E. S. (1967). Measuring social distances. In M. Fishbein (Ed.), *Readings in attitude theory and measurement* (pp. 71–76). New York: Wiley.

Bogardus, E. (1933). A social distance scale. *Sociology and Social Research*, 22, 265–271.

Bower, C. A., Pharmer, J. A., & Salas, E. (2000). When member homogeneity is needed in work teams: A meta-analysis. *Small Group Research, 31*, 305–327.

Brewer, M. B. (2000). Reducing prejudice through cross-categorization: effects of multiple social identities. In S. Oskamp (Ed.), *Reducing prejudice and discrimina-*

tion. The Claremont Symposium on Applied Social Psychology (pp. 165–183). Mahwah, NJ: Erlbaum.

Brief, A. P., Umphress, E. E., Dietz, J., Burrows, J. W., Butz, R. M., Scholten, L. (2005). Community matters: Realistic group conflict theory and the impact of diversity. *Academy of Management Journal, 48*, 830–844.

Caroll, G. R., & Harrison, J. R. (1998). Organizational demography and culture: Insights from a formal model and simulation. *Administrative Science Quarterly, 43*, 637–667.

Chan D. K., & Goto, S. G. (2003). Conflict resolutions in the culturally diverse workgroups: Some data from Hong Kong employees. *Applied Psychology: An International Review, 52*, 441–460.

Cox, T. (2004). Problems with research by organizational scholars on issues of race and ethnicity. *Journal of Applied Behavioral Science, 40*, 124–145.

Cox, T. H., & Blake, S. (1991). Managing cultural diversity: Implications for organizational competitiveness. *Academy of Management Executive, 5* (3), 45–56.

Cramton, C. D., & Hinds, P. J. (2005). Subgroup dynamics in internationally distributed teams: Ethnocentrism or cross-national learning? *Research in Organizational Behavior, 26*, 231–263.

Dahlin, K. B., Weingart, L. R., & Hinds, P. A. (2005). Team diversity and information use. *Academy of Management Journal, 48*, 1107–1123.

De Dreu, C. K. W., Harinck, F., & Van Vianen, A. E. M. (1999). Conflict and performance in groups and organizations. In C. L. Cooper & I. T. Robertson (Eds.), *International review of industrial and organizational psychology* (Vol. 14, pp. 369–414). Chichester, UK: Wiley.

De Dreu, C. K. W., & Weingart, L. R. (2003). Task versus relationship conflict, team performance, and team member satisfaction: A meta-analysis. *Journal of Applied Psychology, 88*, 741–749.

De Dreu, C. K., & West, M. A. (2001). Minority dissent and team innovation: The importance of participation in decision making. *Journal of Applied Psychology, 86*, 1191–1201.

Dekker, H., Malová, D., & Hoogendoorn, S. (2003). Nationalism and its explanations. *Political Psychology, 24*, 345–376.

Dennen, J. M. G. (1987). Ethnocentrism and in-group/out-group differentiation: A review and interpretation of the literature. In V. Reynolds, V. Falger & I. Vine. (Eds.), *The sociobiology of ethnocentrism: Evolutionary dimensions of xenophobia, discrimination, racism and nationalism* (pp. 1–47). London: Croom Helm.

Gibson, C. B., Zellmer-Bruhn, M. E., & Schwab, D. P. (2003). Team effectiveness in multinational organizations: Evaluation across contexts. *Group Organization Management, 28*, 444–474.

Earley, P. C., & Mosakowski, E. (2000). Creating hybrid team cultures: An empirical test of transnational team functioning. *Academy of Management Journal, 43*, 26–49.

Greenwald, A. G., & Banaji, M. R. (1995). Implicit Social Cognition: Attitudes, Self-Esteem, and Stereotypes. *Psychological Review, 102*, 4–27.

Hagendoorn, L., & Kleinpenning, G. (1991). The contribution of domain-specific stereotypes to ethnic social distance. *British Journal of Social Psychology, 30*, 63–78.

Hamilton, D. L., & Sherman, J. W. (1994). Stereotypes. In R. S. Wyer, Jr. & T. K. Srull (Eds.), *Handbook of social cognition* (2nd ed., pp. 1–68). Hillsdale, NJ: Erlbaum.

Harrison, D. A., Price, K. H., & Bell, M. P. (1998). Beyond relational demography: Time and the effects of surface- and deep-level diversity on work group cohesion. *Academy of Management Journal, 41*, 96–107.

Haslam, S. A., Turner, J. C., Oakes, P. J., McGarty, C., & Hayes, B. K. (1992). Context-dependent variation in social stereotyping: I. The effects of intergroup relations

as mediated by social change and frame of reference. *European Journal of Social Psychology, 22*, 3–20.

Hicks-Clarke, D., & Illes, P. (2000). Climate for diversity and its effects on career and organizational attitudes and perceptions. *Personnel Review, 29*, 324–345.

Hinds, P., & Bailey, D. (2003). Out of sight, out of sync: Understanding conflict in distributed teams. *Organization Science, 14*, 615–632.

Hofstede, G. (1983). National cultures in four dimensions: A research-based theory of cultural differences among nations. *International Studies of Management and Organization, 13* (1–2), 46–74.

Homan, A. C., van Knippenberg, D., van Kleef, G. A., & De Dreu, C. K. W. (2007). Bridging faultlines by valuing diversity: Diversity beliefs, information elaboration, and performance in diverse work groups. *Journal of Applied Psychology, 92*, 1189–1199.

Hopkins, N., Regan, M., & Abell, J. (1997). On the context dependence of national stereotypes: Some Scottish data. *British Journal of Social Psychology, 36*, 553–563.

Jehn, K. (1997). A qualitative analysis of conflict types and dimensions in organizational groups. *Administrative Science Quarterly, 42*, 530–557.

Jehn, K. A. (1995). A multidimensional examination of the benefits and detriments of intragroup conflict. *Administrative Science Quarterly, 40*, 256–282.

Jehn, K. A., & Bezrukova, K. (2004). A field study of group diversity, workgroup context, and performance. *Journal of Organizational Behavior, 25*, 703–729.

Jehn, K. A., & Chatman, J. A. (2000). The influence of proportional and perceptual conflict composition on team performance. *International Journal of Conflict Management, 11*, 56–73.

Jehn, K., Greer, L., Rispens, S., Barreto, M., & Rink, F. (2006, August). *The roots and effects of asymmetric conflict perceptions*. Paper presented at the annual meeting of the Academy of Management, Atlanta, GA.

Jehn, K. A., & Mannix, E. (2001). The dynamic nature of conflict: A longitudinal study of intragroup conflict and group performance. *Academy of Management Journal, 44*, 238–251.

Jehn, K. A., Northcraft, G. B., & Neale, M. A. (1999). Why differences make a difference: A field study of diversity, conflict, and performance in workgroups. *Administrative Science Quarterly, 44*, 741–763.

Johnson, D., Terry, D. J., & Louis, W. R. (2005). Perceptions of the intergroup structure and anti-Asian prejudice among white Australians. *Group Processes & Intergroup Relations, 8*, 53–71.

Kenny, D. A. (1994). *Interpersonal perception: A social relations analysis*. New York: Guilford Press.

Kilduff, M., Angelmar, R., & Mehra, A. (2000). Top management team diversity and firm performance. *Organization Science, 11*, 21–34.

Kinket, B., & Verkuyten, M. (1999). Intergroup evaluations and social context: A multilevel approach. *European Journal of Social Psychology, 29*, 219–237.

Kirchmeyer, C. (1993). Multicultural task groups: An account of the low contribution level of minorities. *Small Group Research, 24*, 127–148.

Kirchmeyer, C., & Cohen, A. (1992). Multicultural groups: Their performance and reactions with constructive conflict. *Group & Organization Management, 17*, 153–170.

Kochan, T., Bezrukova, K., Ely, R., Jackson, S., Joshi, A., Jehn, K., Leonard, J., Levine, D., & Thomas, D. (2003). The effects of diversity on business performance: Report of the diversity research network. *Human Resource Management, 42* (1), 3–21.

Kramer, R. M., & Brewer, M. B. (1984). Effects of group identity on resource use in a simulated commons dilemma. *Journal of Personality and Social Psychology, 46*, 1044–1057.

Lalljee, M., Laham, S., & Tam, T. (2007). Unconditional respect for persons: A social psychological analysis. *Gruppendynamik und Organisationsberatung* [*Group Dynamics and Organization Consulting*], *38,* 451–464.
Langfred, C. W. (2004). Too much of a good thing? Negative affects of high trust and individual autonomy in self-managing teams. *Academy of Management Journal, 47,* 385–399.
Lau, D. C., & Murnighan, J. K. (1998). Demography diversity and faultlines: The compositional dynamics of organizational groups. Academy *of Management Review, 23,* 325–340.
Lawrence, B. S. (1997). The black box of organizational demography. *Organization Science, 8,* 1–22.
Manning, M. L. (2000, Winter). Understanding diversity, accepting others: Realities and directions. *Educational Horizons*, pp. 125–127.
Mannix, E., & Neale, M. A. (2005). What differences make a difference? The promise and reality of diverse teams in organizations. *Psychological Science in the Public Interest, 62,* 31–55.
McLeod, P. L., Lobel, S. A., & Cox, T. H. (1996). Ethnic diversity and creativity in small groups. *Small Group Research, 27,* 248–264.
Milliken, F., & Martins, L. (1996). Searching for common threads: Understanding the multiple effects of diversity in organizational groups. *Academy of Management Review, 21,* 402–433.
Mor-Barak, M. E., Cherin, D. A., & Berkman, S. (1998). A tool to expand organizational understanding of workforce diversity: Exploring a measure of inclusion–exclusion. *Administration in Social Work, 22* (1), 47–64.
Ogbonna, E., & Harris, L. C. (2006). The dynamics of employee relationships in an ethnically diverse workforce. *Human Relations,* 59, 379–407.
O'Reilly, C., Caldwell, D., & Barnett, W. (1989). Work group demography, social integration, and turnover. *Administrative Science Quarterly, 34,* 21–37.
Pelled, L. H. (1996). Demographic diversity, conflict, and work group outcomes: An intervening process theory. *Organization Science, 7,* 615–631.
Pettigrew, T. F., & Meertens, R. W. (1995). Subtle and blatant prejudice in Western Europe. *European Journal of Social Psychology, 25,* 57–75.
Phillips, K. W., & Thomas-Hunt, M. C. (2007). Garnering the benefits of conflict: The role of diversity and status distance in groups. In L. Thompson & K. Behfar (Eds.), *Conflict in organizational teams: New directions in theory and practice* (pp. 37–56). Evanston, IL: Northwestern University Press.
Pitts, D. W. (2005). Diversity, representation, and performance: Evidence about race and ethnicity in public organizations. *Journal of Public Administration Research and Theory, 15,* 615–631.
Polzer, J. T., Stewart, K. J. & Simmons, J. L. (1999). A social categorization explanation for framing effects in nested social dilemmas. *Organizational Behavior and Human Decision Processes, 79,* 154–178.
Randel, A. E. (2002). Identity salience: A moderator of the relationship between group gender composition and work group conflict. *Journal of Organizational behavior, 23,* 749–766.
Reade, C. (2001). The antecedents of organizational identification in multinational corporations: Fostering psychological attachment to the local subsidiary and the global organization. *International Journal of Human Resource Management, 12,* 1269–1291.
Rijswijk, W., & Ellemers, N. (2002). Context effects on the application of stereotype content to multiple categorizable targets. *Personality and Social Psychology Bulletin, 28,* 90–101.

Rispens, S., Jehn, K.A., & Thatcher, S. (2005). *Asymmetric conflict in workgroups: Effects on group processes and performance.* Work and Organizational Psychology Conference, Rotterdam, The Netherlands.

Roberson, L., & Block, C. J. (2001). Racioethnicity and job performance: A review and critique of theoretical perspectives on the causes of group differences. *Research in Organizational Behavior, 23*, 247–325.

Segall, M. H., Dasen, P. R., Berry, J. W., & Poortinga, Y. H. (1990). *Human behavior in global perspective: An introduction to cross-cultural psychology*. New York: Pergamon.

Shaw, J. B., & Barrett-Power, E. (1998). The effects of diversity on small work group processes and performance. *Human Relations, 51*, 1307–1325.

Thatcher, S. M. B., & Jehn, K. A. (1998). A model of group diversity profiles and categorization processes in bicultural organizational teams. *Research on Managing Groups and Temas, 1*, 1–20.

Townsend, A. M., & Scott, K. D. (2001). Team racial composition, members' attitudes, and performance: A field study. *International Relations, 40*, 317–337.

Triandis, H. (1994). *Culture and social behavior.* New York: McGraw-Hill.

Tsui, A. S., Egan, T. & O'Reilly, C. A. (1992). Being different: Relational demography and organizational attachment. *Administrative Science Quarterly,* 37, 549–79.

Turner, J. C., Hogg, M. A., Oakes, P. J., Reicher, S. D., & Wetherell, M. S. (1987). *Rediscovering the social group: A self-categorization theory*. Oxford: Blackwell.

Van Knippenberg, D., & Schippers, M. C. (2007). Work group diversity. In M. I. Posner & M. K. Rothbart (Eds.), *Annual review of psychology* (Vol. 58, pp. 515–541). Palo Alto, CA: Annual Reviews.

Verkuyten, M., & Hagendoorn, L. (2002). In-group favoritism and self-esteem: The Role of identity level and trait valence. *Group Processes & Intergroup Relations, 5*, 285–297.

Wagner, G. W., Pfeffer, J., & O'Reilly, C. A. (1984). Organizational demography and turnover in top-management groups. *Administrative Science Quarterly, 29*, 74–92.

Watson, W. E., Kumar, K., & Michaelsen, L. K. (1993). Cultural diversity's impact on interaction process and performance: Comparing homogeneous and diverse task groups. *Academy of Management Journal, 36*, 590–602.

Wiersema, M. F., & Bantel, K. A. (1992). Top management team demography and corporate strategic change. *Academy of Management Journal, 35*, 91–121.

Williams, K. Y., & O'Reilly, C. A. (1998). Demography and diversity in organizations: A review of 40 years of research. *Research in Organizational Behavior, 20*, 77–140.

Zenger, T. R., & Lawrence, B. S. (1989). Organizational demography: The differential effects of age and tenure distributions on technical communication. *Academy of Management Journal, 32*, 353–376.

Current Topics in Management, **Vol. 15, 2011, pp. 41-62**

MODERATING EFFECTS OF GEOGRAPHIC DISPERSION AND TEAM TENURE ON THE TASK–AFFECTIVE CONFLICT RELATIONSHIP

Patricia J. Holahan, Ann C. Mooney, and Laura Finnerty Paul

Advances in information and communication technologies have provided teams the opportunity to communicate virtually, without dependence on face-to-face communication. This has made it possible for organizations to assemble teams from around the globe that wouldn't otherwise be formed. As a result, organizations in almost all fields—e.g., science, engineering, and education—are in a better position to compose teams that leverage and combine diverse knowledge, skills, and resources to innovate and improve performance.

While technology has allowed organizations to capitalize on benefits of comprising more diverse and geographically disperse teams, geographical dispersion also presents formidable challenges to the team's functioning. One of these challenges, researchers have found, is that team conflict often is exacerbated when working in a distributed environment (Kankanhalli, Tan, & Wei, 2006; Staples & Zhao, 2006). Understanding conflict in distributed teams is important because conflict has been shown to have direct effects on decision making processes and outcomes (Amason, 1996). If managed right, task-related conflict can be kept constructive and may improve team outcomes. If left unchecked, conflict may spiral into more destructive personal, or affective, conflict that distracts team members from the tasks at hand and jeopardizes team performance (Mooney, Holahan, & Amason, 2007).

While much of the conflict research has been focused on face-to-face teams, the research on conflict in distributed teams is growing (e.g., Hinds & Mortensen, 2005; Mortensen & Hinds, 2001; Kankanhalli et al., 2006/2007; Polzer, Crisp, Jarvenpaa, & Kim, 2006). Despite this growth, we still have much

to understand. First, few empirical studies of conflict have actually examined conflict in both distributed and co-located teams. Our research is conducted using a sample that includes both geographically distributed teams and co-located comparison teams. Second, one of the areas that has gone largely unexplored in empirical studies of conflict and geographic dispersion is how geographic dispersion impacts an important aspect of conflict and conflict management—the relationship *between* task and affective conflict. In this study, we examine the relationship between task and affective conflict in distributed teams. We suggest the relationship between task conflict and affective conflict is a critical link if distributed teams are to effectively manage conflict. The focus of our research is consistent with the plea by Martins, Gilson, and Maynard (2004) who call for greater research emphasis on the management of conflict in distributed teams. Our research examines two questions. Might the positive linkage between task and affective conflict be stronger in geographically distributed teams—making the management of conflict even more problematic in the distributed context? And, what is the effect of team tenure on the task–affective conflict link?

Literature Review and Hypotheses

Task and Affective Conflict

Managing conflict is not an easy task because conflict is multi-dimensional. Although Conlon and Jehn (2010) recently suggested there may also be additional forms conflict, research to date has focused almost exclusively on two forms. One form of conflict is referred to in the literature as task conflict (Jehn, 1994). Task conflict occurs when team members offer and debate varying perspectives that relate directly to the tasks at hand. The other form of conflict is affective conflict, which occurs when team members offer and debate varying perspectives related to issues that are more personal and emotional in nature (Jehn, 1994).

While a 2003 meta-analysis by DeDreu and Weingart suggested that both task and affective conflict are associated with lower team performance, the studies they reviewed generally examined the effects of task and affective conflict separately, without controlling for the other form of conflict. We suspect that this potentially biased their results because, as we discuss, there is strong evidence that task and affective conflict are difficult to separate. Conlon and Jehn (2010) also argued that the types of teams, tasks, and outcomes in the studies DeDreu and Weingart (2003) reviewed were limited and might have influenced their results.

Indeed, researchers have long argued that task conflict is generally constructive while relationship conflict is generally destructive for team decision making. Task conflict has been shown to be constructive for team decision making because it encourages the exchange of ideas and the surfacing of assumptions,

which ultimately leads to a synthesis of perspectives into a decision by the team that is superior to any individual team member's perspective (Amason, 1996). Accordingly, researchers have found task conflict to relate positively to decision quality and the understanding and acceptance of decisions (Amason, 1996; Jehn, 1997). Affective conflict has been shown to be destructive for team decision making because it distracts the team from critical tasks and degrades the quality and affective acceptance of decisions reached by the team (Amason, 1996).

Thus, the main objective for conflict management is actually rather simple: keep conflict constructive by gaining the benefits of task conflict while avoiding the costs of affective conflict (Amason & Sapienza, 1997). The difficulty comes into play when carrying out this prescription because task and affective conflict are difficult to separate (Eisenhardt, Kahwajy, & Bourgeois, 1997). Task and affective conflict often occur together, as evidenced by the strong positive correlations ($r = .60$ and above) reported in the literature (e.g., Simons & Peterson, 2000).

Researchers seeking to disentangle task and affective conflict have explored the mechanisms by which the two forms of conflict are related. Although other explanations have been offered (e.g., that task and relationship conflict share some similar determinants, Jehn, 1995, 1994), more recent evidence suggests that the effect is largely explained by the tendency for task conflict to trigger affective conflict during decision making (Mooney et al., 2007). These researchers argue that attribution and social judgment processes explain why task conflict and affective conflict are so closely linked.

According to attribution theory, team members constantly try to interpret other team members' intentions and motivations during decision making (Harvey & Weary, 1985). When the perspectives offered by other team members are different from their own, team members have a tendency to rationalize the differing perspectives by making attributions about the individuals who offered the perspectives (Fiske & Taylor, 1991). When team members' viewpoints are viewed as highly subjective and/or difficult to justify, other members may misinterpret those viewpoints and attribute them to being motivated by more sinister intentions, such as political game-playing (Creed & Miles, 1996). This tendency to misinterpret underlying motives when uncertainty is high, or trust is low, is also supported by social judgment theory (Hagafors & Brehmer, 1983). Thus, attribution and social judgment theories provide theoretical rationales for why task conflict may indeed trigger affective conflict.

Geographic Distribution and Task–Affective Conflict Link

While many studies have been published on the topic of team conflict in distributed teams, most have examined conflict in general and have not separated out the different types of conflict (i.e., task and affective conflict) or explored

how the two types of conflict relate to each other. The handful of studies that have examined task conflict and affective conflict in distributed teams have looked at antecedents of conflict (Hinds & Mortensen, 2005; Kankanhalli et al., 2006; Mortensen & Hinds, 2001; Polzer et al., 2006; Staples & Zhao, 2006), moderators of the antecedents of conflict (Hinds & Mortensen, 2005; Mortensen & Hinds, 2001; Polzer et al,. 2006), implications of conflict on outcomes such as performance and attitudes (Hinds & Mortensen 2005, Kankanhalli et al., 2006, Mortensen & Hinds 2001; Staples & Zhao, 2006), and potential moderators of the conflict–performance relationship (Kankanhalli et al. 2006).

Much of the theorizing about team processes in distributed teams is drawn from the literature concerning the effects of technology mediated communication on social information and social influence processes. A fundamental premise of these theories is that communication mediated by technology carries less social information than face-to-face communication (e.g., Lea & Spears, 1992). For example, Sproull and Kielser (1986) argue that compared to face-to-face communication, technology mediated communication contains fewer social context cues.

Cramton (2002, 2001) and Cramton, Orvis, and Wilson (2007) built upon this notion and proposed a link between reduced situational understanding and the attribution process. Cramton et al. (2007) argue that geographically distributed team members rely on dispositional attributions rather than situational attributions as explanations for team members' negative behavior. For example, Cramton et al. (2007) argue that a remote partner would be more likely to conclude that a team member was uncommitted or unreliable in the absence of situational information regarding factors that may have contributed to the observed behavior problem (e.g., a technology problem). Cramton and her colleagues call the absence of situational information that exists in distributed teams "situation invisibility." Cramton et al.'s 2007 study supported the finding that in lieu of observing (or being given information suggesting) situational causes, geographically distributed partners resort to making negative dispositional attributions about their partner's behavior. These findings suggest that in distributed environments, where situation invisibility is high, team members will invoke a greater number of dispositional (versus situational) attributions in their attempts to interpret and understand team member behavior. Thus, it appears members of distributed teams are inclined toward negative dispositional attributions about team members when they lack situational information to help them interpret behavioral shortcomings of their fellow team members (Cramton 2002; Cramton et al., 2007). Based on this theory, it follows that when members of distributed teams disagree, there may be a greater tendency to invoke dispositional attributions—e.g., the other member(s) are stubborn, uncooperative, self-serving, etc.—rather than task-related attributions as the underlying reason for the disagreement.

A second stream of literature that supports the notion that task conflict may lead to more affective conflict in geographically distributed teams is the work on media effects. According to media synchronicity theory (Dennis, Fuller, & Valacich, 2008), communication technologies differ in the extent to which they enable synchronous collaboration and in how "rich" or "lean" they are as communication channels. Richness is defined as "the ability of information to change understanding in a timely manner, or the clarity with which information can be communicated through a specific channel in a way that reduces information ambiguity in a timely manner" (Maruping & Agarwal, 2004, p. 977). For example, desktop videoconferencing is relatively high in media richness and synchronicity, while email is not. Lower levels of synchronicity and richness require more time for comprehension of the information.

Media synchronicity theory proposes that task performance will be improved when the information needs of the task are matched to the medium's information richness (Dennis et al., 2008). For example, media capable of transmitting "rich" information (e.g., face-to-face meetings) are better suited to tasks where there are multiple interpretations or ambiguities in the information and less "rich" or lean media (e.g., email) are better suited to tasks where equivocality or ambiguity in the information is low. As a result, researchers have found that lean communication media (e.g., email) often lead to misinterpretation of communications and consequently affective conflict (Griffith, Mannix, & Neale, 2003). Further, the diminished non-verbal and visual cues associated with leaner and asynchronous communication media have been cited as reasons why distributed teams are less able to make inferences about member's knowledge and are less able to anticipate team members' responses (Cramton, 2002). Thus, when teams debate differing task-related perspectives and attempt to reach mutual understanding and agreement by exploring the nuances of their differing perspectives and reconciling these differences, it is more likely that this process could go awry and invoke more affective conflict in teams where situation invisibility is high and there is greater reliance on lean communication technologies. The effects of lean communication technologies on conflict in geographically distributed teams may be further exacerbated by the fact the geographically distributed teams are often more diverse in composition (e.g., little or no shared work history, greater cultural diversity, greater diversity of functional expertise, etc.), which makes interpretation of meaning in members' communications even more problematic.

Finally, several researchers have observed that uninhibited behavior such as swearing, name-calling, and insults are significantly greater in groups that rely on technology mediated communication than in face-to-face groups (e.g., Siegel, Dubrovsky, Kiesler, & McGuire, 1986; Sproull & Kiesler, 1986). The use of harsh language in geographically distributed teams may result in what started out as task conflict triggering affective conflict (Simons & Peterson, 2000).

Taken together Cramton et al.'s (2007) work on situation invisibility, the work on lean communication media (e.g., Cramton, 2001; Griffith et al., 2003), and the increased use of harsh language in distributed teams (Siegel et al., 1986; Sproull & Kiesler, 1986) support the tendency for task conflict to be more likely to trigger affective conflict during decision making in geographically distributed teams who rely more on technology mediated communication than in co-located teams. Thus, we offer the following hypotheses:

> *Hypothesis* 1: Geographic distribution will moderate the relationship between task conflict and affective conflict, such that the task conflict–affective conflict link will be stronger in geographically distributed teams.

Team Tenure and Conflict

Team tenure (the amount of time a team has been working together) has been shown to be an important determinant of team process (e.g., Tihanyi, Ellstrand, Daily, & Dalton, 2000). Katz (1982) found long tenure to be associated with increased information sharing and reduced conflict in co-located teams. Gersick and Hackman (1990) observed in traditional teams that, over time, as team members develop experience with one another, roles and norms take root. On the other hand, both co-located and distributed teams with little past experience working together, or shared history, have been found to lack effective patterns of information sharing and working together (Gibson & Gibbs, 2006; Mortensen & Hinds, 2001).

While the preponderance of research on how team tenure affects team process has been conducted with co-located teams, it is widely held that socialization processes and the development of shared identity are two factors that relate to teams' ability to effectively manage conflict (Mannix, Griffith, & Neale, 2002; Mortenson & Hinds, 2001; Hinds & Mortenson, 2005). Socialization is a process whereby team members learn and identify with team-level behavioral norms and rules. Team members learn these behavioral norms and rules via exposure to one another, conformity pressures, and by the team's active monitoring and enforcement of these norms—i.e., sanctions are applied when team members violate these norms. When team-level norms are clearly established and conformity to these norms is high, confusion and misattributions about team members' should be reduced. Thus, over time as socialization occurs and team norms take root team members should have a better foundation for making sense of each others' behavior, potentially mitigating harsh attributions and decreasing affective conflict.

Several researchers have documented the importance of shared team identity—team members identifying with one another and the team as whole—in managing conflict and cooperation within teams (Mannix et al., 2002; Moore, Kurtzberg, Thompson, & Morris, 1999). Shared identity impacts the relationship between heterogeneity and conflict. It is widely held that heterogeneous groups

are less integrated, have less communication and experience more conflict (Pelled et al., 1999). Over time, as teams develop shared identity perceived similarities increase and perceived differences decrease. As team members perceive greater similarities, negative attributions among team members decrease and conflict resolution and consensus building are facilitated (Moore et al., 1999). The notion of shared identity is particularly relevant for distributed teams as they tend to be more heterogeneous than co-located teams. Hinds and Mortensen (2005) found that an increase in shared team identity was associated with a decrease in affective conflict for geographically distributed teams. While Mortensen and Hinds (2001) found that an increase in shared team identity was associated with decreases in both task and affective conflict for geographically distributed teams. As teams develop shared identity, we expect the extent to which task conflict triggers affective conflict will lessen. In sum, shared understanding around norms, roles, and goals, and shared identity should lessen the effects geographic distribution and improve the team's ability to keep conflict task-oriented.

The difficulties distributed teams experience in developing shared identity and shared norms are, in part, believed to be the result of the fact that a majority of their communication is technology mediated—i.e., less rich and less synchronous compared to traditional, face-to-face teams. However, Carlson and Zmud's (1999) channel expansion theory proposes that "[lean] communication media can be perceived as being rich…if, over time, communicators become accustomed to using the medium and have developed a system of understanding each other" (Maruping & Agarwal, 2004, p. 981). Thus, as distributed teams develop experience with one another and shared identity and shared norms take root, channel expansion theory would predict that the limitations of less synchronous and lean communication technologies are lessened.

In sum, we propose a three-way interaction, i.e., that team tenure (the amount of time a team has been working together) will moderate the interaction between geographic dispersion and conflict.

> *Hypothesis* 2: Team tenure will moderate the interaction between geographic dispersion and conflict, such that with longer team tenure the task conflict–affective conflict link in geographically dispersed teams will be weakened.

Method

Sample and Procedure

To test our hypotheses, we gathered data from 94 project teams (612 individuals) in 79 companies in the New York metropolitan area, operating in 8 industries, including manufacturing, pharmaceuticals, telecommunications, computer hardware/software, government defense, financial services, consumer products, and consumer electronics. Our use of project teams is consistent

with the type of groups examined in much of the conflict research from which we draw (Jehn, 1994, 1995, 1997; Jehn & Mannix, 2001; Pelled et al., 1999). Findings from studies of top management teams (Amason & Sapienza, 1997; Amason & Mooney, 1999) should also have relevance to the decision making behaviors of the teams in our sample as these teams were focused on complex, strategic issues. Examples of the issues being addressed by the teams in the sample include new product and service development, vendor selection, customer service issues, and order fulfillment problems.

The teams were identified and accessed through team members enrolled in an Executive Master of Technology Management (EMTM) program at a leading university. Participants in this program average 32 years of age and all hold management level positions. Managers in the EMTM program were made aware of the study and asked if a team in which they were involved at their organizations would participate. Each EMTM manager identified a project team within his or her organization. Participation by these teams, however, was voluntary. The manager, referred to in the paper as the "team representative" was the primary contact. On average, we received 6.5 responses per team, with one of those responses being the team representative. Of the 612 individual responses then, 94 (one from each team) were from the EMTM program; the remaining 518 (85%) respondents were not. Since students represented such a small percentage of the overall sample, we are reasonably confident that the program did not bias the responses and study results.

Data were collected via two survey instruments: (1) a team information sheet, and (2) a team member survey. The team information sheet was completed only by the team leader and was used to collect objective, descriptive data about the team and the project. The team member survey was completed by all the team members, including the team leader, and was designed to collect data about team dynamics and team member interactions. The surveys were distributed to the team members, including the team leader, by the team representative.

From each of the 97 teams contacted, we received an information sheet (from each team leader) and team member surveys from multiple team members. In three of the 97 cases, less than one-third of the team responded. As a result, these teams were dropped from the study. The final sample then was 94 teams, which yielded a response rate of 97%. The average size of the teams, as reported by the team leader, was 9.5 members and we received, on average, 6.5 responses per team, a within-team response rate of 68%. For 74 (79%) of the teams, 50% or more of the team responded. Thus, we are reasonably confident that the data represented the collective views of the teams.

Measurement

Task Conflict. Task conflict was measured on the team member survey with four items used by Pelled et al. (1999) and Jehn (1994). Responses were pro-

vided on a 5-point Likert scale ranging from 1 ("none") to 5 ("a great deal"). Sample items included, "How often did the members of your team debate or discuss different ideas about how things should be done? And, "To what extent were there different ideas and opinions expressed during this project?" Cronbach's alpha for the task conflict scale was .79. To justify aggregation we calculated r_{wg}. R_{wg} provides a measure of within group agreement, also referred to as within group inter-rater reliability (James, Demaree, & Wolf 1993). R_{wg} for the task conflict scale was .85

Affective Conflict. Affective conflict was measured on the team member survey with 4 items used by Pelled et al. (1999) and Jehn (1994). Responses were provided on a 5-point Likert scale, ranging from 1 ("none") to 5 ("a great deal"). Sample items included, "How often did people get angry while working in this team? And, "To what extent were there personal clashes within the team during this project?" Cronbach's alpha and r_{wg} for the relationship scale were .88 and .84, respectively.

The resulting r_{wg} for both task and affective conflict suggested a high level of agreement among team members. Thus, we believe we are justified in aggregating individual team member's responses to obtain team-level measures.

Geographic Dispersion. Similar to Hinds and Mortensen (2005), we measured geographic dispersion using self-report information from the team leader which identified the distribution of the team members' office locations. We identified co-located teams as those teams where the team leader indicated the majority of the team's members were located in the same building. Fifty-percent of our sample fell within this classification. We identified geographically dispersed teams as those teams where the team leader indicated the majority of the team's members were not located in the same building. When testing our hypotheses we coded teams where the majority of its team's members were located in the same building as "0"; and all others (distributed teams) as "1."

Team Tenure. We measured team tenure by having the team leader indicate the time the team had worked together in months.

Team Size. Finally, to control for conflict that might arise from the coordination requirements faced by larger teams, we measured team size. These data were collected from the team leaders who indicated the number of team members involved in the project.

Analysis and Results

Descriptive statistics and zero-order correlations are provided in Table 1. Consistent with most studies, task and affective conflict were positively correlated ($r = .61$). To test the discriminant validity of task and affective conflict, we conducted exploratory factor analyses. The scale items loaded onto two distinct factors and the factor loadings suggest a high degree of within-factor convergence and between-factor discrimination.

Table 1
Means, Standard Deviations, and Correlations

Variable	*Mean*	*SD*	1	2	3	4
1. Affective conflict	2.16	.69				
2. Team size	9.58	5.86	.19†			
3. Task conflict	2.94	.61	.61*	.09		
4. Geographic dispersion	.50	.50	–.003	.18	–.03	
5. Team tenure	16.82	13.34	.167	–.01	.16	.07

Note: $N = 94$
* $p < .05$. ** $p < .01$.

Hierarchical Regression Analyses

Hypotheses 1 and 2 were tested using hierarchical regression. Hypothesis 1 stated that the relationship between task and affective conflict would be stronger when teams were geographically dispersed than when teams were co-located. In other words, we expected that geographic dispersion would moderate the relationship between task and affective conflict. To test the moderation, we regressed affective conflict on the predictor (task conflict) and the moderator (geographic dispersion) while controlling for team size (Steps 1 and 2, Table 2). We then included the interaction term, which was formed by multiplying geographic dispersion and task conflict (Step 3, Table 2). Before multiplying the variables included in the interaction term, the variables were centered around the mean to minimize multicollinearity (Aiken & West, 1991). The final model produced an R^2 of .41 and was significant ($p < .01$). As predicted, the interaction term was significant and positive ($\beta = .21, p < .05$). Following Cohen and Cohen (1983), we then graphed the results. As shown in Figure 1, the results were as expected. The positive relationship between task conflict and affective conflict is stronger under conditions of geographic dispersion than under conditions of co-location. Thus, Hypothesis 1 was supported.

Hypothesis 2 stated that team tenure affects the strength of the interaction between conflict and geographic distribution. We theorized that this moderation effect will be stronger for teams with long tenure compared to teams with short tenure. To test the moderation, a moderated hierarchical regression analysis approach (Cohen & Cohen, 1983) was used. According to Jaccard, Wan, and Turrisi (1990), to analyze a three-way interaction, a distinction among the moderator variables is required. In our hypothesis, geographic dispersion would be our first order moderator because we are hypothesizing it to moderate positively

Table 2
Results of Hierarchical Regression Analyses for Hypothesis 1

Predictor Variable	Affective Conflict		
		R^2	ΔR^2
Step 1: Control			
Team size	.14	.04	
Step 2: Main effects of moderators			
Task conflict	.46**		
Geographic dispersion	–.01	.39*	.35*
Step 3: Moderating effects			
Task conflict × Geographic dispersion	.21*	.41*	.02

Note: $N = 94$.
* $p < .05$. ** $p < .01$.

Figure 1
Geographic Dispersion as a Moderator of the Task–Affective Conflict Relationship

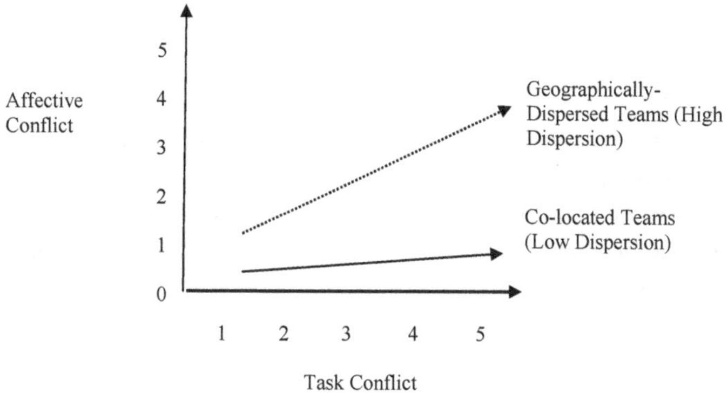

the relationship between task conflict and affective conflict. Team tenure is our second-order moderator because it is thought to affect the strength of the first order moderation. Specifically, we proposed as team tenure increases, the influence of dispersion on the task–affective conflict connection is reduced.

As shown in Table 3, the final model produced an R^2 of .50 and was significant ($p < .01$). As predicted, the interaction term was significant and positive ($\beta = .22, p < .05$) suggesting that the relationship between geographic dispersion and task conflict and affective conflict depends on a third variable—team tenure.

Following Cohen and Cohen (1993), we then graphed the results. As shown in Figure 2a, the results were contrary to our expectations. Figure 2a illustrates

Table 3
Results of Hierarchical Regression Analyses for Hypothesis 2

Predictor Variable	Affective Conflict		
	β	R^2	ΔR^2
Step 1: Control			
Team size	.12	.04	
Step 2: Main effects			
Task conflict	.46**		
Geographic dispersion	–.06		
Team tenure	–.08	.39**	.35**
Step 3: 2-Way interaction			
Task conflict × Geographic dispersion	.17		
Task conflict × Team tenure	–.22*		
Team tenure × Geographic dispersion	.18	.47**	.08*
Step 4: 3-Way interaction			
Task conflict × Geographic dispersion × Team tenure	.22*	.50**	.03*

Note: $N = 94$
* $p < .05$. ** $p < .01$.

that task conflict was *more* likely to lead to affective conflict in geographically dispersed teams when teams had higher tenure. Thus, Hypothesis 2 was not supported. Interestingly, the reverse was found for co-located teams. For co-located teams the relationship between task and affective conflict was weakened as the team gained experience working with one another (see Figure 2b).

Discussion

We believe this study makes a contribution to our understanding of conflict in geographically distributed teams. First, our study is one of only a few comparative studies on conflict that actually examines conflict in both distributed and co-located teams. Second, while past research has focused primarily on antecedents and outcomes of conflict in distributed teams, we examined how geographic dispersion may impact the relationship *between* task and affective conflict. Specifically, we confirmed our hypothesis that the linkage between task and affective conflict was more positive in geographically distributed teams than in co-located teams. Additionally, we examined whether team tenure weakened this moderation effect. Contrary to our expectations, our results showed when teams were geographically dispersed, task conflict was more strongly correlated

Figure 2 (a)
The Relationship between Task Conflict and Affective Conflict for Geographically-Dispersed Teams with High and Low Team Tenure

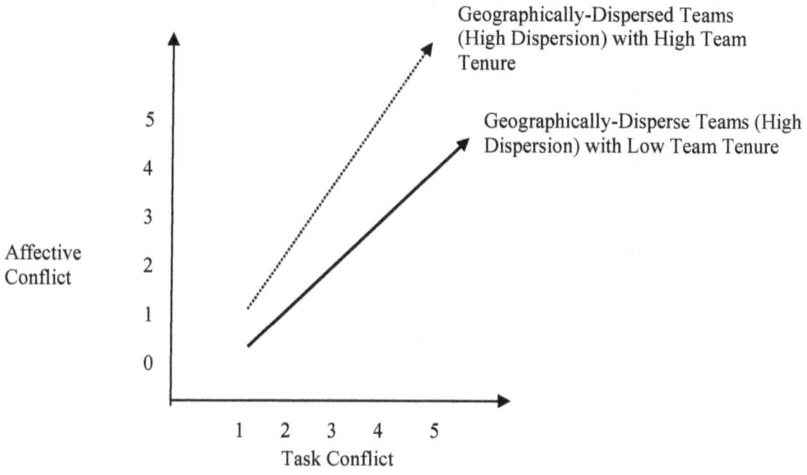

Figure 2 (b)
The Relationship between Task Conflict and Affective Conflict for Co-Located Teams with High and Low Team Tenure

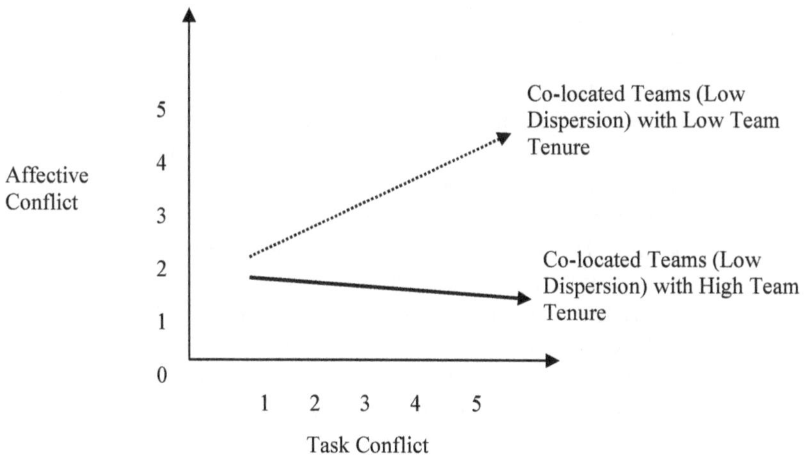

with affective conflict when teams had higher team tenure than when they had lower team tenure. In other words, experience working together didn't seem to help and may have even hurt the ability of geographically dispersed teams to keep conflict task-oriented. However, this relationship did not hold for co-located teams. For co-located teams, long team tenure was associated with a weakening of the correlation between task and affective conflict. Taken together, these findings suggest that effectively managing conflict in distributed teams may be even more problematic than in co-located teams, an issue we argue is worth further exploration.

The research literature suggests several factors that may contribute to why task conflict seems more likely to trigger affective conflict when teams are geographically dispersed. First, high situation invisibility (Cramton et al., 2007), which is characteristic of geographically- distributed teams, may make team members more likely to attribute disagreement to dispositional characteristics. Faced with conflict and lacking rich contextual information, members of geographically distributed teams may more readily attribute difficulties in resolving conflict and reaching agreement to personality issues. That is, distributed team members may be more inclined to judge their fellow members negatively, e.g., as stubborn, self-serving, etc. These negative attributions in turn may result in affective conflict.

Second, keeping team conflict task-oriented and developing convergence or consensus from it is a process that requires highly collaborative behaviors—i.e., the open exchange of differing views with the goal being to develop a convergence of shared meaning and understanding among team members. Geographically distributed teams' greater reliance on technology mediated communication may make the task of engaging in open dialogue and developing shared meaning more difficult. When team members debate differing task-related perspectives and attempt to reach agreement by understanding their differing perspectives and reconciling these differences, it is more likely that misunderstanding and miscommunication will creep into this process when communicating via less synchronous and leaner communication technologies. This diminished capacity for rich communication coupled with the tendency to make dispositional attributions may result in what started out as task-related conflict degrading into affective conflict.

Finally, the stronger relationship observed between task and affective conflict in geographically distributed teams may be the result of more contentious communication. Individuals are less inhibited and have a tendency to use harsher language when communications are mediated via technology versus communicating face-to-face (Siegel, Dubrovsky, Kiesler, & McGuire, 1986; Sproull & Kiesler, 1986). Simons and Peterson (2000) found some support for contentious communication as a moderator of the relationship between task conflict and affective conflict—the more contentious the communications the stronger the relationship between task and affective conflict. Thus, it may be that in the face

of disagreement, distributed teams' communications have a greater tendency to take on an air of contentiousness which may allow what began as task related conflict to devolve into more affective oriented conflict. Taken together, these three factors—situation invisibility, the greater use of less synchronous and less rich communication media, and the tendency for individuals to use harsher language when communication is mediated by technology—may account for the stronger relationship observed between task and affective conflict in geographically distributed teams compared to co-located teams.

We also predicted that long team tenure would lessen the effects of geographic dispersion on the task–affective conflict link. For traditional teams, it has been found that long team tenure can facilitate team processes, helping teams overcome communication and collaboration challenges (Tihanyi et al., 2000). Interestingly, this finding held true for the traditional, co-located teams in our sample, but not for the geographically dispersed teams. That is, the strong positive relationship between task and affective conflict persisted over time for the geographically dispersed teams, but weakened for the co-located teams. These findings imply that over time, teams operating in a face-to-face environment may indeed learn how to better manage conflict. However, for distributed teams, managing conflict constructively may be more difficult.

The observation that the relationship between task and affective conflict in geographically dispersed teams does not weaken over time would seem to imply that the development of a shared team identity and socialization processes may be more problematic in distributed teams. Shared identity has been found to facilitate conflict resolution and consensus building and to decrease negative attributions among team members (Moore et al., 1999). Socialization—whereby team members adopt a common set of behavioral norms and rules—has been found to counter the effects of diversity by promoting behavioral similarity among team members and to facilitate the establishment of a shared team identity. It may well be that distributed teams as compared to co-located teams experience less socialization and less shared identity as a result of less exposure to one another, weaker interpersonal ties, and unshared context. Further, geographically distributed teams tend to be more diverse in their composition with a greater variety of work experience, functional expertise, and cultural/national differences. This heightened diversity may also impede the development of a shared team identity and team socialization processes.

Implications for Management

When teams stimulate debate and the open exchange of conflicting ideas (i.e., task conflict), they may be inadvertently stimulating affective conflict as well; and our results suggest that this is even more common in geographically distributed teams. As a consequence, conflict may be more difficult to manage

when teams are geographically dispersed. Managers and team members should be aware of this tendency and should seek out conditions that mitigate it.

While it is premature to offer exact prescriptions for how geographically distributed teams can manage conflict effectively, past research offers some preliminary suggestions. For example, researchers have proposed that team members' experience with the media channel (e.g., email, discussion boards, video conferencing) may diminish the negative effects of the communication channel on communication processes (Dennis et al., 2008; Maruping & Agarwal, 2004). As team members become more experienced with a given information technology, they are likely to become more comfortable with its shortcomings and adapt it accordingly, in essence "enriching" it (Carlson & Zmud, 1999). Thus, we propose that formal training in the technology may result in adapting the technology in ways that enrich it, lessening to some extent the drawbacks of lean communication technologies. In addition, as team members gain experience with specific communication technologies and adapt them to their needs, it is possible that they will adapt them in ways which include more social and/or contextual cues, thereby weakening the negative effects of geographic distribution on the attributions made by team members.

Second, it may be that team development is even more important for distributed teams than co-located teams. The context in which distributed teams operate may make socialization processes and development of a shared team identity problematic. Shared team identity and socialization processes have been shown to be critical to co-located teams' ability to effectively deal with conflict (Moore et al., 1999). Thus, interventions that enable a shared team identity and promote the establishment of a common set of team norms that guide the team's behavior are recommended. Interestingly, there has been little research examining the creation of a shared social identity in distributed teams. However, in co-located teams a clear, collective team goal, feelings of accountability for team outcomes, high task interdependence, and low member turnover have been found related to shared team identity (Mortensen & Hinds, 2001). One possible intervention to promote socialization processes in geographically distributed teams is to offer team building opportunities that help team members gel. When starting to work together, co-located team members make assessments of trustworthiness and develop norms that tend to get reinforced in future interaction (Gersick & Hackman, 1990). Thus, the addition of team building opportunities at the beginning of the project which assist distributed members in developing trust and developing a set of shared norms may be particularly helpful for distributed teams. The crux of the matter is these team building efforts may be more effective if done face-to-face as such interaction may allow for the development of closer and more positive relationships and stronger social norms. However, we acknowledge that conducting face-to-face team building activities may not be feasible for distributed teams. Thus a current management challenge is how to conduct these activities virtually. The

increasing accessibility of communication technologies such as Skype and other means of "rich" communication media may offer promising alternatives.

Directions for Future Research

As we discuss above, we acknowledge that our research stops short of examining empirically *why* task conflict relates more positively to affective conflict in geographically distributed teams. While we offer several theoretical explanations—such as the effects of situation invisibility, the lack of richness in technology mediated communications, more contentious communication—these mechanisms should be explored more explicitly in future research. For example, our research supports the notion that negative dispositional attributions or social judgments may be more prevalent in geographically distributed teams. Future research should look more closely at this process to better understand how attributions affect the interpretation of disagreement in distributed teams.

Future research should also explore potential moderators that might help distributed teams keep conflict task-oriented and avoid affective conflict. In the research on co-located teams both trust and behavioral integration have been found to negatively moderate the task-affective conflict link (Mooney et al., 2007; Simons & Peterson, 2000). Interestingly, several researchers examining distributed teams have noted that collaborative norms, such as those that comprise behavioral integration, and trust may be harder to establish in distributed teams (e.g., Jarvenpaa, Knoll, & Leidner, 1998). Future research should take into account how the above factors—i.e., situation invisibility/dispositional attributions, lean and asynchronous communication technologies, trust, and behavioral integration—interrelate to affect conflict management in distributed teams.

Study Strengths and Limitations

Although our study offers several new insights, some limitations should be noted. First, the study's design is cross-sectional, which limits our ability to draw causal inferences. Indeed, a longitudinal design may capture more effectively the process by which task conflict ignites affective conflict. On the other hand, we suspect that the process by which task conflict triggers affective conflict occurs rather quickly, often within the course of a single discussion. Capturing such a process would be difficult even in a multi-period study.

A second limitation is the risk of common method variance—i.e., the risk that employing single-source methodology produces artificially high intercorrelations (Avolio, Yammarino, & Bass, 1991). This concern is minimized however by having the team leader (via the team information sheet) provide the data for geographic dispersion and team tenure (two fairly objective constructs) while the team (via the team survey) provided the data for task and affective conflict.

Third, several of our theoretical arguments rely on the assumption that geographically distributed teams use less rich communication media than co-located teams. That is, we infer that because team members are remotely located that they have less face-to-face interaction and therefore rely more heavily on computer and telecommunication technologies to mediate their interactions. Future research on distributed teams should measure the extent to which these teams do in fact rely on technology mediated communication and the richness of these media.

Finally, DeDreu and Weingart (2003) conducted a meta-analysis and raised the issue that, contrary to findings by Amason (1996) and several others, both task and affective conflict can be damaging to team performance. A number of methodological issues with their study notwithstanding, we accept that in some cases task conflict may relate negatively to some performance outcomes in teams. At the same time, we argue that task conflict has consistently been reported to have more beneficial effects than affective conflict. Moreover, we suspect that DeDreu and Weingart's (2003) findings reflect much of what we propose. Specifically, that the effects of task and affective conflict have been so hard to separate because researchers have overlooked the possibility that task conflict actually triggers affective conflict. Indeed, the research they reviewed generally examined the effects of task and relationship conflict on performance without controlling for the effects of the other form of conflict. As noted by Jehn (2010), the studies reviewed by DeDreu and Weingart (2003) also only considered a limited number of outcomes and team tasks, and the teams in the studies' samples were limited to mostly large firms. Finally, although DeDreu and Weingart's paper may at present call into question the positive effects of task conflict, consensus still exists that teams should avoid affective conflict. Thus, even if our premise (and the premise of many other researchers) that task conflict is generally good for teams is somewhat faulty; our research is meaningful in that it sheds more light on the conditions under which affective conflict can become more exacerbated in teams.

Despite these limitations, we believe our study helps us to better understand conflict in distributed teams. Our findings suggest there may be important differences between the functioning of co-located and distributed teams. These findings, coupled with others findings that distributed teams are indeed different from their face-to-face counterparts (e.g., McLeod & Liker, 1992; Straus & McGrath, 1994) call into question whether existing models of team behavior can be applied to distributed teams. In sum, there is a need for greater use of comparative field research to better understand exactly how and why distributed teams differ from their co-located counterparts.

References

Aiken. L. S., & West, S. G. (1991). *Multiple regression: Testing and interpreting interactions*. Thousand Oaks, CA: Sage.

Amason, A. C. (1996). Distinguishing the effects of functional and dysfunctional conflict on strategic decision making: Resolving a paradox for top management teams. *Academy of Management Journal, 39*, 123–148.

Amason, A. C., & Mooney, A. C. (1999). The effects of past performance on top management team conflict in strategic decision making. *International Journal of Conflict Management, 10*, 340–359.

Amason A. C., & Sapienza, H. J. (1997). The effects of top management team size and interaction norms on cognitive and affective conflict. *Journal of Management, 23*, 495–516.

Avolio, B. J., Yammarino, F. J., & Bass, B. M. (1991). Identifying common methods variance with data collected from a single source: An unresolved sticky issue. *Journal of Management, 17*, 571–587.

Brehmer, B. (1976). Social judgment theory and the analysis of interpersonal conflict. *Psychological Bulletin, 83*, 985–1003.

Carlson, J. R., & Zmud, R. W. (1999). Channel expansion theory and the experiential nature of media richness perceptions. *Academy of Management Journal, 42*, 153–170.

Cohen, J., & Cohen, P. (1983). *Applied multiple regression/correlation analysis for behavioral sciences* (2d ed.). Mahwah, NJ: Erlbaum.

Conlon, D. E., & Jehn, K. A. (2010) Behind the music: Conflict, performance, longevity, and turnover in punk and new wave rock bands. *Current Topics in Management, 14*, 13–48.

Cramton, C. D., Orvis, K. L., & Wilson, J. M. (2007). Situation invisibility and attribution in distributed collaborations. *Journal of Management*, 33, 525–546.

Cramton, C. D. (2002) Attribution in distributed work groups. In P. M. Hinds & S. Kiesler (Eds.), *Distributed work* (pp. 191–212). Cambridge: MIT Press.

Cramton, C. D. (2001). The mutual knowledge problem and its consequences for dispersed collaboration. *Organization Science, 12*, 346–371.

Creed, W. E. D., & Miles, R. E. (1996). Trust in organizations: A conceptual framework linking organizational forms, managerial philosophies, and the opportunity costs of controls. In R. M. Kramer & T. R. Tyler (Eds.), *Trust in organizations: Frontiers of theory and research,* (pp. 16–39). CA: Sage.

DeDreu, C. & Weingart, L. (2003). Task versus relationship conflict, team performance, and team member satisfaction: A meta-analysis. *Journal of Applied Psychology, 88*, 741–749.

Dennis, A. R., Fuller, R. M. & Valacich, J. S. (2008). Media, tasks, and communication processes: A theory of media synchronicity. *MIS Quarterly,* 32, 575–600.

Eisenhardt, K. M., Kahwajy, J. L., & Bourgeois III, L. J. (1997). How management teams can have a good fight. *Harvard Business Review, 75* (4), 77–85.

Fiske, S. T., & Taylor, S. E. (1991). *Social cognition* (2nd ed.). New York: McGraw Hill.

Gersick, C. J. G., & Hackman, J. R. (1990). Habitual routines in task-performing groups. *Organizational Behavior and Human Decision Processes, 47*, 65–97.

Gibson, C. B., & Gibbs, J. L. (2006) Unpacking the concept of virtuality: The effects of geographic dispersion, electronic dependence, dynamic structure, and national diversity on team innovation. *Administrative Science Quarterly, 51*, 451–495.

Griffith, T. L., Mannix, E. A., & Neale, M. A. (2003) Conflict and virtual teams. In T. L. Griffith, E. A. Mannix, & M. A. Neale (Eds.) *Virtual teams that work* (pp. 213–233). San Francisco: Jossey-Bass.

Hagafors, R., & Brehmer, B. (1983). Does having to justify one's judgments change the nature of the judgment process? *Organizational Behavior and Human Performance, 31*, 223–232.

Harvey, J. H. & Weary, G. (1985). *Attribution: Basic issues and applications*. New York: Wiley.
Hinds, P. J., & Mortensen, M. (2005). Understanding conflict in geographically distributed teams: The moderating effects of shared identity, shared context, and spontaneous communication. *Organization Science, 16*, 290–307.
Jaccard, J., Wan, C. K., & Turrisi, R. (1990). The detection and interpretation of interaction effects between continuous variables in multiple regression. *Multivariate Behavioral Research, 25*, 467–478.
James, L. R., Demaree, R. G., & Wolf, G. (1993). An assessment of within-group interrater agreement. *Journal of Applied Psychology, 78*, 306–309.
Jarvenpaa, S. L., Knoll, K., & Leidner, D. E. (1998). Is anybody out there? Antecedents of trust in global virtual teams. *Journal of Management Information Systems, 14*, 29–64.
Jehn, K. A. (1997). A qualitative analysis of conflict types and dimensions in organizational groups. *Administrative Science Quarterly, 42*, 530–557.
Jehn, K. A. (1995). A multimethod examination of the benefits and detriments of intragroup conflict. *Administrative Science Quarterly, 40*, 256–282.
Jehn, K. A. (1994). Enhancing effectiveness: An investigation of advantages and disadvantages of value-based intragroup conflict. *International Journal of Conflict Management, 5*, 223–228.
Jehn, K. A., & Mannix, E. A. (2001). The dynamic nature of conflict: A longitudinal study of intragroup conflict and group performance. *Academy of Management Journal, 44*, 238–251.
Kankanhalli, A., Tan, B. C., & Wei, K. (2006). Conflict and performance in global virtual teams. *Journal of Management Information Systems, 23*, 237–274.
Katz, R. (1982). The effects of group longevity on project communication and performance. *Administrative Science Quarterly, 27*, 81–104.
Lea, M., & Spears, R. (1992). Paralanguage and social perception in computer-mediated communication. *Journal of Organizational Computing, 2*, 321–341.
Mannix, E. A., Griffith, T. L., & Neale, M.A. (2002). The phenomenology of conflict in virtual work teams. In P. J. Hinds & S. Kiesler (Eds.), *Distributed work* (pp. 213–233). Cambridge, MA: MIT Press.
Martins, L. L., Gilson, L. L. & Maynard, M. T. (2004). Virtual teams: What do we know and where do we go from here? *Journal of Management, 30*, 805–835.
Maruping, L. M., & Agarwal, R. (2004). Managing team interpersonal processes through technology: A task-technology fit perspective. *Journal of Applied Psychology, 89*, 975–990.
McLeod, P. L., & Liker, J. K. (1992). Electronic meeting systems: Evidence from a low structure environment. *Information Systems Research, 3*, 195–223.
Mooney, A. C., Holahan, P. J., & Amason, A. C. (2007). Don't take it personally: Exploring cognitive conflict as a mediator of affective conflict. *Journal of Management Studies, 44*, 733–758.
Moore, D. A., Kurtzberg, T. R., Thompson, L. L., & Morris, M. W. (1999). Long and short routes to success in electronically mediated negotiations: Group affiliations and good vibrations. *Organizational Behavior and Human Decision Processes, 77*, 22–43.
Mortensen, M. & Hinds, P. J. (2001). Conflict and shared identity in geographically distributed teams. *International Journal of Conflict Management, 12*, 212–238.
Pelled, L. H., Eisenhardt, K. M., & Xin, K. R. (1999). Exploring the black box: An analysis of work group diversity, conflict, and performance. *Administrative Science Quarterly, 44*, 1–28.

Polzer, J. T., Crisp, C. B., Jarvenpaa, S. L., & Kim, J. W. (2006). Extending the faultline model to geographically dispersed teams: How colocated subgroups can impair group functioning. *Academy of Management Journal, 49*, 679–692.

Siegel, J., Dubrovsky, V., Kiesler, S., & McGuire, T. W. (1986) Group processes in computer-mediated communication. *Organizational Behavior and Human Decision Processes, 37*, 157–187.

Simons, T., & Peterson, R. (2000). Task conflict and relationship conflict in top management teams: The pivotal role of intragroup trust. *Journal of Applied Psychology, 85*, 102–112.

Sproull, L. & Keisler, S. (1986). Reducing social context cues: Electronic mail in organizational communication, *Management Science*, *32*, 1492–1513.

Staples, D. & Zhao, L. (2006). The effects of cultural diversity in virtual teams versus face-to-face teams. *Group Decision and Negotiation, 15*, 389–406.

Straus, S., & McGrath, J. E. (1994). Does the medium matter? The interaction of task type and technology on group performance and member reactions. *Journal of Applied Psychology, 79*, 87–97.

Tihanyi, L., Ellstrand, A. E., Daily, C. M., & Dalton, D. R. 2000. Composition of the top management team and firm international diversification. *Journal of Management, 26*, 1157–1177.

Current Topics in Management, Vol. 15, 2011, pp. 63-92

FAIRNESS AND CONSUMER BEHAVIOR: A WWJD (WHAT WOULD JUSTICE DO?) ANALYSIS

Kelly Schwind Wilson, Donald E. Conlon, and Joel Koopman

From its original roots in law and social psychology (e.g., Thibaut & Walker, 1975), work on organizational justice or fairness (we use the terms interchangeably in this chapter—see below) has moved into the domain of organizations (e.g., Folger & Greenberg, 1985). In fact, many studies in the last two decades have examined how outcomes, procedures, information, and interpersonal treatment by organizations or their agents influence employee attitudinal and behavioral reactions (for reviews see Colquitt, Conlon, Wesson, Porter, & Ng, 2001; Greenberg & Colquitt, 2005). Even more recently, a number of studies have begun to reach beyond the consideration of employee reactions by focusing on the reactions of parties external to the organizations. One area that has received considerable attention is that of how customers react to their encounters with organizations or service providers, and how their fairness judgments might influence their attitudes and behaviors.

A central goal of this paper is to examine the influence of justice in consumer behavior settings. In particular, we identify areas in the customer-service provider interaction where fairness concerns are likely to arise, and discuss the implications of these fairness concerns. We conclude with recommendations for researchers and practitioners, along with a discussion of some of the limitations in the research on this topic.

In approaching this topic, we offer three caveats for the reader to keep in mind. First, we will review research from a variety of different contexts with an awareness that the context itself is likely an important moderator of relationships between fairness and customer outcomes such as satisfaction, trust, repatronage behavior, and positive or negative word of mouth. There are likely to be critical

contextual differences between such situations with important implications for how justice influences important customer outcomes.

Our second caveat is that we will consider examples of both *typical* and *atypical* service interactions. Many service exchanges are unremarkable in the sense that customers receive exactly the service they were expecting to get. However, sometimes customers receive "atypical" service, which often means that the customer received service that did not meet expectations, though we note that atypical service could involve situations where customers receive service that exceeds expectations. Many studies have focused on the role of fairness in reaction to service *failures*, and while we will consider this work, we also examine the customer service relationship more broadly and include situations where service meets or exceeds expectations.

Third, we will do our best as we discuss studies to identify whether a particular type of justice is being considered, or whether an overall judgment of justice is the focus of attention. As many readers may know, the organizational justice literature frequently views justice in terms of four dimensions: distributive, procedural, interpersonal, and informational justice (cf., Colquitt et al., 2001). Applied to a service context, we might define distributive justice as the fairness of the outcome (e.g., product) received in return for the price paid. Procedural justice could be defined as the fairness of the procedures used or transactions followed in a service exchange situation. Interpersonal justice focuses on the fairness of the interpersonal treatment one receives from service providers during the course of their contact, and informational justice focuses on the fairness of the communication characteristics (e.g., explanations for events, relevance of a service provider's communicated response) that occur as part of the service exchange. In contrast to this multidimensional approach to justice, other studies discuss justice as a general, overarching characteristic of a situation. These studies might simply ask, "Is this fair?" Such an approach is consistent with some authors who argue that fairness may be better understood as a global reaction because it can be difficult in many situations for people to disentangle perceptions of outcomes, procedures, treatment, or information from each other.

Some of the studies we will review will use global fairness judgments as their point of reference; other studies will draw finer distinctions between various types of justice and discuss how these nuanced justice judgments influence attitudes and behaviors. Which approach is better is a subject of some debate (e.g., Ambrose & Arnaud, 2005; Dulebohn, Conlon, Sarinopoulos, Davison, & McNamara, 2009) but is also not central to the present review. The focus of our review is how consumers perceive the various aspects of a service exchange with an eye toward the implications therein for managers and organizations. As a result, we believe our contribution is not negated by lack of cohesion in the measures used to assess consumer perceptions. We hope our review will allow scholars to target areas where relationships still need to be studied, while

also helping managers and organizations gain an understanding of the current research on this topic.

A Simple Model of the Customer-Service Provider Interaction

In viewing the literature that exists between fairness and customer service outcomes, we will follow a simplified temporal or process based-approach that approximates the events individuals typically experience during service exchanges (e.g., Pisharodi & Langley, 1990). Our model is presented in Figure 1. As the model suggests, the general pattern of a service exchange can be described as occurring in five stages. Stage 1 consists of events that occur even before customers enter a particular service setting (e.g., a store, a restaurant, an office). This is because customers often have prior expectations about a focal service provider, and/or prior experience with the focal service provider. These expectations or experiences could influence customer judgments of (a) what the experience with the service provider will be like, (b) the product or service they will receive, and (c) the price of the product or service.

Obviously, during later stages of the model, events that transpire could confirm or violate customer expectations or previous experiences. Consider what could happen in Stage 2, where the customer enters the service environment. The physical environment may include many signals or cues that the customer may process, leading to changes in customer judgments and inferences even before they formally interact with a service provider. Such input may come from their own scan of the physical setting (perhaps alerting them to a change in price or in service), or it could come from social information that presents itself to the customer (e.g., overhearing conversation between other customers, or between other customers and service providers, as might be the case when one is waiting in line to talk to a service provider). Stage 3 consists of the formal interaction the customer has with the service provider.

Figure 1
A Model of the Interaction Process between Customers and Service Providers

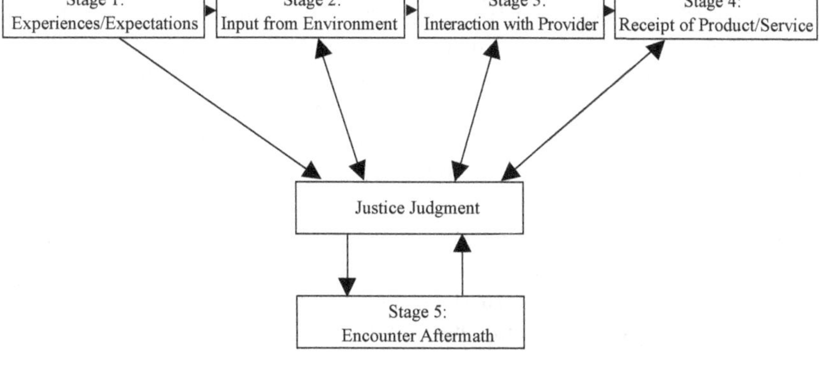

Stages 2 and 3 are described above in terms of what we might call a traditional customer service interaction, i.e., one that might involve the customer entering the service provider's location (Stage 2) and then subsequently interacting with the service provider or an agent on behalf of the service provider (Stage 3). Of course, with the increase in online purchases, traveling to the service provider location may be nothing more than sitting at one's home and going online, and the "salesperson" may be virtual rather than human.

In Stage 4, the product or service in question is purchased and, depending on the product or service, is subsequently received. "Received" may be operationalized as consumed (as in a meal), experienced (as in a massage), used (clothing, cars), and depending on the product or service, there may be a temporal separation between payment and receipt of the item. The exact sequence with which these events occur can vary depending on the context (e.g., at many formal restaurants, a customer-service provider exchange might consist of the following order of events: The customer is greeted and seated by a host or hostess [service provider 1 (SP 1)]; a waiter or waitress (SP 2) takes their food order; a cook (SP 3) prepares their meal, which is then delivered to the customer, sometimes by another person (SP 4); the food is then eaten, and the customer then pays for the meal [sometimes interacting with SP 2, other times with yet another unique service provider, the cashier (SP 5)]. On the other hand, at many "fast food" restaurants, the food is cooked even before the customer arrives; many times the customer is greeted, orders food, pays for the food, and is served the food by a single service provider. Such an ordering obviously involves far fewer service providers, which may make uniform service provision easier to accomplish (Salancik & Leblebici, 1988).

Stage 5 can be described as the post-service rumination phase. In many service experiences, receipt of the product or service may be the end of the customer-service provider interaction. This is most likely the case when the product or service meets expectations, and perhaps when the interaction is of little consequence or occurs so frequently that it is not thought about much (e.g., the monotony of fueling your car at the same gas station, or the regularity of getting your morning coffee at the same cafe). Depending on the product or service, there may be little active rumination, in fact the customer may never think of the experience again. However, sometimes the experience may lead to a variety of thoughts about the product, the service provider and the customer's own affective reactions and future behavioral intentions.

We label this last phase the "service encounter aftermath" stage. It could include customer judgments of satisfaction and trust directed at multiple targets (e.g., the specific item or service, as well as the service provider), as well as statements and behaviors they engage in after the service interaction. Companies are of course interested in the immediate proximal reactions of customers (such as customer satisfaction and trust), but they are also interested in more distal customer behaviors—especially their repatronage, and their word of mouth to

others (potential customers). The aftermath stage could contain many interactions between customers and service providers. For instance, when service providers receive a complaint, they often provide a response to the customer (this may include an explanation for the service received and could also include actions such as refunding the price of the product, or providing the customer a discount on the service purchased or perhaps a future service).

Note from the model that events at any of the five stages can trigger justice reactions. Also note that as a result, pre-existing justice reactions could color or frame expectations and influence customer reactions at any other stage of the model (i.e., something deemed unfair that is noted by a customer at Stage 2 might influence their reactions to events at stage 3). This is why the model presents bidirectional arrows between justice judgments and stages 2–5 of the model. It is crucial to note that at each of the five stages outlined above, events can occur that will cue fairness considerations that could impact whether the customer continues with the transaction or opts out, though some contexts make it quite difficult for the customer to exit the service setting (Conlon, Van Dyne, Milner, & Ng, 2004). In an attempt to organize our review of the literature, we will follow the process outlined above, beginning with studies that investigate individuals' prior knowledge of the service provider or characteristics of the service.

Stage 1: Prior Experiences or Expectations

Even before entering a service setting (e.g., a store, a restaurant, etc.), people often have information about a service provider (e.g., reputation) or aspects of a service (e.g., price, quality) that comes from one of three sources. People may have information drawn from prior personal experiences with the service provider in question. People may also have indirect experiences with a service provider. Following Sawyer, Kernan, Conlon and Garland (1999), we define indirect experience as information acquired through networks of friends, peers, and reference groups, and research has documented the influence that such communication has on attitudes and behaviors (e.g., Salancik & Pfeffer, 1978). Finally, people may acquire information through impersonal, mass-media sources that could include newspapers, radio, television, e-mail, etc. While direct personal experiences are usually weighed more heavily by decision makers than indirect or mass media information, this does not mean that these other information sources do not play a role in customer fairness judgments and subsequent evaluations, especially when one is intentionally seeking to try a new product or service (e.g., a new restaurant).

Central to many studies in consumer behavior are reactions to price information. This variable is obviously salient to justice researchers as price fairness would in many cases appear analogous to a distributive justice judgment. Many of the studies of pricing in the consumer behavior literature mention

"fairness" in a general sense, but do not differentiate or specify exactly what type of fairness they are referring to (distributive, procedural, interpersonal, informational, or overall). While these studies rarely use the typical distributive justice questions we might find in other areas of research, they remain highly informative of the significant role distributive justice often plays in customer service settings.

In perhaps the most well-referenced study examining price fairness (cited over 600 times in the Social Science Citation Index as of April, 2010), Kahneman, Knetsch, and Thaler (1986) published a series of household survey data sets examining reactions to changes in pricing. For instance, in one of their studies respondents were told of a hardware store that normally sold snow shovels for $15; the morning after a large snowstorm however, respondents were told that the store raised the price to $20. Most (82%) of the respondents viewed this as unfair. Kahneman et al. (1986) note that whether prices are viewed as unfair or not depends on a variety of contextual factors including reference transactions (e.g., relevant precedents or comparisons) and the outcomes to the firm (e.g., moving car sale prices from list price to $200 above list price is seen as unfair, but moving the price from $200 below list price up to list price is seen as fair). Building on the Kahneman et al. (1986) results, Piron and Fernandez (1995) found that consumers will retaliate by withholding their repatronage (by not returning to a retailer) when a firm is seen as unfair (e.g., raising the price of a snow shovel after a big snow storm).

Extending the Kahneman et al. (1986) findings related to comparison information, Bearden, Carlson, and Hardesty (2003) used undergraduate business students to examine how the presence or absence of invoice price information (the cost to the seller) in an advertised offer affected customer judgments. Invoice price information would be viewed as a relevant comparison point using the language of Kahneman et al. (1986). The results indicate that higher invoice prices increased customer ratings of transaction value, acquisition value and offer fairness. Bearden et al. (2003) also noted that invoice price moderated the relationship between sale price and offer fairness, such that the negative relationship between sale price and offer fairness was lessened by the provision of a higher invoice amount.

Moving away from discussing the antecedents and consequences of distributive justice and into the consideration of other justice forms, we note that explanations for price variations have also received some attention. While Kahneman et al.'s (1986) seminal work was not construed in terms of its impact on informational justice judgments, their work does speak to this construct as they also examined how explanations (in their case, a justification) might influence overall fairness judgments. For example, their research found that if respondents were told that the grocer's cost for lettuce rose by 30 cents a head, respondents then believed that charging customers 30 cents more per head of lettuce was fair.

Vaidyanathan and Aggarwal (2003) used attribution theory to examine consumers' perceptions of the fairness of price increases. They conducted three experiments in which participants read scenarios about firms' abilities to control pricing. Their results suggest that cost-justified price increases can be perceived as unfair when there is an internal locus of cause for the seller and/or when the price increase is seen as within the control of the seller (e.g., if competitors' prices remain the same, the cost increase is viewed as less fair). Similarly, Bolton, Warlop, and Alba (2003) used a scenario study design and found that consumer knowledge of prices, profits, and costs contribute to perceptions of price unfairness, consistent with some of the findings of Kahneman et al. (1986). Interestingly, in what might be a corollary of the well-known fundamental attribution error, consumers underestimate the effects of inflation (external factors) and tend to attribute price differences to profits (internal factors) rather than costs. However, consumers judge price differences as most fair when price variations are attributed to quality differences.

In a study that manipulated a company's intentions and reputation, Campbell (1999) examined the antecedents and consequences of a company's inferred motives for increasing prices. In the first study, participants were asked to read a scenario in which a company was portrayed as having a positive or negative motive for increasing the price of a good (a child's toy). In the positive motive condition, the firm was described as using profits for a daycare center; in the negative motive condition the firm appeared to take advantage of consumers by not donating any profits. Participants then completed fairness evaluations. In the second study, participants read scenarios in which a company was portrayed as having either a good or bad reputation. Positive (negative) reputation is operationalized using the following description (Campbell, 1999): "Store X is a large retailer that has been established for many years and is (is not) highly regarded in the community … this store seems to have a good (bad) reputation with its customers, employees, and the community at large" (p. 194). One might view such a manipulation as similar to online reviews consumers read before deciding to visit a store.

The results suggest that both motives and reputation influence customer reactions to price increases. When a company was seen as having a positive motive, a price increase was perceived as more fair than when a company was seen as having a negative motive. In addition, when a company was portrayed as having a good reputation, consumers inferred a more positive motive. For firms with a poor reputation, a negative motive was inferred regardless of whether the firm profited from the price increase. Finally, Campbell (1999) demonstrated that perceived price unfairness mediates the effects of inferred motive and relative price on consumers' shopping intentions. That is, perceived unfairness led to lower future shopping intentions.

Oh and Jeong (2004) conducted an on-line survey to investigate how lodging consumers process brand and price information. Brand awareness was positively

associated with price fairness, consistent with the idea that some brands (e.g., Ritz Carlton, Four Seasons) might provide better outcomes to customers than others (e.g., Motel 6, Sleep Inn), even when controlling for price. In addition, higher levels of perceived price fairness were associated with higher levels of value perceptions. Oh and Jeong (2004) conclude, "The role of price fairness is noticeable in particular. Consumers seem to evaluate the appropriateness of a charged price for given product quality, and the resulting perceptions tend to affect value perceptions in the positive direction" (p. 356).

While many of the studies above link price fairness to customer attitudes and intentions, it is the rare study that links price fairness to behavioral outcomes. Verhoef, Franses, and Hoekstra (2002) collected data from 1,986 insurance company customers. Their findings suggest payment equity (perceived fairness of price), along with a variety of other attitudes (customer trust, affective commitment, satisfaction) were positively related to customer recommendations to others. Of particular interest here is that price fairness was significantly related to customer recommendations to others and number of services purchased by the customer.

Daskalopoulu and Petrou (2006) modeled consumer fairness perceptions of retailers to determine the effect of those perceptions on repurchase decisions. Using questionnaires in major Greek cities, they found that respondents' fairness perceptions have an effect on the amount of money spent at the retailer. In addition, Homburg, Hoyer, and Koschate (2005) found that repurchase intentions decreased as price levels increased, however satisfaction with the purchase moderated this effect. These authors also demonstrated that perceived intentions play a role in behavioral outcomes. They also found that satisfaction moderates the relationship between perceived motive fairness and repurchase intentions, such that repurchase intentions were higher when the motive for the price increase was perceived as fair and the effect of perceived motive fairness was stronger when customers were more satisfied.

Finally, Kimes, and Wirtz (2003) examined the perceived fairness of "rate fences" in the restaurant industry. Rate fences, also called demand-based pricing, entails varying selling prices such that lower prices are offered at off-peak times. Such pricing variations can be accomplished through a variety of different means. Kimes and Wirtz (2003) found that demand-based pricing in the form of coupons, time-of-day pricing, and lunch/dinner pricing were perceived as fair. On the other hand, weekday/weekend pricing was seen as neutral to slightly unfair and table location pricing was seen as somewhat unfair. Why the difference in opinion? Perhaps consumers are already accustomed to paying different prices for movies at different times of the day and having differently priced lunch/dinner menus whereas the other contexts presented novel instances of price variations. It could also be merely a matter of perspective. Courty and Pagliero (2008) found that consumers were averse to pricing variations, even when the result was lower expected prices. It could also be an example of natural reference points influencing reactions. Kimes and

Wirtz (2003) noted that, consistent with prospect theory, demand-base pricing framed as a discount lead to higher judgments of fairness than demand-based pricing framed as a surcharge.

Stage 2: Entering the Physical Setting

Stage 2 of our model recognizes that merely by entering the physical (or virtual) setting, customers may receive cues or information from their initial environmental scan that could create new fairness judgments, or change existing fairness judgments. Thus, Stage 2 recognizes that environmental stimuli (perhaps in the form of a sign on a wall, perhaps in the form of conversations overheard between customers, or between other customers and the service provider) can lead to fairness judgments and increase or decrease important service outcomes like patronage, repatronage, positive or negative word of mouth, etc. However, in our survey of the literature, we could find almost no research that has examined customer reactions at this stage (i.e., without continuing on to stage 3).

One can find evidence of the potential for events at Stage 2 to be impactful even without going to Stage 3 however. Consider the uproar that occurred at Geno's Steaks (Associated Press, 2006). The South Philadelphia restaurant, famous for its "philly cheesesteak" sandwiches, posted signs on their walls in 2006 that stated "This is America: When ordering speak English." While the restaurant owner viewed the signs as an attempt to help customers learn English, some customers viewed the signs as evidence of racism or xenophobia. It is likely such signs aroused interpersonal justice reactions in some people.

Another setting in which events at Stage 2 may be important is when customers visit on-line retail websites. When a potential consumer visits a website and reaches the front page, a completed transaction has not yet occurred, however the consumer is already processing information about the site and company. Are the desired links easy to find? Are there sales on the front page? Is the customer's desired item more expensive than s/he thought it would be? Consumers who navigate away from a webpage without purchasing represent lost sales for the company, and their decisions to "click elsewhere" may sometimes be traced to perceptions of unfairness.

As we said, empirical studies that stop the customer-service provider process at Stage 2 and collect data appear to be rare, though there may be the occasional scenario study that could be described in this fashion. For instance, Huppertz, Arenson, and Evans (1978) investigated consumer perceptions of inequity in negative retail exchange situations (e.g., the price of an item was 40% higher than a shopper had seen elsewhere). When the price was greater than expected (high price inequity), participants perceived the situation as less fair and when this inequity was present, participants indicated they would leave the store and/or complain about the price or service.

Customers also find themselves in Stage 2 dilemmas from time to time when they are waiting to be served. What we have learned is that direct communication need not take place for an injustice to be perceived by a customer. Zhou and Soman (2008) conducted a scenario study in which they assessed justice perceptions of customers who imagined themselves being forced to wait in a line. These authors found that if consumers felt that their wait time was unfair, and that the delay was the fault of the service provider, their satisfaction with the transaction was reduced.

Stage 3: Interactions with Sales Personnel

The next stage of a service exchange typically involves interacting with a sales person. Depending on the frequency with which a customer contracts for a product or a service, and depending on whether the customer knows the service provider from prior exchanges, customers often have little information regarding with whom they will interact when entering a retail establishment. In contrast with prices or brand reputation—information that is researchable or generally static—an interaction with another human being can be highly idiosyncratic. The customer has no control over which employees will be working that day, what mood the employee is in or, often, which employee will assist them. An emerging area of research is on the quality of the relationships established between customers and salespersons and the effect of these relationships on the fairness perceptions of the exchange. Aurier and Siadou-Martin (2007) state "consumers who experience higher levels of perceived justice are more likely to engage in relationship behavior and, as a consequence, to become and remain loyal customers" (p. 464). Of course, this also means that customers who experience hostile rather than pleasant interactions will perceive less fairness and be less loyal.

On the hostile side, consider Doucet's (2004) study of a telephone service center of a large retail bank. Hostile behavior in this study was defined in terms of overt actions by one party that a target perceives as malevolent, unfavorable, or even warlike toward himself or herself. Hostility was measured using coders who rated the service provider's tone of voice on each speaking turn for whether there was a presence or absence of hostility. An overall measure of hostility included the average hostility rating across all of the service provider's speaking turns in a given interaction with a customer. Findings suggest that service provider hostility was most detrimental to customer service quality evaluations when customers had a high utility for the service (e.g., the importance of aspects of the service interaction to the customer) and technical performance was low (e.g., whether the customer received the information they requested). We would argue that the instances of service provider hostility in Doucet's (2004) study are antecedents to low interpersonal justice perceptions on the part of the customer. Of course hostility can be a two way street, with customers expressing

hostility toward employees as well. Skarlicki, Van Jaarsveld and Walker (2008) examined customer service representatives at a Canadian call center and found that interpersonal injustice committed by the customer toward the employee led to employee sabotage directed at the customer.

Babin, Griffin, and Boles (2004) investigated how interactions with a salesperson generate ethical perceptions that affect consumer emotions. They defined "moral equity" as the inherent rightness/wrongness or perceived justice of some action. These authors found in their study using graduate and undergraduate students that individuals experience higher levels of negative affect when they perceive they were not treated fairly. Furthermore, they found that a perception of injustice had an effect on future patronage intentions and that this effect was mediated by both positive and negative affect created by the interaction. These authors end by stating, "It becomes increasingly evident that customer perceptions of equity are critically important in helping encourage consistent behavior patterns that lead to loyalty" (Babin et al., 2004, p. 1161).

On the pleasant side, Maxwell, Nye, and Maxwell (1999) primed fair interpersonal treatment in one-on-one price negotiations and found that when fairness is primed, various positive outcomes are evident. In general, fairness-primed buyers demonstrated more cooperative behavior, made more concessions that lead to faster agreement, held more positive attitudes toward the seller, and were more satisfied with the outcome. In a follow-up study, Maxwell, Nye, and Maxwell (2003) investigated how fairness-primed buyers react to reciprocity. That is, what happens when sellers reciprocate or fail to reciprocate cooperative behavior on the part of buyers? When sellers reciprocated, buyers were more cooperative in the negotiation, more satisfied, perceived the settlement as more fair, and were more willing to negotiate with the seller in the future. In addition, when there was a lack of reciprocation, buyers sought revenge. That is, when fairness is primed in a negotiation and sellers do not reciprocate cooperative behavior, buyers sought to punish sellers by becoming extremely competitive.

Oliver and Swan (1989) conducted a field study regarding new automobile purchasers' perceptions of equity and satisfaction. Their findings suggest that interpersonal and distributive fairness (i.e., items included "I was treated fairly by my salesperson" and "The deal I agreed on with the salesperson was fair") and advantageous inequity (inequity in the customer's favor) influence buyer outcomes. For instance, perceptions of favorable interpersonal and economic outcomes (i.e., received a lot of help, got a good deal, etc.) are related to high levels of both interpersonal (e.g., "I was treated fairly by my salesperson") and distributive (e.g., "The deal I agreed on with the salesperson was fair") justice. In addition, distributive and interpersonal justice items predicted satisfaction. Thus, even when the item to be purchased is quite expensive, perceptions of interpersonal fairness (and not just distributive fairness) appear to be important determinants of consumer evaluations and satisfaction.

Holbrook and Kulik (2001) examined the effects of strong and weak relational ties on bank loan applicants' perceptions of three forms of justice (distributive, procedural, and interactional) in service transactions. The findings show outcome favorability (i.e., customers who had a greater amount of their loan request funded), opportunity for voice, and interpersonal treatment all enhance the perceived fairness of loan outcomes. In addition, weak-tie customers had more extreme reactions—more positive fairness perceptions of favorable outcomes and more negative fairness perceptions of unfavorable outcomes—compared to strong-tie customers. In the same year, Masterson (2001) investigated organizational justice perceptions in service employees and customers (operationalized as college teachers and students, respectively). Her results indicate that instructors who perceive high distributive and procedural justice at work report higher organizational commitment. In turn, students reported higher levels of instructor effort, instructor prosocial behavior (e.g., the instructor was available to meet outside of class), fairness, and more positive reactions (i.e., satisfaction, repatronage intentions, and word-of-mouth recommendations) toward the instructor.

A study by Raimondo, Miceli, and Costabile (2008) extends the above concepts of fairness and relationships in a study about the tenure of the relationship and the resultant effect on customer loyalty. In a study of cellular phone users in Italy, these authors found support for the effect of relational equity on customer loyalty—a stronger effect than either satisfaction or trust. These authors also found that over time, satisfaction plays less of a role in loyalty than does relational equity. Thus, fairness (relational equity) in a service relationship both builds loyalty early on and contributes to a continuation of the relationship and hence the loyalty of the consumer.

Another area of recent interest is when customers assist in the production process. Auh, Bell, McLeod, and Shih (2007) characterize such "co-production" as "constructive customer participation in the service creation and delivery process" (p. 361) and clarify that it requires meaningful, cooperative contributions to the service process. Examples of co-production include prospective homebuyers independently researching properties to engage in value creating discussions or avoid wasting time during face-to-face meetings with their realtor. Thus, co-production can increase value for both clients and the organization. These authors theorize that clients engaging in co-production are likely to display increased loyalty to the company. Furthermore, these authors argue that organizations can influence the extent to which clients engage in co-productive behavior through interpersonal justice. Both hypotheses were supported in a study of high-value clients of a financial firm, suggesting that interpersonal justice may play a role in building loyalty and creating value for organizations.

Consistent with the fundamental attribution error, consumers tend to overestimate the role that people play in controlling outcomes (Gilbert & Malone,

1995). Campbell (2007) performed several experiments to determine how the source of price information (human or nonhuman) may moderate the relationship between price changes and perceived fairness by manipulating a price change for a desired item as well as the source of the new price. Participants were told that they had shopped for a rug the previous week and, upon returning to the store to purchase it, the price had either increased or decreased by 25%. Furthermore, the source of the new price was either a salesperson (human) or price tag (nonhuman). She found that, in general, participants felt that a price increase was less fair when the new price was communicated by the salesperson as opposed to a price tag.

Stage 4: Receipt or Consumption of Goods or Services

This stage in the service exchange should be the payoff for the customer; the reason the customer engaged in a service exchange in the first place. After all, the goal is not to merely price shop (stage 1) or get to the service environment (Stage 2) or talk to an employee (stage 3), but to receive the desired outcome. However, much as is the case with Stage 2 in our model, it is rare that customer reactions are actually procured during the receipt or consumption of the goods or services contracted for. In some respects, this is logical (who wants to be interrupted during their meal at a restaurant and be asked to complete a survey?). However, there are some instances where goods and services are continuously utilized that would fall into this stage of our model and that we can examine.

In the case of services that can be continually utilized (e.g., cable television service, cell phones, etc.) future usage levels can be predicted based upon the perceived fairness of the original agreement and previous amount of usage. Bolton and Lemon (1999) found that customers plan their future usage of a continuous service by reflecting on the fairness of the exchange relationship. Customers evaluate their prior usage and the price of the service and adjust their future usage accordingly. This suggests, for example, that customers who feel they are not getting their money's worth are likely to increase their future usage to achieve an equitable balance of price and usage.

A study by Aurier and Siadou-Martin (2007) with French consumers found that perceived injustice in the receipt of a service is strongly related to dissatisfaction with the entire exchange. Utilizing the critical incident method, these authors surveyed French consumers and evaluated the extent to which justice perceptions with service receipt influenced perceptions of the quality of outcomes or the interaction, as well as subsequent trust-based outcomes (credibility and benevolence) with the service. Aurier and Siadou-Martin (2007) found that distributive justice was related to outcome quality and both procedural and interpersonal justice were related to interaction quality. Furthermore, distributive justice was related to subsequent credibility perceptions and distributive and interpersonal justice were related to subsequent benevolence perceptions.

Hui, Zhao, Fan, and Au (2004) examined variations in customer-service provider relationship age, process quality, and outcome quality on service evaluations. The experiments asked participants to role-play a scenario where a company representative was purchasing computers for his or her employer. Their first experiment confirmed the expectation that process quality and outcome quality interact to affect consumers' post-consumption behavior (measured here as satisfaction and repatronage intentions). "Process quality" (considerate versus rude interpersonal treatment during the ordering process) had a stronger effect on satisfaction and repatronage intent when outcome quality was favorable (e.g., on-time delivery of an order) compared to unfavorable (e.g., delay in delivery). In their second study, which involved the computers failing to work properly, the authors found support for the hypothesis that when consumers feel uncertain about the service outcome prior to consumption, they use process quality as a proxy in their assessment of the trustworthiness of the service provider.

Oliver, Shor, and Tidd (2004) also studied consumer satisfaction and its relationship with inequity in the form of over-benefiting or under-benefiting. These authors recruited student participants to a fictitious website via email lists and online ads. The context of their study included buying a gift on-line in which some participants received a coupon (overbenefit) while others received an empty coupon field (underbenefit). Receiving a coupon had positive effects on purchase completion, satisfaction, and repatronage intentions, while receiving an empty coupon field had strong negative effects on the aforementioned outcomes.

One concept that is important for organizations to focus on in providing goods or services to consumers is the importance of choice and representation in the offerings and fairness in the provision of outcomes. Greenwell, Brownlee, Jordan, and Popp (2008) conducted a study in which students were put in a position of having a dissatisfying encounter with a ticket office for a campus sporting event. The ticket policy was manipulated as having been determined by either a representative group of students or by the athletic department with no student input. These authors found that dissatisfaction with the ticket policy was weaker when the tickets were free (distributive justice) or when the policy had been designed by student representatives (procedural justice). Thus, dissatisfaction with outcomes may be reduced given increased procedural or distributive justice perceptions.

Stage 5: Service Aftermath

The final stage in our model recognizes that customer reactions to the receipt of a product or service can range from positive to negative (including having a neutral or indifferent reaction). Not surprisingly, the vast majority of fairness research in the service aftermath stage considers what happens when there

is a service failure—meaning that some element of the service exchange did not go as the customer expected it to. Service failures are the leading cause of customer switching behaviors (Keaveney, 1995) and thus are of considerable concern to firms. However, we begin by reviewing evidence related to service events that are not necessarily service failures.

Consider the custom of tipping after receiving a service—a sixteen billion dollar yearly event in the United States (Seligman, 1998). Tipping provides an opportunity to assess a behavioral outcome relevant to the quality of the service. Probably the most common environment in which tipping is customary is dining. Lynn and McCall (2000) conducted a meta-analysis of the relationship between a variety of aspects of customer restaurant experiences and tipping behavior. Their analysis of 13 studies involving over 2500 customers at a variety of restaurants (including Red Lobster, Chi-Chi's, Bennigans, and Olive Garden) documented that customers who perceived that they received better service left proportionately larger tips. The association between the service received from the waitperson and tip size received from the customer was significant even when controlling for other possible explanations such as quality of the food or customer mood. Moreover, while regular customers (those who have a service relationship with the waitstaff) tip proportionately more than infrequent customers (those who have a service exchange with the waitstaff), this factor does not eliminate the enhancement in tips received as a function of service. Thus, receiving quality interpersonal treatment (high interpersonal justice) as part of the dining experience pays off for service providers.

Nance and White (2009) conducted a study with undergraduates looking at the relationship between justice and service quality perceptions. Using a sample composed of individuals from both Central & Eastern Europe as well as the United States, these authors evaluated the effects of justice on service performance perceptions. The authors found that procedural, interpersonal and informational justice were positively related to perceptions of service performance. In addition, the relationship between interpersonal justice and service performance was stronger for the European participants.

Perhaps the greatest amount of research in the consumer behavior literature related to justice surrounds the dynamics of problematic service exchanges. Numerous studies have investigated how goods or services failures influences consumer satisfaction. The good news for organizations is that, in general, perceptions of justice in the recovery process are associated with increased satisfaction (e.g., Smith, Bolton, & Wagner, 1999; Tax, Brown, & Chandrashekaran, 1998).

Voorhees and Brady (2005) used a telephone sample of individuals in a southeastern metropolitan area to examine the antecedents of future complaining behavior and made some surprising discoveries. After a failed service encounter, customer perceptions of distributive and procedural justice actually increase future intentions to complain. That is, the higher the customer's perceived

level of justice, the more likely that consumer is to complain in the future. The authors surmise that this result indicates that consumers who believe they have received positive outcomes feel a stronger affinity for the organization, and therefore will complain should a future encounter go wrong, thus giving the organization an opportunity to rectify the situation. This is preferable to a customer who receives a poor outcome and never brings it to the attention of the firm, thus allowing whatever caused the negative situation to continue unchecked.

A study of business students by Saxby, Tat, and Johansen (2000) measured consumer perceptions of fairness in a complaint context. They found evidence that respondents were able to distinguish the extent to which the individual they were speaking with was listening to their complaint. Respondents also cared whether their complaint was handled with honesty and consistency, and they desired the ability to refute or appeal the outcome of the complaint. The authors believe these findings suggest "consumers form perceptions of their complaint fairness experience based on an amalgam of indicators rather than on discrete and identifiable dimensions" (p. 214). We agree and note that their study considers elements of both procedural justice (consistency and correctability) and interpersonal justice (honesty).

Bradley and Sparks (2009) looked more closely at the types of explanations (excuses, justifications, referential, apologies) used in a recovery situation. Using a sample of undergraduate students, they found that customer satisfaction and perceived justice depended on the explanation received for a service failure. Referential accounts (attempts to minimize the failure by making references to others worse off) negatively impacted customer satisfaction. In addition, different types of explanations had effects on different forms of justice. Apologies were related to interpersonal justice (and were the most favorable explanation overall in terms of outcomes), justifications were related to informational justice and excuses predicted procedural justice.

Collie, Bradley, and Sparks (2002), using a sample of undergraduate psychology students, investigated the effects of different forms of justice on customer satisfaction in a service recovery setting (a special offer of a discounted meal was disputed). A manipulation in the experiment revolved around participants knowledge of the outcomes of other customers. Surprisingly, perceptions of fairness did not seem to hinge on either distributive or procedural characteristics, but on interpersonal justice. The authors surmise that the "interpersonal treatment of customers … has significant effects on customer evaluations of outcome fairness and satisfaction" (Collie et al., 2002, p. 552).

Dunning, Pecotich, and O'Cass (2004) used mall-intercept and door-to-door techniques to investigate the adequacy of an explanation in unsatisfactory sales encounters. The findings suggest that explanation adequacy is positively related to perceptions of the fairness of the resolution and external attributions of blame (i.e., "no one is really to blame"). When individuals could place ex-

ternal blame, their perceptions of the justice of the resolution were increased. Similarly, when internal blame (i.e., agents of the company can be blamed) could be placed, consumer's emotional reactions were increased. Finally, justice perceptions of the resolution were negatively related to emotional reactions by the consumer.

Maxham and Netemeyer (2002) collected data from two samples of customers who complained about their banking service and new home construction. The findings suggest that distributive and interpersonal justice was related to satisfaction with both the recovery and the firm overall. In addition, firm satisfaction increased with procedural justice. Additionally, the authors found that satisfaction with recovery affects intentions to recommend the firm and overall satisfaction with the firm. Overall satisfaction with the firm, in turn, has an effect on repatronage intentions. In a follow up field study involving customer complaints, Maxham and Netemeyer (2003) found that customer ratings of distributive, procedural and interpersonal justice affect customer satisfaction with recovery situations, overall firm satisfaction, future purchase intent and recommendations to others.

Several studies have used the travel and vacation industries as the context in which to study fairness. Using a sample of airport travelers, Sindhav and colleagues (Sindhav, Holland, Rodie, Adidam, & Pol, 2006) studied passenger reactions to airport security and found that satisfaction with the service received (airport security) was most strongly related to procedural justice, followed closely by distributive justice. Importantly, however, all four types of justice studied (procedural, distributive, interpersonal and informational) were all significantly related to overall satisfaction with the service.

McCollough, Berry, and Yadav (2000) also investigated consumer satisfaction following service failure and recovery using survey data collected from airline passengers waiting in an airport. Participants were asked to respond to a scenario dealing with airline delays in which both distributive and interpersonal justice were manipulated. Results show that high perceptions of distributive as well as interpersonal justice are related to high post-service recovery satisfaction. There furthermore was an interactive effect of distributive and interpersonal justice predicting post-recovery satisfaction above and beyond either form of justice by themselves.

Park, Lehto, and Park (2008) examined a sample of complaints taken from online customer complaint sites referring to a family vacation or similar reference. Their results revealed that customer justice perceptions after service failures differed across industries, and reactions also depended on when in the vacation the service failure occurred. In the cruise industry for example, customer complaints reflected more significant interpersonal injustices whereas in hotel accommodation and airline travel, complaints were more associated with distributive injustices (e.g., price paid did not equal quality of room received). In addition, service failures occurring before the trip lead to perceptions of

procedural injustice, while service failures after a travel-related event were more related to interactional injustice. Finally, customers had different preferences for service recovery actions based on the injustice they received. Those customers who felt high distributive injustice preferred monetary compensation while customers who experience interpersonal injustice wanted the company warned or punished (via negative word-of-mouth).

Finally, a couple of studies have looked at reactions to booking travel-related activities using online intermediaries. In a laboratory simulation of an online purchasing decision, Humphrey, Ellis, Conlon, and Tinsley (2004) examined how customers' bids, recommendations, and repatronage behavior were affected by characteristics of the purchasing context. The setting required participants to offer a price for a hotel through an intermediary, which was then either accepted or rejected by the other party (similar to the structure of PriceLine.com, linking potential customers and hotels). Humphrey et al. (2004) found that negotiation structures (when ultimatum structures were expected) reduced distributive justice and informational justice, long waiting times for a system response reduced procedural, interpersonal, and informational justice, and rejected bids reduced all four types of justice judgments. Subsequent analyses revealed that injustice perceptions (particularly informational and distributive injustice) negatively influenced customers' recommendations to others and their repatronage intentions.

In a follow-up study, Ellis, Humphrey, Conlon, and Tinsley (2006) found that justifications or explanations should only be provided in a service recovery situation, and not as a general business practice. These authors examined customer reactions to having their electronic bids for a hotel room accepted or rejected by the intermediary. A manipulation varied whether the participants received a justification that discussed how procuring or not procuring a hotel room was a function of both room supply and the price offered by the customer along with the information about their accepted or rejected offer. While receipt of a justification improved customer reactions (distributive and interpersonal justice, as well as recommendation intentions) when their bids for the hotel were rejected, they reduced these same judgments when bids for hotels were accepted. These authors theorized that when customers receive a favorable outcome from such exchanges, they want to psychologically take credit for the outcome and do not want to consider that their success might partly be due to factors outside their control such as room availability.

Using videotaped scenarios and student subjects, Bradley and Sparks (2000) assessed likely customer reactions to staff empowerment (autonomy and discretion) to resolve problems in a hotel context. Subjects viewed service failures (delayed check-in, wrong room type, wrong amenity package) and subsequent service provider responses, and were then asked to rate aspects of the service delivery while imagining that they were the customer depicted in the videotape. They found that when service staff are fully empowered to handle the problem,

participants were more satisfied. In addition, participants rated the full empowerment condition as that most likely to lead to fair outcomes. Study 2 replicated the findings of the first study, and also made an important revelation in terms of the communication style of the employee. When the employee was accommodating (informal and personal) in their communication style, consumers had higher satisfaction than if the employee was not fully empowered. However, when the employee was not accommodating (formal and impersonal) there was no significant difference between satisfaction with empowered or unempowered employees. This continues to suggest that the interpersonal interaction in the service recovery phase is extremely important.

In service recovery settings, problem resolution often involves some sort of compensation or refund (Conlon & Murray, 1996). Many organizations feel that a refund is a small price to pay for customer retention, especially because the cost of gaining new customers exceeds that of retaining current ones (Hart, Heskett, & Sasser, 1990; Schneider, White, & Paul, 1998). However, the research on monetary compensation in recovery is mixed in this regard. Smith et al. (1999) found that compensation enhanced distributive justice in customers, which led to increases in satisfaction. Mattila and Cranage (2005) found support for the importance of compensation and the importance of an apology in a recovery situation. In a study using undergraduates, the authors found that both compensation and an apology increased distributive fairness, a finding confirmed through a 2-way interaction of the variables.

However, this does not seem to be a universal phenomenon. In an extension of the Smith et al. (1999) study, Sparks and McColl-Kennedy (2001), used local business and community group members to look at consumer satisfaction using video scenarios of a hotel service failure. These authors noted that higher satisfaction occurred when customers received a refund due to the service provider adhering to a company policy, rather than when the service provider was seen as doing a special favor for the customer. In the later situation, perhaps the customers felt the special favor was an admission of guilt, rather than a policy designed to maintain and enhance customer satisfaction. However, when customers received a more token compensation measure (e.g., drink vouchers), the participants expressed higher satisfaction if the service provider was doing a special favor.

While most of the studies in this area have used U.S. samples, there are a few studies that have examined issues related to justice and services cross-culturally. Mattila and Patterson (2004) examined the impact of compensation and explanations on perceptions of fairness and satisfaction using samples of undergraduate students in Asia and the United States (i.e., collectivist and individualist cultures, respectively). The participants read scenarios describing a service failure in a restaurant (e.g., slow service and an incorrect order). This study suggests that both compensation and explanations (a discount and an apology) are especially effective in restoring distributive and interpersonal

justice perceptions in American consumers. Offering an explanation for the service failure also had a positive effect on consumer perceptions regardless of one's cultural background. Finally, the results also suggest that both types of justice are directly linked to consumer satisfaction.

Au, Hui, and Leung (2001) conducted a cross-cultural study to investigate the effects of voice, compensation and responsibility on consumer attributions of blame, justice perceptions and post-complaint behavior (e.g., repatronage intentions and recommendations to others). The findings suggest that voice (i.e., a manager gives the customer a chance to air their complaint by listening patiently, asking questions regarding details of the complaint, etc.) fails to reduce consumer attributions of blame. However, offering compensation actually increases customers' blame on the service provider. Cross-cultural effects suggest that collectivists blame the service provider more than individualists and that responsibility (blame) attribution mediates the relationship between culture and justice perceptions and post-complaint behaviors.

Extending the cultural focus of recovery tactics, Patterson, Cowley, and Prasongsukarn (2006) used samples from Thailand and Australia to look at individual characteristics generally associated with one's culture such as power distance, uncertainty avoidance and collectivism and determine the role played by these characteristics in fairness perceptions of a service recovery. Their results are intriguing for managers; customers with a higher power distance orientation felt greater distributive justice when an apology was provided by an employee of higher status, while those in a low power distance orientation reported no difference in justice perception. However, those individuals with low power distance orientation perceived more procedural and interpersonal justice when a low status employee delivered an apology. The authors also found a main effect of service recovery initiation whereby customers (regardless of their orientation) felt a higher sense of interpersonal justice when the organization initiated the service recovery. In addition, when customers had a collectivist orientation, they perceived greater procedural justice when the organization initiated the recovery. Furthermore, customers with higher uncertainty avoidance orientation felt more procedural and distributive justice when they were kept informed during the recovery process.

Hui and Au (2001) investigated justice perceptions of three methods of handling complaints during the service recovery phase: voice, compensation and apology, using a Chinese and a Canadian sample. The results suggest that overall both voice and compensation were related to higher perceived fairness of outcomes in both samples while only voice had an affect on the perceived fairness of the process in general. Additionally, an apology also had an effect on the perceived fairness of the complaint-handling process for both nationalities. However, there were cultural differences as to which nationality responded stronger to one method of handling complaints or another, suggesting the need for managers to take heed of who their customers are.

Discussion

Implications for Researchers

We hope that this review, while not exhaustive, paints a very clear picture of the current status of justice research as it relates to consumers. In terms of attempting to summarize the research as it relates to our model, we note that in Stage 1 of the service exchange we found no research that explicitly relied on any of the four specific forms of justice we outlined at the beginning of the chapter. Instead, the studies in this section tend to rely on a more global, holistic conception of the fairness of a given situation (even though the focus of many of these studies is in the area of price fairness, i.e., distributive justice). The reliance on global fairness measures makes it difficult for us to address exactly what predictors need to be managed to increase fairness.

The potential to apply our fourfold model of justice is even greater in Stage 2. Recall that this stage consists of the consumer entering the service setting and attending to cues in the environment; however a social interaction has not yet occurred. It may well be that some critical justice judgments are formed in this stage and once formed, they could be very resistant to change, despite new information learned in later stages (cf. Van den Bos, 1997). Research focused on Stage 2 of the service exchange is practically non-existent, save some recent studies examining the effects of waiting in line for a service. While we provide some anecdotes regarding the type of injustices that may be encountered in this stage, as a field we know very little about justice in this stage. This is definitely an area waiting for further investigation.

Stage 3 focuses on the social interaction that a consumer has with the service provider. This stage is well represented with studies that examine three of the four types of justice. Research at this stage has most heavily emphasized the interpersonal justice domain, though some work has been done on distributive and procedural justice as well. The one justice type not frequently examined by studies classified into this stage is informational justice. However, we think explanations often form part of the social interaction between service providers and customers, and that customers can evaluate the candidness and truthfulness of communications in this stage. Thus, it is curious that informational justice judgments are rarely procured at this stage.

Stage 4 presents fewer studies, but with a frequency pattern similar to Stage 3 in that we could find studies in this stage that examined distributive, procedural, and interpersonal justice more often than studies that examined informational justice. Research at this phase would seem to be fruitful and, furthermore, would directly speak to justice perceptions at Stage 5 in which the most research has been conducted. Stage 5 involves the aftermath of service consumption. Although this stage encompasses both positive and negative post-consumption experiences, the bulk of the research has tended toward a recovery

situation—an unsurprising situation considering that service failures are among the leading cause of customer switching (Keaveney, 1995) and thus, alleviating that failure may result in the retention of that consumer. As the service recovery phase often involves discussions of compensation and company policies, it is no surprise to see distributive and procedural justice so well represented. Explanations and interpersonal treatment are also of great relevance to events in this stage and as a result both informational and interpersonal justice are also well represented.

Turning to a consideration of the variables typically measured in these studies, we find further potential for significant contributions in this field. The bulk of the research conducted in Stage 1 considers fairness perceptions themselves as the end variable of interest (i.e., the dependent variable); price changes and satisfaction are the typical independent variables. In stage 2, the one study that we did review considered repatronage intentions as the dependent variable. In stage 3, repatronage, satisfaction, and word-of-mouth recommendations are the typical dependent variables. When fairness is considered as the dependent variable, it is usually only in studies examining price changes as the independent variable. In stage 4, satisfaction is the most prevalent dependent variable studied, whereas favorable outcomes are the most commonly studied independent variable. In stage 5, where the bulk of research has been conducted, many dependent variables have been studied: repatronage intention, satisfaction, word-of-mouth recommendation, satisfaction, etc. Rarely is fairness considered as the dependent variable in this stage.

In sum, though certain dependent variables are represented in multiple stages, their presence is not consistent. Stages 2 and 4, and stage 3 to some extent, have received relatively little research attention compared to stages 1 and 5 and thus contributions can be made by conducting research in stages 2–4 using the variables typically found in stages 1 and 5.

Implications for Management

Each of the five stages of the service exchange provides a different set of challenges for managers and organizations. It is important for organizations to make the consumer aware of their brand (Stage 1), get the consumers to the store (Stage 2), arrange an interaction with an associate (Stage 3), make the sale (Stage 4) and hopefully avoid post-sale complications and the need for a service recovery (Stage 5). In conceiving a strategic plan for an organization, managers must pay attention to the justice implications of each stage in order to run a profitable enterprise.

At stage 1, consumers have a number of different options for the goods or services they wish to consume. Managers must be aware that consumers have perceptions of the price of goods or services before ever setting foot inside the service setting. Furthermore, consumers are very sensitive to price changes

at this point. This presents a problem for managers because price changes are necessary; the costs of goods increase regularly and often these increases are beyond the control of management. If the cost of goods increases, management should attempt to convey that these increases were beyond their control, and furthermore, prices should be increased only by the additional cost.

Furthermore, management should closely monitor the reputation of their firm, as those reputation effects can have significant implications for consumer justice perceptions. In fact, along with a reputation for good service and prices, managers might want to cultivate their store's reputation for fairness. To put it another way, consumers are more likely to give the benefit of the doubt to a firm with a good reputation as opposed to a poor reputation. Finally, the use of rate fences or demand-based pricing seems to be a practice that consumers will accept, given certain conditions. Though weekday/weekend pricing differences may make economic sense, consumers may be unwilling to accept those. Furthermore, the use of demand-based pricing should be framed as a discount as opposed to a surcharge, given what the literature on framing has taught if linked to surprises such as high costs, may lead to very upset customers.

We have few suggestions to make for managers regarding consumer experiences at stage 2, given the lack of research conducted at this stage. It would seem that consumers who encounter a price significantly higher than they expected upon entering a store are prone to leave, perhaps without ever giving the store a chance to correct the situation. For a firm, this situation is dire, as they may have lost a customer without ever knowing it. A suggestion for managers is to augment price information with information justifying the price—in other words, combine informational justice information with the information that communicates distributive justice information. Augmenting the price with interpersonal justice could also be helpful. The take-home message from the anecdote about Geno's Steaks would suggest that customers may be so offended by a sign that they switch their patronage without the firm ever having the chance to engage in recovery. Finally, we note that the speed with which customers are served also appears to be important, and may perhaps be even more important for online customers. Long waits can lead customers to perceive interpersonal injustice, and subsequent decrements in repatronage and increases in negative word of mouth. Here, the answer might be to neutralize the delay by offering compensation or some other reward that grows larger as the delay in service grows longer.

Stage 3 demonstrates the criticality of the consumer's interaction experience with a sales associate. In general, it would seem that organizations recognize the importance of friendly associates as evidenced by the recent interest in the emotional labor construct (e.g., Grandey, 2000, 2003). Management should understand that these interactions are highly idiosyncratic and that during this phase, anything can happen. During this stage, perceptions of justice tend to lead to increased consumer satisfaction and future repatronage intentions. The

extent to which these interactions can affect subsequent consumer behaviors, as well as the potential for variability in interactions during this stage suggests the need for explicit training of sales associates on how to manage these interactions and ensure that the consumers feels that they have been treated justly.

Stage 4 represents the payoff for the consumer, the desired end-state of consumption of the good or service. For the consumer, this stage is the most important and thus justice perceptions at this stage should be of particular interest to managers. Success at this stage may preclude the need to advance to stage 5 and recovery and therefore, attention should be focused on this stage to prevent the need for subsequent stages. Research at this stage suggests that the quality of the outcome is extremely important to justice perceptions. Managers must ensure that the good or service delivered is of the expected quality. In addition, research at this stage shows that little extras such as a coupon may increase consumer justice perceptions. Furthermore, that coupon may ensure that the consumer engages in repatronage in order to take advantage of the discount.

Judging by the bulk of research in this area, stage 5 seems to be of the utmost importance to managers. However, managers likely would be unanimous in agreeing that they would prefer to never have to be in this stage because, generally speaking, this stage of the consumer service exchange implies that something has gone wrong. However, the research indicates that all is not lost and that recovery can occur, problems can be corrected, and consumers can feel justice in this stage. The most important requirement of this stage is for the consumer to bring the problem to the attention of management; if the consumer does not do this, the problem cannot be corrected and consumer attrition may occur. Research indicates that those consumers who feel an affinity to the organization or have in the past had favorable experiences are more likely to give the organization a chance to recover. Thus, as in stage 1, brand reputation is very important. Furthermore, managers should ensure that consumer complaints are handled promptly and with a degree of humility on the part of the organization. It makes no difference if the organization was in the right; if the consumer feels injustice then attrition is likely to occur. Research has indicated that some form of a favorable distributive outcome can increase justice perceptions here, however the context is important.

Coupons or other forms of reimbursements such as refunds have been found to increase satisfaction and loyalty, however, this is not a panacea. Some research has shown that a full refund (perhaps preferable to the organization to keep the customer, see: Hart et al., 1990; Schneider et al., 1998) may lead the consumer to perceive the recovery as an admission of guilt and attribute full blame to the organization and reduce satisfaction. In addition, when the refund was attributed to a "special favor" as opposed to company policy, consumers felt more injustice, possibly because they believe in another situation perhaps they would not have received the same compensation. The take-home message for managers in this situation is that reimbursement as a form of recovery can be a tricky situation

and, if that is the policy of the company, this policy should be clearly spelled out to the customer and an apology should be issued as well.

Limitations and a Look to the Future

Our review also highlights where improvements can be undertaken to facilitate our understanding of how justice judgments influence aspects of the consumer behavior context. It is safe to say that the majority of studies in this area appear to be field surveys or laboratory-based scenario studies. While these methods have provided a wealth of information, it would seem that the time is ripe for other methodologies to be used. For example, very few studies incorporate video, when it seems that by doing so, the context could be made more realistic. This might especially be the case for investigating issues related to interpersonal justice, where elements observable on video (tone of voice, facial expressions, body language) cannot be seen when one is reading a scenario vignette. It also seems that clever researchers could design field experiments using different store franchise locations as the units of manipulation. We are not suggesting that franchise owners create conditions of gross injustice at one store (which might irreparably harm sales), but perhaps individual stores can be chosen to try out procedures or policies intended to enhance fairness perceptions. For instance, employees could be trained to exhibit greater interpersonal sensitivity, which should enhance interpersonal justice and potentially lead to a variety of more favorable customer reactions.

A second area worthy of additional work involves the relationship of emotions to justice and customer outcomes. Emotions are currently a hot topic in the organization sciences (Brief & Weiss, 2002; Elfenbein, 2007), however research linking emotion reactions or emotional displays to justice perceptions has not occurred with much frequency. Emotional displays could come from the customer, the service provider, other customers, or other service providers. How would seeing a manager publicly berate (versus publicly praise) an employee influence your attitudes about shopping at a store? How would seeing another customer express anger at a store employee influence your reactions? Incorporating emotions more fully into our discussions of fairness and consumer behavior would be a fruitful arena for future research.

The importance of justice perceptions regarding consumer reactions and behavior has been the subject of much recent research. A central goal of this chapter was to examine the influence of justice in consumer behavior settings. By reviewing a large number of studies published in a disparate sample of journals, we have painted a picture of the current state of research in this arena. Furthermore, by identifying the research that has been conducted, we have illuminated areas in which theoretical and empirical contributions can be made. Finally, we discussed the potential implications of the current research for managers and organizations, as well as some areas in need of additional research.

References

Ambrose, M., & Arnaud, A. (2005). Are procedural justice and distributive justice conceptually distinct? In J. Greenberg & J. A. Colquitt (Eds.), *Handbook of organizational justice* (pp. 59–84). Mahwah, NJ: Erlbaum.

Associated Press. (2006, June 08). Philadelphia's Geno's Steaks adopts English-only ordering policy. Retrieved from http://www.foxnews.com/story/0,2933,198757,00.html.

Au, K., Hui, M. K., & Leung, K. (2001). Who should be responsible? Effects of voice and compensation on responsibility attribution, perceived justice, and post-complaint behaviors across cultures. *International Journal of Conflict Management, 12,* 350–364.

Auh, S., Bell, S. J., McLeod, C. S., & Shih, E. (2007). Co-production and customer loyalty in financial services. *Journal of Retailing, 83,* 359–370.

Aurier, P., & Siadou-Martin, B. (2007). Perceived justice and consumption experience evaluations. *International Journal of Service Industry Management, 18,* 450–471.

Babin, B. J., Griffin, M., & Boles, J. S. (2004). Buyer reactions to ethical beliefs in the retail environment. *Journal of Business Research, 57,* 1155–1163.

Bearden, W. O., Carlson, J. P., & Hardesty, D. M. (2003). Using invoice price information to frame advertised offer. *Journal of Business Research, 56,* 355–366.

Bolton, L. E., Warlop, L., & Alba, J. W. (2003). Consumer perceptions of price (un)fairness. *Journal of Consumer Research, 29,* 474–491.

Bolton, R. N., & Lemon, K. N. (1999). A dynamic model of customers' usage of services: Usage as an antecedent and consequence of satisfaction. *Journal of Marketing Research, 36,* 171–186.

Bradley, G. L., & Sparks, B. A. (2000). Customer reactions to staff empowerment: Mediators and moderators. *Journal of Applied Social Psychology, 30,* 991–1012.

Bradley, G. L., & Sparks, B. A. (2009). Dealing with service failures: The use of explanations. *Journal of Travel & Tourism Marketing, 26,* 129–143.

Brief, A. P., & Weiss, H. M. (2002). Organizational behavior: Affect in the workplace. *Annual Review of Psychology, 53,* 1120–1128.

Campbell, M. C. (1999). Perceptions of price unfairness: Antecedents and consequences. *Journal of Marketing Research, 36,* 187–199.

Campbell, M. C. (2007). "Says who?!" How the source of price information and affect influence perceived price (un)fairness. *Journal of Marketing Research, 46,* 261–271.

Collie, T., Bradley, G., & Sparks, B. A. (2002). Fair process revisited: Differential effects of interactional and procedural justice in the presence of social comparison information. *Journal of Experimental Social Psychology, 38,* 545–555.

Colquitt, J. A., Conlon, D. E., Wesson, M., Porter, C., & Ng, K. (2001). Justice at the millennium: A meta-analytic review of 25 years of organizational justice research. *Journal of Applied Psychology, 86,* 425–445.

Conlon, D. E., & Murray, N. M. (1996). Customer perceptions of corporate responses to product complaints: The role of explanations. *Academy of Management Journal, 39,* 1040–1056.

Conlon, D. E., Van Dyne, L., Milner, M., & Ng, K. Y. (2004). The effects of physical and social context on evaluations of captive intensive service relationships. *Academy of Management Journal, 47,* 433–445.

Courty, P., & Pagliero, M. (2008). Do consumers care about how prices are set? *International Journal of the Economics of Business, 15,* 27–43.

Daskalopoulou, I., & Petrou, A. (2006). Consumers' expenditures and perceived price fairness. *International Journal of Social Economics, 33,* 766–780.

Doucet, L. (2004). Service provider hostility and service quality. *Academy of Management Journal, 47,* 761–771.

Dulebohn, J. H., Conlon, D. E., Sarinopoulos, I., Davison, R. B., & McNamara, G. (2009). The biological bases of unfairness: Neuroimaging evidence for the distinctiveness of procedural and distributive justice. *Organizational Behavior and Human Decision Processes, 110,* 140–151.

Dunning, J., Pecotich, A., & O'Cass, A. (2004). What happens when things go wrong? Retail sales explanations and their effects. *Psychology and Marketing, 21,* 553–572.

Elfenbein, H. A. (2007). Emotion in organizations: A review and theoretical integration. *Academy of Management Annals, 1,* 315–386.

Ellis, A. P., Humphrey, S. E., Conlon, D. E., & Tinsley, C. H. (2006). Improving customer reactions to electronic brokered ultimatums: The benefits of prior experience and explanations. *Journal of Applied Social Psychology, 36,* 2293–2324.

Folger, R., & Greenberg, J. (1985). Procedural justice: An interpretive analysis of personnel systems. In K. Rowland & G. Ferris (Eds.), *Research in personnel and human resources management* (Vol. 3, pp. 141–183). Greenwich, CT: JAI Press.

Gilbert, D. T., & Malone, P. S. (1995). The correspondence bias. *Psychological Bulletin, 117,* 21–38.

Grandey, A. A. (2000). Emotion regulation the workplace: A new way to conceptualize emotional labor. *Journal of Occupational Health Psychology, 5,* 95–110.

Grandey, A. A. (2003). When "the show must go on": Surface acting and deep acting as determinants of emotional exhaustion and peer-rated service delivery. *Academy of Management Journal, 46,* 86–96.

Greenberg, J. (Ed.), & Colquitt, J. A. (Ed.). (2005). *Handbook of organizational justice.* Mahwah, NJ: Erlbaum.

Greenwell, T. C., Brownlee, E., Jordan, J. S., & Popp, N. (2008). Service fairness in spectator sport: The importance of voice and choice on customer satisfaction. *Sport Marketing Quarterly, 17,* 71–78.

Hart, C. W. L., Heskett, J. L., & Sasser, W. E. (1990). The profitable art of service recovery. *Harvard Business Review, 68* (4), 148–156.

Holbrook, R. L., & Kulik, C. T. (2001). Customer perceptions of justice in service transactions: The effects of strong and weak ties. *Journal of Organizational Behavior, 22,* 743–757.

Homburg, C., Hoyer, W. D., & Koschate, N. (2005). Customers reactions to price increases: Do customer satisfaction and perceived motive fairness matter? *Journal of the Academy of Marketing Science, 33,* 36–49.

Hui, M. K., & Au, K. (2001). Justice perceptions of complaint-handling: A cross-cultural comparison between PRC and Canadian customers. *Journal of Business Research, 52,* 161–173.

Hui, M. K., Zhao, X., Fan, X., & Au, K. (2004). When does the service process matter? A test of two competing theories. *Journal of Consumer Research, 31,* 465–475.

Huppertz, J. W., Arenson, S. J., & Evans, R. H. (1978). An application of equity theory to buyer–seller exchange situations. *Journal of Marketing Research, 15,* 250–260.

Humphrey, S. E., Ellis, A. P. J., Conlon, D. E., & Tinsley, C. H. (2004). Understanding customer reactions to brokered ultimatums: Applying negotiation and justice theory. *Journal of Applied Psychology, 89,* 466–482.

Kahneman, D., Knetsch, J., & Thaler, R. (1986). Fairness as a constraint on profit seeking: Entitlements in the market. *American Economic Review, 76,* 728–741.

Keaveney, S. M. (1995). Customer switching behavior in service industries: An exploratory study. *Journal of Marketing, 59,* 71–82.

Kimes, S. E., & Wirtz, J. (2003). Has revenue management become acceptable?: Findings from an international study on the perceived fairness of rate fences. *Journal of Service Research, 6,* 125–135.

Lynn, M., & McCall, M. (2000). Gratitude and gratuity: A meta-analysis of research on the service-tipping relationship. *Journal of Socio-Economics, 29,* 203–214.

Masterson, S. S. (2001). A trickle-down model of organizational justice: Relating employees' and customers' perceptions of and reactions to fairness. *Journal of Applied Psychology, 86,* 594–604.

Mattila, A. S., & Patterson, P. G. (2004). Service recovery and fairness perceptions in collectivist and individualist contexts. *Journal of Service Research, 6,* 336–346.

Mattila, A. S., & Cranage, D. (2005). The impact of choice on fairness in the context of service recovery. *Journal of Services Marketing, 19,* 271–279.

Maxham, J. G., & Netemeyer, R. G. (2002). Modeling customer perceptions of complaint handling over time: The effects of perceived justice on satisfaction and intent. *Journal of Retailing, 78,* 239–252.

Maxham, J. G., & Netemeyer, R. G. (2003). Firms reap what they sow: The effects of shared values and perceived organizational justice on customers' evaluations of complaint handling. *Journal of Marketing, 67,* 46–62.

Maxwell, S., Nye, P., & Maxwell, N. (1999). Less pain, some gain: The effects of priming fairness in price negotiations. *Psychology and Marketing, 16,* 545–562.

Maxwell, S., Nye, P., & Maxwell, N. (2003). The wrath of the fairness-primed negotiator when the reciprocity norm is violated. *Journal of Business Research, 56,* 399–409.

McCollough, M. A., Berry, L. L., & Yadav, M. S. (2000). An empirical investigation of customer satisfaction after service failure and recovery. *Journal of Service Research, 3,* 121–137.

Nance, W., & White, D. (2009). Service performance and procedural justice: The mediating roles of family life cycle and culture. *Journal of Services Marketing, 23,* 195–207.

Oh, H., & Jeong, M. (2004). An extended process of value judgment. *International Journal of Hospitality Management, 23,* 343–362.

Oliver, R. L., Shor, M., & Tidd, S. T. (2004). Induced over-benefiting and under-benefiting on the Web: Inequity effects on feelings and motivations with implications for consumption behavior. *Motivation and Emotion, 28,* 85–106.

Oliver, R. L., & Swan, J. E. (1989). Consumer perceptions of interpersonal equity and satisfaction in transactions: A field survey approach. *Journal of Marketing, 53,* 21–35.

Patterson, P. G., Cowley, E., & Prasongsukarn, K. (2006). Service failure recovery: The moderating impact of individual-level cultural value orientation on perceptions of justice. *International Journal of Research in Marketing, 23,* 263–277.

Park, O., Lehto, X., & Park, J. (2008). Service failures and complaints in the family travel market: A justice dimension approach. *Journal of Services Marketing, 22,* 520–532.

Piron, R., & Fernandez, L. (1995). Are fairness constraints on profit-seeking important? *Journal of Economic Psychology, 16,* 73–96.

Pisharodi, R. M., & Langley, C. J. (1990). A perceptual process model of customer satisfaction based on cybernetic/control theory. *Journal of Business Logistics, 11,* 26–49.

Raimondo, M. A., Miceli, G., & Costabile, M. (2008). How relationship age moderates loyalty formation: The increasing effect of relational equity on customer loyalty. *Journal of Service Research, 11,* 142–160.

Salancik, G. R., & Leblebici, H. (1988). Variety and form in organizing transactions: A generative grammar of organization. In S. Bachrach (Ed.), *Research in the sociology of organizations* (Vol. 6, pp. 1–34). Greenwich, CT: JAI Press.

Salancik, G., R., & Pfeffer, J. (1978). A social information processing approach to job attitudes and task design. *Administrative Science Quarterly, 23*, 224–253.

Sawyer, J., Kernan, M., Conlon, D., & Garland, H. (1999). Responses to the Michelangelo computer virus threat: The role of information sources and risk homeostasis theory. *Journal of Applied Social Psychology, 29*, 23–51.

Saxby, C. L., Tat, P. K., & Johansen, J. T. (2000). Measuring consumer perceptions of procedural justice in a complaint context. *Journal of Consumer Affairs, 34,* 204–216.

Schneider, B., White, S. S., & Paul, M. C. (1998). Linking service climate and customer perceptions of service quality: Tests of a causal model. *Journal of Applied Psychology, 83,* 150–163.

Seligman, D. (1998, December 14). Why do you leave tips? *Forbes,* pp. 138–140.

Sindhav, B., Holland, J., Rodie, A. R., Adidam, P. T., & Pol, L. G. (2006). The impact of perceived fairness on satisfaction: Are airport security measures fair? Does it matter? *Journal of Marketing Theory and Practice, 14,* 323–335.

Skarlicki, D. P., van Jaarsveld, D. D., & Walker, D. D. (2008). Getting even for customer mistreatment. The role of moral identity in the relationship between customer interpersonal injustice and employee sabotage. *Journal of Applied Psychology, 93,* 1335–1347.

Smith, A. K., Bolton, R. N., & Wagner, J. (1999). A model of customer satisfaction with service encounters involving failure and recovery. *Journal of Marketing Research, 36,* 356–372.

Sparks, B. A., & McColl-Kennedy, J. R. (2001). Justice strategy options for increased customer satisfaction in a services recovery setting. *Journal of Business Research, 54,* 209–218.

Tax, S. S., Brown, S. W., & Chandrashekaran, M. (1998). Customer evaluations of service complaint experiences: Implications for relationship marketing. *Journal of Marketing, 62,* 60–76.

Thibaut, J., & Walker, L. (1975). *Procedural justice: A psychological analysis.* Hillsdale, NJ: Erlbaum.

Vaidyanathan, R., & Aggarwal, P. (2003). Who is the fairest of them all? An attributional approach to price fairness perceptions. *Journal of Business Research, 56,* 453–463.

Van den Bos, K. (1997). Procedural and distributive justice: What is fair depends more on what comes first than what comes next. *Journal of Personality and Social Psychology, 72*, 95–104.

Verhoef, P. C., Franses, P. H., & Hoekstra, J. C. (2002). The effect of relational constructs on customer referrals and number of services purchased from a multiservice provider: Does age of relationship matter? *Journal of the Academy of Marketing Science, 30,* 202–216.

Voorhees, C. M., & Brady, M. K. (2005). A service perspective on the drivers of complaint intentions. *Journal of Service Research, 8,* 192–204.

Zhou, R., & Soman, D. (2008). Consumers' waiting in queues: The role for first-order and second-order justice. *Psychology & Marketing, 25,* 262–279.

PART II

LEADERSHIP, SOCIAL CAPITAL, AND PERSONALITY

Current Topics in Management, **Vol. 15, 2011, pp. 95-116**

OBAMA VS. CLINTON: A STUDY EXPLORING THE IMPACT OF LEADERSHIP LANGUAGE

Diana Hargrove, Phyllis A. Duncan, Mark T. Green, Charles Salter, and John M. Trayhan

The 2008 United States presidential election presented many challenges to voter decisions and opportunities for analysis. It was an historical election year with many firsts, including the first time since the 1928 election that neither an incumbent president nor incumbent vice president ran for their party's nomination. It was the first time since 1952 that neither was a candidate in the general election. It was the first time that two sitting senators ran against each other for president and both were born outside the continental United States. It was the first time a woman and an African–American ran for president ("United states presidential," n.d.). In addition to all of the firsts, there were many issues for the voter to take into consideration including the state of the economy, the war in Iraq, threat of terrorism, social security, unemployment, healthcare, and increasing food and fuel costs. How does a voter begin to decide? One place to start, as suggested by George Stephanopoulos (2008, June 29), was to focus on what the candidates did, but more importantly, what they said, especially when under pressure.

Leaders and Leadership

Characteristics of ideal leaders had been described throughout history, even as early as Plato's analysis of philosopher–kings (Burns, 1995). Northouse (2001) describes a leader as the person who takes responsibility for initiating and maintaining a relationship and communication linkage with a follower. However, a leader could be any person who was expected to perform the

specialized leadership role (Yukl, 2002). Leaders must commit to a goal with mind, body, and soul to make change happen (Denning, 2007). "Leadership is one of the most observed and least understood phenomena on earth" (Burns, 1995, p. 9).

Not all scholars agree as to the leadership qualities of politicians. Judgments about presidential leadership were often based on images of the office and not reality (Neustadt, 1991). Denning's (2007) qualitative analysis of political leaders pointed out that a successful politician must get elected and/or re-elected to a political office. However, the qualities required to achieve this goal were not necessarily leadership, especially transformational leadership. A successful politician was willing to fight, needed to be well armed/funded, was willing to play hardball, flexible, pursued issues with existing electorate consensus, and was ambiguous about his/her commitment to change.

Until the 2008 presidential election, public prejudices and perceived presidential traits had limited the diversity of the presidential candidates. No Catholic had been elected until 1960. The first African–American and female nomination did not occur until 2008. Additionally, health, age, finances, family connections, and family life could be influencing factors in the nominating process (Edwards & Wayne, 2003).

Language of Leadership, Politics, and Gender

Bennis and Nanus (1985), Kotter (1996), Bass and Riggio (2006), and Denning (2007) all suggest a leader should communicate in a language that expresses the urgency of a communication, an exciting vision of a future state, and that this communication should be reinforced through narratives and other communications, which model the action required to attain the desired future.

As noted by Hart (2002) and Tulis (as cited by Beasley, 2004), the language of politicians is not much askew from those cited above. Political leaders should engage in rhetoric, which inspires their constituents and leads them to reflect on a desired future state. Hackman and Johnson (2000) and Bligh, Kohles, and Meindl (2004) suggest that verbal and non-verbal communication were a fundamental of political leadership.

In business organizations, sports metaphor and military language define the culture of business. The normal processes of communications and language in these environments are controlled and can be associated with the culture of upper-class, White males (Lakoff, 2000; Eagley & Carli, 2007). Lakoff (1975) stated women speak in a powerless language, which avoids strong opinion or commitment. Eckert and McConnell-Ginet (2003) suggest that the attitude stated by Lakoff (1975) led to women utilizing more assertive language and behavior. Eagley (2007) suggests that the recent findings on transformational leadership, whose constructs include, what was previously thought of as less

masculine behaviors, such as individualized consideration, have resolved some of the conflicts associated with female leadership behavior.

Content Analysis

Neuendorf (2002) defined content analysis as the systematic, objective, quantitative analysis of messages ranging from spoken language, newspaper articles, television shows, to advertisements. The ability to make inferences from text to their contexts was the defining feature of content analysis (Krippendorf & Bock, 2009). Krippendorf (2004) indicates that content analysis has been used as a research tool since the seventeenth century, when Church officials and the state wanted to censor text. By the twentieth century, scholars were utilizing content analysis to exam mass media and to conduct literary studies. Words and concepts are analyzed and inferences are made about the messages within the texts, sometimes about the audience and even the culture. Texts can include a variety of media including books, book charters, essays, interviews, articles, speeches and other media. The text is studied by the researcher by breaking it down into manageable parts. The parts are then examined using conceptual analysis or relational analysis (Colorado State, 2010).

In computer-assisted content analysis, all words and phrases from the texts analyzed can be tallied and sorted. Then, using a feature commonly called Key Word in Context, frequently used words and phrases can be further examined to ascertain the context in which they are being used. If a word or phrase is representative of a theme being analyzed, it is then considered a meaning unit. Systematically, a large number of meaning units is added to themes to be used in the subsequent content analysis.

Statement of the Problem

The words a politician uses during a campaign could tell us a great deal about that person, including the leadership style we might expect him or her to utilize once in office. However, too often voters make their decisions and cast their ballots without knowledge of what leadership actually was or regard for the type of leadership that would be provided in the future, but rather based upon party affiliation, mass media portrayal of sound bites, or the never ending polls. Leaders were chosen for their style rather than their substance, for their image instead of their integrity (George, 2006).

Purpose of the Study

The purpose of this study was to determine the leadership language reflected in the campaign speeches of the 2008 Democratic Party presidential candidates Senator Hillary Rodham Clinton and Senator Barack Hussein Obama through

the use of non-intrusive, empirical quantitative text analysis software, as opposed to relying on the qualitative viewpoints of the press based on gender, race, religion, and political experience. The fundamental purpose of the study was to explore the possible impact of leadership language in the candidates' success or failure in achieving the party nomination. Additionally, the study context and candidates provided the backdrop to examine gender and ethnicity differences in leader language and voter response.

Method

Operational Definitions for Dependent Variables

The dependent variables transformational leadership language, transactional leadership language, and passive leadership language were operationalized with custom dictionaries created by the researchers. A custom dictionary was a set of words, phrases, parts of speech, or other word-base indicators used as a basis for a search of texts (Neuendorf, 2002). Initially, the researcher identified the following issue themes frequently addressed in the candidate's speeches: economy, health care, education, and foreign policy. Economy, health care, and foreign policy were identified as important issues by the voters during Democratic primary exit polls ("ABC News 2008," n.d.). Therefore, in keeping with the exit polls and for the purposes of this study, education issues theme was dropped and the following dictionaries were created: transformational language, transactional language, passive language, economic issues themes, health care issues themes, and foreign policy issues themes.

Procedure

Content analysis should follow a set of procedures that were common for research in the scientific method (Insch, Moore, & Murphy, 1997; Krippendorf, 2004; Neuendorf, 2002; Weber, 1990). Therefore, the literature was first reviewed for relevant theory and previous research to develop research questions and constructs. Theoretical rationales were developed for why a construct would manifest itself in text and why word counts would represent a measurement of the construct. Next, a search for availability of candidate speeches revealed the official website for each candidate posted the speeches they made along the campaign trail. Since the use of computers makes analysis at the detailed level less cumbersome, and this study utilized computer aided content analysis, the basic unit of analysis was individual words (Insch, Moore, & Murphy, 1997).

The value added to content analysis was the classification of units into categories that were derived from the research questions, underlying theories, and constructs. The Full Range of Leadership Model (Bass, 1985) was the

basis for defining the characteristics of leadership language. The dictionaries were created using single classification, or classifying each keyword in the category where it best fits and prior to a detailed examination of the text. A published content analysis dictionary was used as the initial basis for the transformational, transactional, passive, economy issues, and health care issues dictionaries (Saldivar Hodgson, 2007). Each category was reviewed to assess the face validity, or correspondence between the concept definitions and the category definitions, of the words assigned to reflect the concept (Insch, Moore, & Murphy, 1997). To ensure the validity, the researchers examined the lists of keywords placed in each category assuring they related to the category, as recommended by Weber (1990).

Results

This research investigated the relationship between Democratic presidential candidates and the percentage of transformational language, transactional language, passive language, economy issues, health care issues, and foreign policy issues words and phrases used in the candidates' speeches when controlling for month of campaign, audience, and subject matter of the speech.

This content analysis used Analysis of Covariance (ANCOVA), mean frequencies, and Pearson correlation to address the research questions. The study consisted of 148 items (speeches) communicated by Senator Hillary Rodham Clinton and Senator Barack Hussein Obama during the 2008 Democratic presidential primary campaign. Since the number of campaign speeches was relatively small, all of the speeches posted to each candidate's official website were included in the study. Seventy-two of Senator Hillary Rodham Clinton's speeches were collected from her official website, http://www.hillaryclinton.com. Seventy-six speeches were collected from Senator Barack Hussein Obama's official website, http://www.barackobama.com.

Research Question 1: Transformational

The first research question asked if there was a difference in the percentage of transformational language used by Senator Hillary Rodham Clinton and Senator Barack Hussein Obama in their campaign speeches from the time candidacy was declared until the 2008 presumptive Democratic nominee was named.

To understand the influence of the independent variables candidate (C), audience (A), and speech topic (T) on the percentage of the use of transformational language, a three-way ANCOVA was conducted. Campaign month was used as a covariate. The results showed significant main effects for candidate, F (1, 122) = 4.40, $p < .04$ and speech topic, F (4, 122) = 3.04, $p < .02$.

To further understand the use of transformational language by each candidate communicating the speeches, the mean frequencies were compared. Hillary

Figure 1
Transformational Language Used by Each Candidate

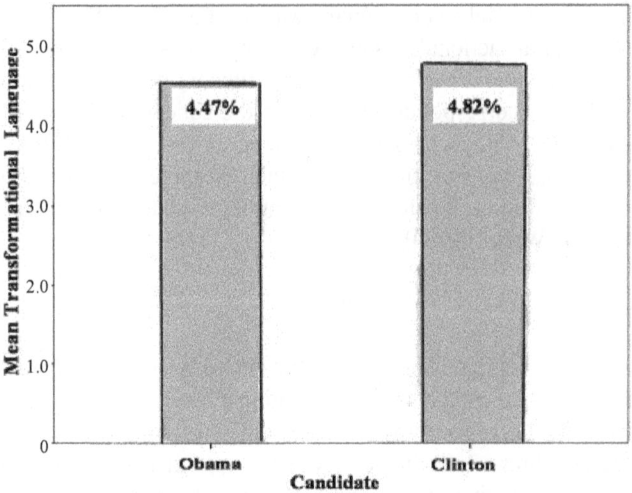

Clinton used a greater percentage (M = 4.82%) of transformational words than Barack Obama (M = 4.47%).

To further understand the use of transformational language by speech topic, the mean frequencies of transformational language as a result of topic of the speech were compared using a Scheffe post-hoc analysis. More transformational words were used in speeches with a foreign policy topic (M = 4.97%) than in speeches with an economy topic (M = 4.19%), $p < .00$. More transformational words were used in speeches with a combination of topics (economy, health care, and foreign policy) (M = 4.80%) than speeches with an economy topic (M = 4.19%), $p < .00$. In addition, more transformational words were used in speeches with other topics (M = 4.68%) than speeches with an economy topic (M = 4.19%), $p < .03$.

Research Question 2: Transactional

The second research question asked if there was a difference in the percentage of transactional language used by Senator Hillary Rodham Clinton and Senator Barack Hussein Obama in their campaign speeches from the time candidacy was declared until the 2008 presumptive Democratic nominee was named.

The results of a three-way ANCOVA showed significant main effects for topic, F (4, 122) = 3.00, $p < .02$ and audience, F (3, 122) = 3.38, $p < .02$. In addition, the results showed significant interactions between candidate and speech topic (C – T), F (4, 122) = 2.69, $p < .03$, as well as between audience and speech topic (A – T), F (6, 122) = 2.92, $p < .01$.

Figure 2
Transformational Language Used by Speech Topic

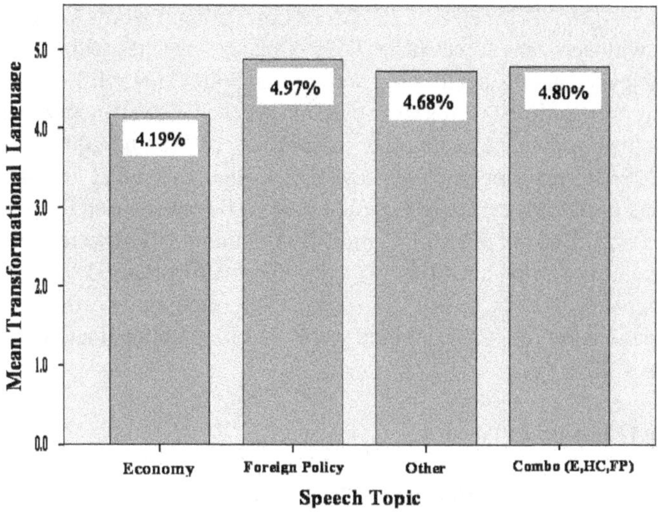

Figure 3
Transactional Language Used by Speech Topic

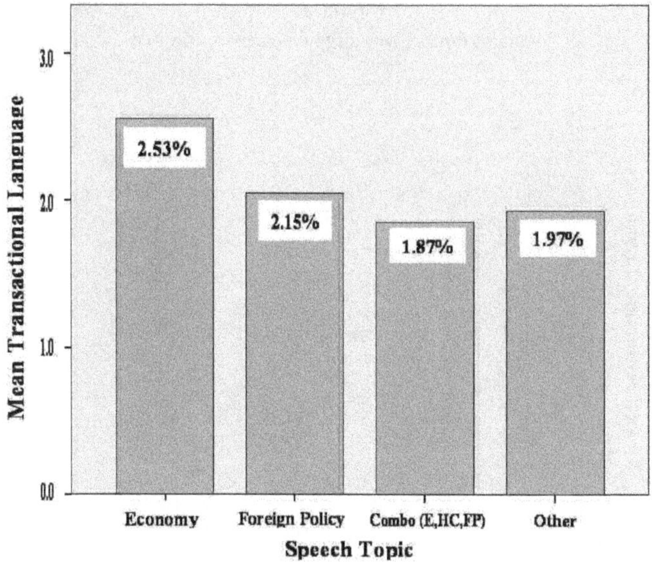

To further understand the use of transactional language by speech topic a Scheffe post-hoc analysis was performed. More transactional words were used in speeches with economy topics ($M = 2.53\%$) than in speeches with foreign policy topics ($M = 2.15\%$), $p < .03$. More transactional words were used in speeches with economy topics ($M = 2.53\%$) than in speeches with a combination of topics (economy, health care, and foreign policy) ($M = 1.87\%$), $p < .00$. Also, more transactional words were used in speeches with economy topics ($M = 2.53\%$) than in speeches with other topics ($M = 1.97\%$), $p < .00$.

The Scheffe post-hoc analysis revealed further that more transactional words were used for local audiences ($M = 2.16\%$) than were used for statewide audiences ($M = 1.66\%$), $p < .01$ and more transactional words were used when the audience was an organization ($M = 2.30\%$) than were used for statewide audiences ($M = 1.66\%$), $p < .00$. Also, more transactional words were used for an organization ($M = 2.30\%$) than were used for a national audience ($M = 1.69\%$), $p < .02$.

Research Question 3: Passive

The third research question asks if there was a difference in the percentage of passive language used by Senator Hillary Rodham Clinton and Senator Barack Hussein Obama in their campaign speeches from the time candidacy was declared until the 2008 presumptive Democratic nominee was named.

Figure 4
Transactional Language Used by Audience

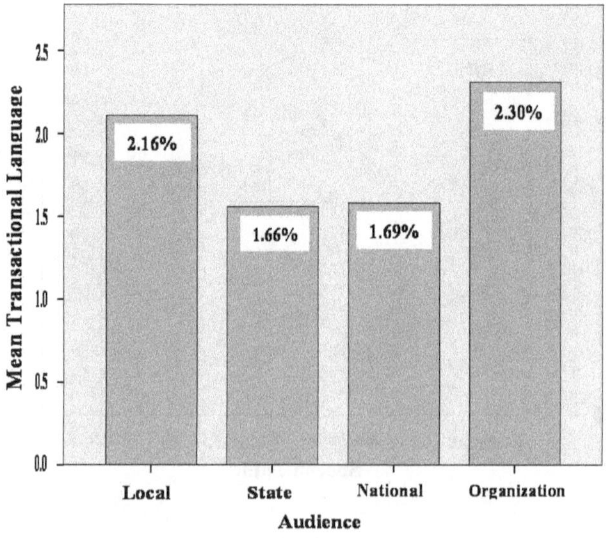

A three-way ANCOVA showed significant main effects for candidate, F (1, 122) = 5.27, $p < .02$; and speech topic, F (4, 122) = 3.42, $p < .01$. The mean frequencies were compared to highlight use of passive language by each candidate. Barack Obama used a greater percentage (M = .41%) of passive words than Hillary Clinton (M = .28%).

To further understand the use of passive language by speech topic, the mean frequencies of passive language as a result of topic of the speech were compared using a Scheffe post-hoc analysis. More passive words were used in speeches with economy topics (M = .42%) than speeches with health care topics (M = .25%), $p < .01$. More passive words were used in speeches with economy topics (M = .42%) than speeches with a combination of topics (economy, health care, and foreign policy) (M = .33%), $p < .04$. Similarly, more passive words were used in speeches with economy topics (M = .42%) than speeches with other topics (M = .29%), $p < .00$. In addition, more passive words were used in speeches with foreign policy topics (M = .44%) than in speeches with health care topics (M = .25%), $p < .01$. Finally, more passive words were used in speeches with foreign policy topics (M = .44%) than in speeches with other topics (M = .29%), $p < .01$.

Research Question 4: Economic Issues

The fourth research question asks if there was a difference in the percentage of economic issues language used by Senator Hillary Rodham Clinton and Sena-

Figure 5
Passive Language Used by Each Candidate

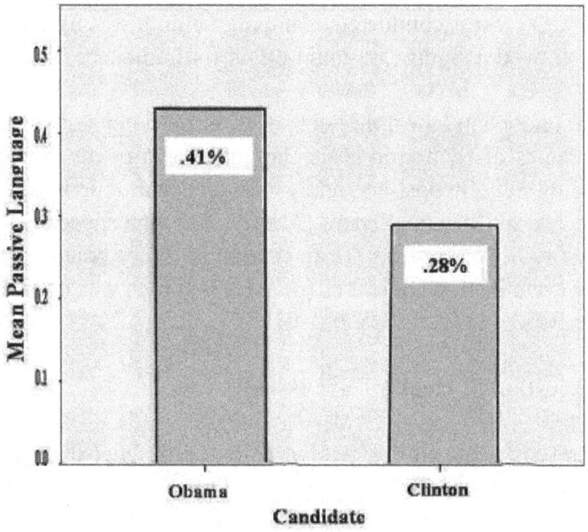

Figure 6
Passive Language Used by Speech Topic

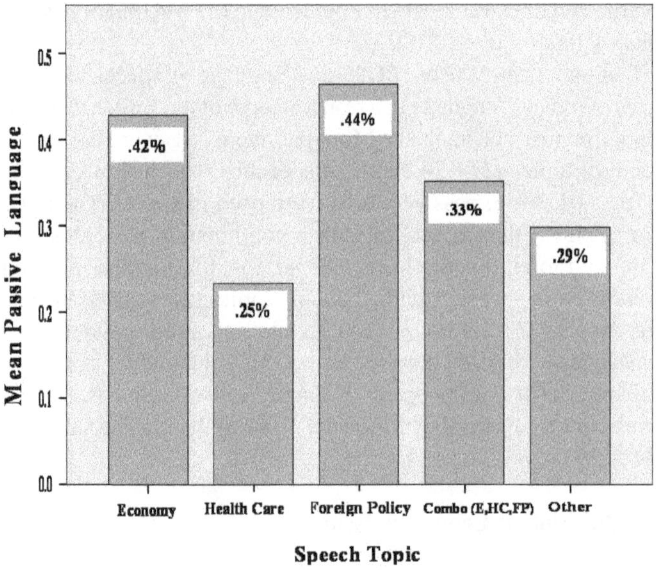

tor Barack Hussein Obama in their campaign speeches from the time candidacy was declared until the 2008 presumptive Democratic nominee was named.

To understand the influence of the independent variables candidate (C) and audience (A) on the percentage of the use of economic issues language, a two-way ANCOVA was conducted. Campaign month was used as a covariate. The results showed a significant main effect for audience, F (3, 139) = 3.18, $p < .03$.

To further understand the use of economic issues language by audience, the mean frequencies of economic issues language as a result of audience were compared using Scheffe post-hoc analysis. More economic issues words were used in speeches for local audiences (M = 2.17%) than speeches for statewide audiences (M = .89%), $p < .00$. More economic issues language was used in speeches for organization audiences (M = 1.97%) than was used in speech for statewide audiences (M = .89%), $p < .02$.

Research Question 5: Health Care Issues

The fifth research question asks if there was a difference in the percentage of health care issues language used by Senator Hillary Rodham Clinton and Senator Barack Hussein Obama in their campaign speeches from the time candidacy was declared until the 2008 presumptive Democratic nominee was named.

Figure 7
Economic Issues Language Used by Audience

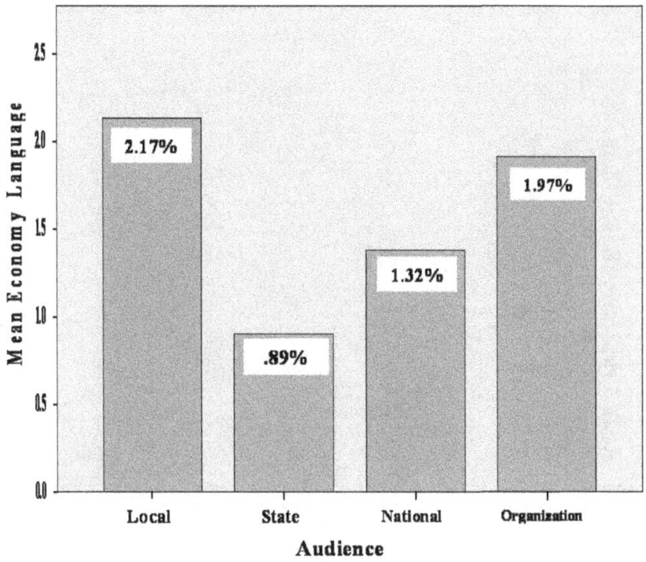

A two-way ANCOVA was conducted. Campaign month was used as a covariate. The results showed a significant interaction between candidate and audience (C – A), F (3, 139) = 3.30, $p < .02$.

Research Question 6, 9–11: Foreign Policy Issues, Passive, Economic, and Health Care Language

This study found no significant differences in the percentage of foreign policy issues language used, the percentage of passive language utilized, the change in percentage of the economic language discussed, or the change in the percentage of health care language used by the candidates during the study period.

Research Question 7: Transformational Change

The seventh research question sought to determine if there was a change in the percentage of transformational language used by Senator Hillary Rodham Clinton and Senator Barack Hussein Obama in their campaign speeches from the time candidacy was declared until the 2008 presumptive Democratic nominee was named. To better understand the magnitude and direction of the relationship between transformational language and campaign month, a Pearson correlation was run. There was a overall positive correlation ($r = .23, p < .00$) between the

Figure 8
Relationship between Transformational Language and Campaign Month for Candidates

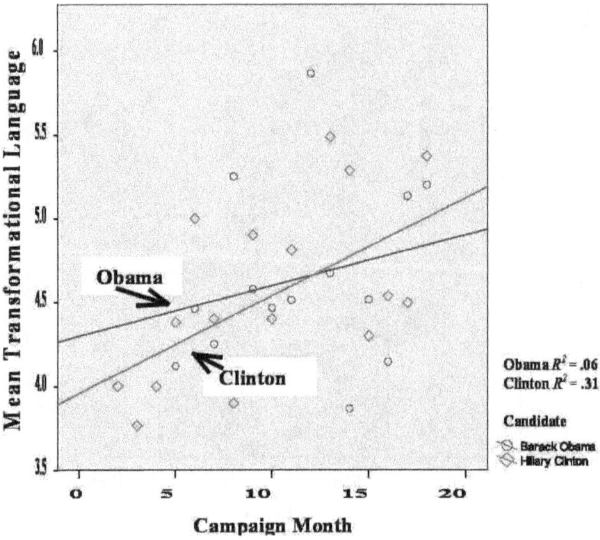

percentage of transformational language used by the candidates and campaign month. In addition, there was a positive correlation ($r = .30, p < .01$) between the percentage of transformational language used by Hillary Clinton and campaign month, but the relationship was not significant for Barack Obama.

Research Question 8: Transactional Change

The eighth research question sought to determine if there was a change in the percentage of transactional language used by Senator Hillary Rodham Clinton and Senator Barack Hussein Obama in their campaign speeches from the time candidacy was declared until the 2008 presumptive Democratic nominee was named. To further explore the change by campaign month, the mean frequency percentages of transactional language by campaign month was run. The average candidates' use of transactional language ranged from a low in May, 2008 (M = 1.67%) to a high in April, 2007 (M = 4.30%). The results were significant, F (16, 131) = 1.88, $p < .03$. Hillary Clinton had the highest average use of transactional language (M = 4.30%) in April, 2007, and the lowest average (M = 1.43%) in June, 2008.

To better understand the magnitude and direction of the relationship between transactional language and campaign month, a Pearson correlation was run. There was a significant negative correlation ($r = -.26, p < .00$) between per-

Figure 9
Change in Transactional Language by Campaign Month

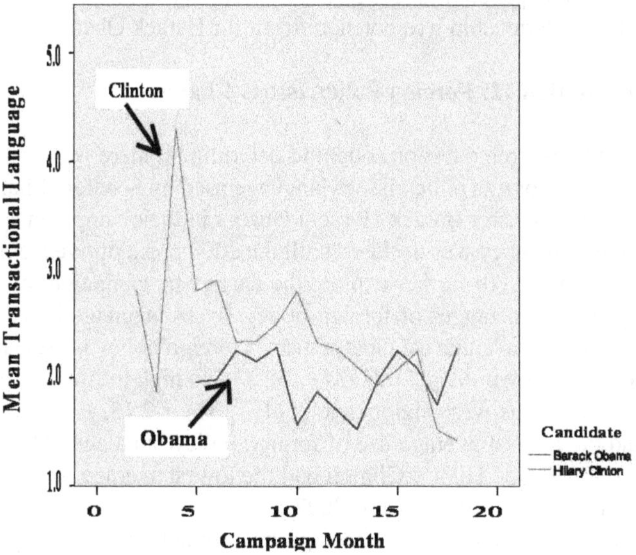

Figure 10
Relationship between Transactional Language and Campaign Month for Candidates

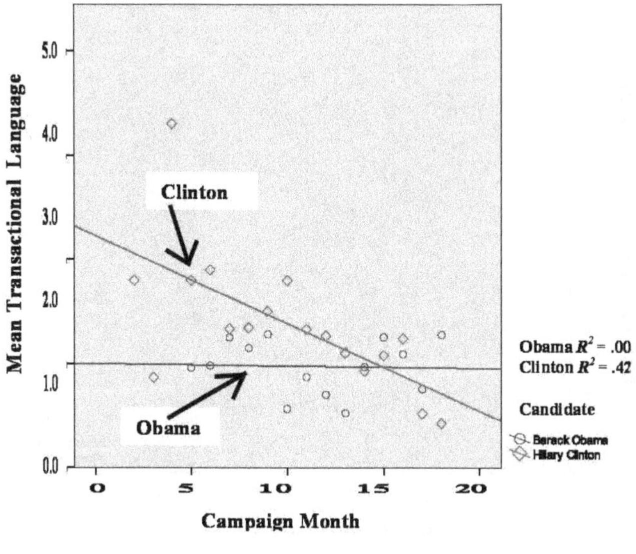

centage of transactional language used by the candidates and campaign month. In addition, there was a negative correlation ($r = -.44$), $p < .00$ between the percentage of transactional language used by Hillary Clinton and campaign month, but the relationship was not significant for Barack Obama.

Research Question 12: Foreign Policy Issues Change

The twelfth research question sought to determine if there was a change in the percentage of foreign policy issues language used by Senator Hillary Rodham Clinton and Senator Barack Hussein Obama in their campaign speeches from the time candidacy was declared until the 2008 presumptive Democratic nominee was named. To further explore the change by campaign month, the mean frequency percentages of foreign policy issues language by campaign month was run. The average candidates' use of foreign policy issues language ranged from a low by in May, 2007 ($M = .52\%$) to a high in August, 2007 ($M = 5.25\%$). The results were significant, $F(16, 131) = 2.13, p < .01$. Barack Obama had the highest average use of foreign policy language ($M = 5.25\%$) in August, 2007, while Hillary Clinton had the lowest average use of foreign policy language ($M = .30\%$) in May, 2007.

A Pearson correlation showed nonsignificant results for a change in the percentage of foreign policy issues language used by the candidates by campaign month.

Figure 11
Change in Foreign Policy Language by Campaign Month

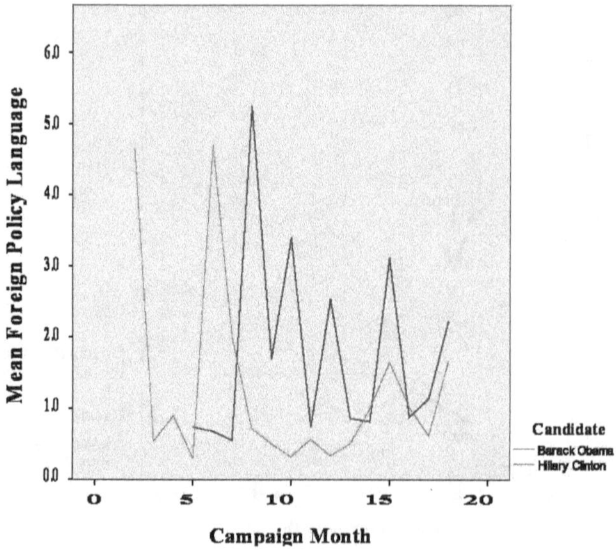

Discussion

Running a national political campaign for the office of president is a complex activity. Certainly a host of variables contribute to opinions that the citizenry develop about a candidate. One of these variables is undoubtedly language. As time went on during the campaign, Clinton began to utilize transactional leadership language less with less frequency and transformational language to a greater degree. Research suggests crisis is needed before transformational leadership emerges (Weber, 1947; Bass & Avolio, 1994; Bass & Riggio, 2006). Gardner (1987) states that every effective leader engages in transactional and transformational behavior, in order to better confront the challenges within their responsibilities. Hoyt and Blascovich (2003) findings suggest higher quantitative performance was experienced under a transactional leader and higher qualitative group performance was associated with transformational leaders. Cavanaugh, Gelles, Reyes, Civielo, and Zahner, (2008), Bass (2008), and Katz (1977), further suggest that directive behavior or transactional behavior is sought by followers in times of turmoil and uncertainty. This suggests leaders should engage in both transformational and transactional language in order to satiate the security needs of their constituents. Bass and Riggio (2006) explain that transformational language communicates a vision of a better time and a confidence the crisis can be averted or overcome. The same authors suggest the leader's vision promotes a quailing of constituents' fears.

Transactional language, or a litany of required actions, reinforces the confidence in a better tomorrow and grows constituent confidence in the leader as the one who not only envisions a better tomorrow, but also knows the steps required to achieve that vision. Barone (2008) even suggests that the calmer the leader's demeanor in communicating this needed Transformational and Transactional message, the more confidence the leader will convey and the more constituents' fears will be assuaged. From this discussion it is intuitive to suggest that Clinton's failure to engage in more transactional language or 'what we need to do to fix this' statements, might have not communicated to constituents a direct course of transaction needed to successfully triumph over their fears of crisis.

Pulitzer Prize winning journalist and media critic, Walter Lippmann (1922), argued that people were more likely to believe the pictures in their heads than to make decisions based on critical thinking. Willis (2007) extended Lippmann's position by equating these pictures in our heads to our thoughts, which were put there by the news media. Willis claimed Americans did not discern the difference between the monologues of David Letterman, opinions of Oprah Winfrey or Dr. Phil, and what comes across the evening news. Also, Americans did not differentiate between the pictures and the real world. Unfortunately, these media implanted pictures fueled our behavioral reactions and influenced our political decisions, including how we voted. If the media falsely portrayed

the candidates, the voters' real-world response, their vote, may have been inconsistent with their political beliefs.

The purpose of this study was to utilize an analytical tool, content analysis, to critically evaluate the campaign speeches of the Senators Hillary Rodham Clinton and Barack Hussein Obama. The goal was to determine if the media portrayal of their leadership style was congruent with the leadership language of their rhetoric. This research investigated the differences and changes in transformational, transactional, passive, economic issues, health care issues, and foreign policy issues language used by the candidates while campaigning against each other.

Findings

The frequency of Senator Hillary Clinton's (M = 4.82%) overall use of transformational leadership language was significantly greater than Senator Barack Obama's (M = 4.47%). Although, Senator Clinton used a higher overall frequency percentage of transformational language, Barack Obama (M = 5.87%) had the highest average use in December, 2007, while Hillary Clinton (M = 3.77%) had the lowest average use in March, 2007. For Hillary Clinton, the relationship of her use of transformational language was positively correlated to the month of the campaign (r = .30). The speech topic had a significant influence on the percentage of transformational language used, when campaign month was used as a covariate.

As the campaign progressed Senator Clinton decreased her use of transactional leadership language, resulting in a negative correlation (r = –.44) between campaign month and percentage of transactional language. Although not significant, the relationship of Senator Obama's use of transactional language to campaign month was consistently low at about two percent throughout the campaign.

Audience, speech topic, the interaction of candidate and speech topic, and the interaction of audience and speech topic had a significant effect of the percentage of the use of transactional language.

The research indicates that as the campaign progressed Senator Clinton's language became more transformational and less transactional. These findings were consistent with those reported by Saldivar Hodgson (2007) when comparing First Lady Hillary Clinton's leadership language used in speeches by term of office where she started off communicating with more transactional language during the first term in office and ended with communicating more transformational language during the second term of office.

Senator Obama's use of transformational language increased throughout the campaign, but not as much as Senator Clinton's. Senator Obama's use of transactional language remained rather flat throughout the campaign. This finding was contrary to the media portrayal of Barack Obama as the transfor-

mational leader (Salter et al., 2009). Barack Obama's speaking style, the way he connected with his audience through the use of facial expressions, frequent use of "you", and restrained body language had a lot to do with this portrayal of Obama as a transformational leader (Weissman, 2009).

Overall Senator Obama (M = .41%) used a greater percentage of passive language than Senator Clinton (M = .28%). For both candidates, although the relationship was not significant, more passive language was used at the beginning of the campaign than at the end of the campaign.

The use of economic issues language was significant depending on the audience, which was greater before local audiences (M = 2.17%) than before statewide audiences (M = .89%). In addition, there was a greater percentage of economic issues language used before organizations (M = 1.97%) than before statewide audiences (M = .89%).

Implications for Management

Leadership Styles and Politics. A transforming leadership style, where a leader adjusted his or her style to be most effective with their constituents, was consistent with the relationship between the politician and the followers (Burns, 1978; Gardner, 1990). Since the Democratic candidates for the 2008 presidential primary represented a never experienced phenomenon, it stood to reason that there were no studies on female, or African–American presidential candidates available. Therefore, it was reasonable to infer the existing studies involving U.S. politicians were applicable. Examples included a rating of the leadership behaviors of U. S. political figures including charismatic leadership scores of U.S. presidents (Bass, 1985), or the effect of crisis conditions on perceptions of President George W. Bush's charismatic leadership style (Merolla, Ramos, & Zechmeister, 2007). Both studies indicated charisma, a transformational leadership factor, could be measured for U.S. presidents, just as this study measured the frequency of transformational language used by U.S. presidential candidates.

The study found that Hillary Clinton used more transformational language than Barack Obama; Obama used more passive language than Clinton. For Clinton, transformational leadership language was positively correlated with campaign month, while transactional language was negatively correlated with campaign month. Key findings were that Senator Obama's use of transformational and transactional leadership language was more consistent throughtout the campaign, while Senator Clinton's variability in use of transformational and transactional leadership language appeared to be adjustments to her opponent and the campaign.

Leadership Styles and Gender. Several studies had measured the differences in leadership style based on gender. Eagly and Johnson (1990) performed a meta-analysis of the available research in an attempt to reconcile the conflicting

conclusions of the social scientists and generalizations of the practitioners. Their findings showed that women tended to be more democratic or participative, while men tended to be more directive leadership style. Bass and Avolio (1994) performed a study that found that women were rated higher on transformational leadership factors, while men were rated higher on transactional and passive leadership behaviors. These findings supported Eagly's and Johnson's (1990) conclusion that women and men do exhibit different leadership styles. Bass, Avolio, and Atwater (1996) conducted a study to examine follower descriptions of the differences between men and women full range model leadership styles. The results showed that women leaders were rated as more transformational than male leaders.

In summary, the existing research supported the generalization that there were differences in the leadership styles of women and men. Generally, the literature indicated women were either perceived to be, or were actually more transformational in their leadership behaviors than men. While the research supported the findings of this study, it was counter to the perceptions conveyed by the media and political consultants. Hillary Clinton was portrayed as a warrior, who considered a show of human feelings as a sign of failure (Sheehy, 2008). Barack Obama was seen as the candidate who could speak more from the heart than the head (Todd & Gawiser, 2009).

Directions for Future Research

The first recommendation for future research would be to study the population of Senator Hillary Clinton's and Senator Barack Obama campaign speeches using Hart's (2002) DICTION content analysis software. This would provide an alternative quantitative view of the campaign based on the certainty, optimism, activity, realism, and commonality variables operationalized in the DICTION dictionaries.

With readily available recorded, or streaming video via the Internet, and video processing tools, future research that incorporates analysis of communication behaviors would provide additional insight into the leadership styles of political candidates. Communication behaviors could include: (a) the body language of leadership, including eye contact, body stance, and gestures; (b) tone and pace of the speech, and (c) narrative techniques, such as alliteration and anecdotes, The research could potentially provide the critical thinking voter additional information to assess the leadership style of the candidate.

Limitations of the Study

Although computer-aided content analysis was a widely used and accepted research tool, final decisions on concepts to measure and how to measure through creation of customized dictionaries was up to the discretion of the

researchers. Therefore, the study was subject to face and content validity issues. All speeches posted to each candidate's official website were utilized in the study. However, the possibility existed that these collections of speeches might not include the entire population of campaign speeches. If only speeches judged to be the best were posted, the study would lack external validity and the results would not be generalizable to other speeches. Also, the dictionaries of language depicting the Full Range of Leadership Model factors (Bass, 1985) of transformational, transactional, and passive leadership styles used for the analysis were researcher defined. In addition, only economic issues, healthcare issues, and foreign policy issues themes were analyzed.

This study did not take into account other intervening variables applicable to the media's portrayal of the democratic primary presidential frontrunners based upon the candidates' position on the war in Iraq, the voters' desire for change versus experience, the results of the Iowa caucus, or the amount of campaign funds. Senator Clinton voted to authorize the Bush administration to take military action in Iraq in 2002, while a centerpiece of Senator Obama's campaign was his opposition to the war. Many voters were ready for the change promised by Senator Obama, while others valued Senator Clinton's experience. Historically, the Iowa Caucus has been a predictor of the Democratic primary where in 2008 Senator Clinton finished third behind Senator Obama and Senator Edwards. Early on Senator Obama demonstrated his ability to raise extensive campaign funds, while Senator Clinton found herself loaning personal funds to her campaign efforts.

References

ABC News 2008 Democratic Primary Exit Poll Results – Key Groups (n.d.). Retrieved February 1, 2009, from http://abcnews.go.com/images/PollingUnit/08DemPrimaryKeyGroups.pdf.

Barone, M. (2008, Nov. 9). Obama's temperament, not policy, triumphs. *Detroit News*. Available at http://www.detnews.com/apps/.

Bass, B. M. (1985). *Leadership and performance beyond expectations*. New York: Free Press.

Bass, B. M., & Avolio, B. J. (1994). Shatter the glass ceiling: Women may make better managers. *Human Resource Management, 33* (4), 549–560.

Bass, B. M., Avolio, B. J., & Atwater, L. (1996). The transformational and transactional leadership of men and women. *Applied Psychology: An International Review, 45* (1), 5–34.

Bass, B. (2008). *The Bass handbook of leadership: Theory, research, and managerial applications,* (4th ed.), New York: Free Press.

Bass, B., & Riggio, R. (2006). *Transformational leadership*. Mahwah, NJ: Lawrence Erlbaum.

Beasley, V. B. (2004). *You, the people: American national identity in presidential rhetoric*. College Station, TX: Texas A&M University Press.

Bennis, W. G., & Nanus, B. (1985). *Leaders: The strategy for taking charge*. New York: Harper and Row.

Bligh, M., Kohles, J., & Meindl, J. (2004). Charting the language of leadership: A methodological investigation of President Bush and the crisis of 9/11. *Journal of Applied Psychology, 89* (3), 562–574.
Burns, J. M. (1978). *Leadership*. New York: Harper.
Burns, J. M. (1995). The crisis of leadership. In J. T. Wren (Ed.), *The leader's companion: Insights on leadership through the ages* (pp. 8–10). New York: Free Press.
Cavanaugh, J. C., Gelles, M. G., Reyes, G., Civiello, C. L., & Zahner, M. (2008). Effectively planning for and managing major disasters. *The Psychologist–Manager Journal, 11* (2), 221–239.
Colorado State University. (2010). *Writing guides: Content analysis.* Retrieved from http://writing.colostate.edu/guides/research/content/pop2a.cfm.
Denning, S. (2007). *The secret language of leadership: How leaders inspire action through narrative.* San Francisco: Wiley.
Eagly, A. H. (2007). Female leadership advantage and disadvantage: Resolving the contradictions. *Psychology of Women Quarterly, 31* (1), 1–12.
Eagly, A. H., & Carli, L. L. (2007). *Through the labyrinth: The truth about how women become leaders.* Boston: Harvard Business School Press.
Eagly, A. H., & Johnson, B. T. (1990). Gender and leadership style: A meta-analysis. *Psychological Bulletin, 108* (2), 233–256.
Eckert, P., & McConnell-Ginet, S. (2003). *Language and gender*. Cambridge, UK: Cambridge University Press.
Edwards, G. C., III, & Wayne, S. J. (2003). *Presidential leadership: Politics and policy making,* (6th ed.). Belmont, CA: Wadsworth/Thomson Learning.
Gardner, J. (1987). *Attributes and context* (Leadership Papers, No. 6). Washington, DC: Leadership Studies Program, Independent Sector.
Gardner, J. N. (1990). *On leadership.* New York: Free Press.
George, B. (2006, October 30). Truly authentic leadership. *U. S. News & World Report.* Retrieved October 12, 2008, from http://www.usnews.com/usnews/news/articles/061022/30authentic_print.htm.
Hackman, M. Z., & Johnson, C. E. (2000). *Leadership: A communication perspective* (3rd ed.), Prospect Heights, IL: Waveland Press.
Hart, R. P. (2002). *Campaign talk: Why elections are good for us*. Princeton, NJ: Princeton University Press.
Hoyt, C. L., & Blascovich, J. (2003). Transformational and transactional leadership in virtual and physical environments. *Small Group Research, 34* (6), 678–715.
Insch, G. S., Moore, J. E., & Murphy, L. D. (1997). Content analysis in leadership research: Examples, procedures, and suggestions for future use. *Leadership Quarterly, 8*, 1–25.
Katz, R. (1977). The influence of group conflict on leadership effectiveness. *Organizational Behavior and Human Performance, 20,* 265–286.
Kotter, J. P. (1996). *Leading change*. Boston, MA. Harvard Business School Press.
Krippendorf, K. (2004). *Content analysis: An introduction to its methodology*. Thousand Oaks, CA: Sage.
Krippendorf, K., & Bock, M. (2009). *The content analysis reader.* Thousand Oaks, CA: Sage.
Lakoff, R. (1975). *Language and woman's place*. New York. Harper .
Lakoff, R. T. (2000). *The language war.* Berkeley, CA: Berkeley University of California Press.
Lippmann, W. (1922). *Public opinion.* New York: Free Press.
Merolla, J. L., Ramos, J. M., & Zechmeister, E. J. (2007). Crisis, charisma, and consequences: Evidence from the 2004 U.S. presidential election. *Journal of Politics, 69* (1), 30–42.

Neuendorf, K. A. (2002). *The content analysis guidebook.* Thousand Oaks, CA: Sage.
Neustadt, R. E. (1991). *Presidential power and the modern presidents: The politics of leadership from Roosevelt to Reagan.* New York: Free Press.
Northouse, P. (2001). *Leadership: theory and practice*. Thousand Oaks, CA: Sage.
Saldivar Hodgson, M. N. (2007). *A content analysis of leadership language in selected speeches communicated by America's First Ladies Hillary Rodham Clinton and Laura Welch Bush.* Unpublished doctoral dissertation, Our Lady of the Lake University, San Antonio, TX.
Salter, C. R., Green, M., Ree, M., Carmody-Bubb, M., & Duncan, P. A. (2009). A study of follower's personality, implicit leadership perceptions, and leadership ratings. *Journal of Leadership Studies, 2* (4), 48–60.
Sheehy, G. (2008). Hillaryland at war: Politics & power. *Vanity Fair*. Retrieved July 1, 2008 from http://www.vanityfair.com/politics/features/2008/08/clinton200808.htm.
Stephanopoulos, G. (2008, June 29). How to be a better voter. *Parade*, pp. 4–5.
Todd, G., & Gawiser, S. (2009). *How Barack Obama won*. New York: Vintage Books.
United States presidential election 2008. (n.d.) Retrieved July 9, 2008, from http://en.wikipedia.org/wiki/United_States_presidential_election,_2008.
Weber, M. (1947). *The theory of social and economic organizations.* (T. Parsons, trans.). New York: Free Press. (Original work published 1924).
Weber, R. P. (1990). *Basic content analysis* (2nd ed.). Newbury Park, CA: Sage.
Weissman, J. (2009). Improve your speaking style: Learn from President Obama. *Bottom Line Personal, 30* (6), 8.
Willis, W. J. (2007). *Media effect: How the news influences politics and government.* Westport, CT: Praeger.
Yukl, G. (2002). *Leadership in organizations* (5th ed.). Upper Saddle River, NJ: Prentice-Hall.

Current Topics in Management, Vol. 15, 2011, pp. 117-136

SOCIAL CAPITAL VIA LEADER–MEMBER EXCHANGES: AN AVENUE TO HUMAN CAPITAL?

E. Edward Stark and Francis L. Jeffries

Within the past decade, the concept of "strategic human resource management" has received increasing attention from practitioners and academics alike. This perspective advocates that human resource management (HRM) is a potential source of sustained competitive advantage when firms create value in a way that is rare and difficult for competitors to emulate (Becker & Gerhart, 1996; David, 2008). As the mainstream theory has evolved, it has postulated that the organization's internal resources constitute "the foundation of strategy" wherein "unique bundles of resources generate competitive advantages that lead to wealth creation" (Brush, Green, & Hart, 2001). This assumes that the collective knowledge, skill, and behavior of employees constitute an appropriate and convertible form of capital. The challenge facing HRM is how to best create and use this capital to further the strategic interests of the firm (Barney, 1995; Uhl-Bien, Graen, & Scandura, 2000).

HRM professionals are confronted with ensuring that employees combine their knowledge, skills, and work related behavior in a synergistic, integrative manner to create human capital. Uhl-Bien et al. (2000) proposed to scholars that realization of human capital at the firm level is not likely to occur until HRM professionals recognize the pivotal role of social capital. Babcock (2007) made this same claim directly to HRM professionals in arguing that relational capital is now the newest differentiator of organizational competitiveness. However, the collective actions of employees as human capital may well be continually underutilized until all understand that the linkage of human capital to firm performance is predicated by adequate levels of social capital.

The Call to Link Social Capital with Human Capital

Uhl-Bien et al. (2000) forcefully argued that in order to realize the expected value of human capital HRM strategy should first address the building of social capital. Portes (1998) defined the concept of social capital as an ability of actors to secure benefits by virtue of membership in social networks or other social structures. Kostova and Roth (2003) enlarged on this concept by stating that social capital is the sum of the actual and potential resources that social actors can mobilize for achieving their goals and that are available to actors because of their social relationship with others. The good will one member has toward another in an organization is a valuable resource because it facilitates exchange of other resources through generation of feelings of gratitude, respect, friendship, and through contacts and connections. Thus, as Adler and Kwon (2002) note, social capital represents a long-term asset that can be invested in with the expectation of a future, but uncertain, flow of benefits.

As a "private good," social capital is considered an asset that individuals can spend to better their own situation (Kostova & Roth, 2003). While much of the theoretical work in social capital has focused on the private good accruing to those who "own" social capital, there is an emerging consensus that social capital also represents a "larger good." As Kostova and Roth (2003) observed, social capital becomes a larger good when it is available to, and could potentially benefit, not only those who have created it but also group members at large. This form of social capital resides at the organizational level and is a collective asset of the organization. From an organizational perspective, the generation of social capital facilitates achievement of outcomes that would be otherwise impossible (Nahapiet & Ghosal, 1998) such as eliciting stronger commitment from employees, attracting and retaining more desirable top level employees, maintaining organizational flexibility, managing collective action (Bulino & Turnley, 2003) all of which should contribute toward realization of high levels of human capital.

To date, we have found no studies that have explicitly linked social capital to human capital although Dess and Shaw (2001) published a theory piece linking social capital to firm performance and included human capital in the discussion. Shaw, Duffy, Johnson, and Lockhart (2005) tested the theory and found that social capital losses adversely impact performance and create inefficiencies in terms of human capital deficits. Further, they suggested that lost relationships in networks and the resultant inefficiencies created are part of the cost of turnover. Finally, Subramaniam and Youndt (2005) observed that human capital interacts in some manner with social capital to positively influence radical innovative organizational capability.

The objective of this study was to investigate the possibility that high quality leader-member exchange (LMX) relationships may represent a measure of social capital and thus predict variance in possible indicators of human capital. We proceed by briefly reviewing the LMX literature as it applies to

development of social capital. This is followed by discussion of theoretical reasons why subordinate cadre status in LMX should be considered an indicator of the presence of social capital. Next, we present our research hypothesis followed by a description of the measures, sample, methods, and the results of our study. Finally, we discuss the findings of our study and suggestions for future research.

Social Capital and LMX

Social capital has been defined as "a person's or group's sympathy toward another person or group that may produce a potential benefit, advantage, and preferential treatment for another person or group of persons beyond that expected in an exchange relationship" (Robison, Schmid, & Siles, 2002, p. 6). It has also been operationalized as "the knowledge embedded within, available through, and utilized by interactions among individuals and their networks of interrelationships" (Nahapiet & Ghoshal, 1998, p. 451). For our purposes, we will combine the two and consider social capital as: The knowledge embedded within, available through, and utilized by interactions among individuals and their networks of interrelationships that can produce potential advantage beyond that expected in an exchange relationship.

Within organizational settings, social capital is a resource that is derived from the relationships among individuals (Bolino, Turnley, & Bloodgood, 2002), and social capital results from expectations of actors that have formed as a result of being part of social structures and the nature of their relationships in the structures. Central to these relationships are ongoing exchanges that generate norms of reciprocity along with other components of a close relationship such as trust, respect, and mutual obligation (Uhl-Bien et al., 2000). Consider that a job incumbent and his/her immediate superior are initially motivated toward interpersonal relationships and high quality exchanges that often reflect the presence of social capital. For example, new hires or transfers enter a position with some sense of a psychological contract between themselves and the firm resulting from their interpretation of job related information communicated through formal organizational channels such as job descriptions and job interviews. Unfortunately, formal channels usually emphasize the physical characteristics of the job rather than the social environment in defining "job reality" (Illgen & Hollenbeck, 1991). Once on the job, the incumbent finds job reality concealed by ambiguity and/or conflict, neither of which can be resolved through reference to a traditional job description (Cook, Hepworth, Wall, & Warr, 1981). This creates dissonance, and the incumbent frequently seeks out the most immediate organizational agent in an attempt to negotiate a "realistic" contract for behavior that will be mutually satisfying to him/herself and the organization (Graen & Scandura, 1987). By far the most accessible and complex organizational agent available to the job incumbent is the immediate manager, supervisor, or leader.

S/he is in a unique position to make or break the subordinate's psychological understanding of the employment relationship (Rosseau & Schalk, 2000) in that the leader can mitigate effects of unmet expectations by cutting special deals, creating opportunities, and providing emotional support and confidence building (Major, Kozlowski, Chad, & Gardner, 1992).

Social capital evolves from ongoing resource exchanges between actors that generate norms of reciprocity (Uhl-Bien et al., 2000). Tjosvold (1989) observed that leaders are generally interested in exchanging organizational resources under their control for obligated behavior from subordinates that goes beyond the traditional job paradigm, and Graen (1976, 2003) suggested that leaders make offers and followers accept depending on their growth need strength. In such exchanges, the leader customarily offers outcomes highly valued by the subordinate (e.g., increased job latitude, assignment to challenging projects, increased mentoring, etc.) in exchange for expertise, collaboration, loyalty, commitment, effort, and the sharing of administrative duties beyond what is normally associated with contractual work behavior (Yukl, 1998). These obligations represent a capital that can assist in accomplishing unstructured goals and objectives of a high priority (Schyns, Paul, Mohr, & Blank, 2005; Harris & Kacmar, 2006). This implies that those with aspirations for advancement self-select into high exchange relationships to advance their careers. The capital represented by such exchanges certainly meets the definition of a private good in that it is owned jointly by the parties in the relationship, it is not easily traded, and it enables achievement of outcomes impossible in its absence (Nahapiet & Ghosal, 1998).

We assert that creation of social capital is likely a critical objective of this most fundamental of organizational relationships, the leader-member dyad. This is consistent with findings showing that higher quality relationships are developed when both parties in a leader-member dyad invest relatively equally in the relationship (Maslyn & Uhl-Bien, 2001) and there is consensus regarding high levels of leader-member exchange (LMX) being positively related to contribution and satisfaction (Schyns, 2006).

We use the label "cadre" first associated with LMX by Graen and Uhl-Bien (1995) to identify subordinates engaged in on-going high levels of exchange with their leader (LMX) resulting in obligated role behavior. Attention should be given to cadre subordinates because such subordinates have been shown to demonstrate levels of behavior beyond those called for in the formal job agreement in exchange for scarce (but prized) resources provided by the leader (Wayne, Shore, & Linden, 1997). Gerstner and Day (1997) found consistent results linking high LMX from cadre subordinates with job performance, satisfaction, commitment, role perceptions, and turnover intentions in their meta-analysis. Additionally, commitment, self-efficacy (Schyns et al., 2005), and satisfaction (Schyns, 2006) have been shown to be positively related to cadre like behaviors resulting from high levels of LMX. We advance the assumption

that the unique role behaviors observed in cadre subordinates represents a form of social capital to a leader because the subordinate becomes obliged to make contributions involving knowledge, skill, or work related behaviors that are unavailable under customary understandings of the employment relationship.

The term cadre was defined at one point in time (1968) as "a nucleus around which an expanded organization can be built" (Webster's New World Dictionary of the American Language), and this somewhat dated definition certainly implied a potential for realization of human capital. A more current definition is "being a small group of people equipped for a special purpose" (New Oxford American Dictionary, 2008). At the level of private goods, this small group of people equipped for a special purpose provides a leader with ownership of capital that enables achievement of organizational outcomes that are not attainable when such capital is lacking. Thus we argue, the obligation associated with cadre status signals the presence of high levels of social capital (Kostova & Roth, 2003) that, theoretically, can facilitate realization of human capital.

Fostering cadre like leader-member exchange relationships has an influence on the organization beyond the focal dyad. It has been shown that a high level of LMX is a strong predictor of co-worker exchange (CWX) (Sherony & Green, 2002). So, strong LMX behavior likely has positive CWX spillover effects. It is a logical assumption that LMX and CWX are the primary sources for generation of social capital in an organizational setting. If there is truly a linkage between the evolution of social capital and ultimate realization of human capital, it would appear to be to the organization's advantage to encourage leaders to quickly develop high quality LMX relationships with subordinates in an attempt to foster quality CWX relationships and create greater social capital.

We would note the need to clearly distinguish behaviors associated with cadre status in an ongoing LMX from those associated with the more widely reported concept of organizational citizenship. While both cadre status and organizational citizenship result in behavior not commonly called for in the formal job contract, behavior at the center of organizational citizenship is typically limited to incidental acts of good will exercised by one organizational member toward another (Van Dyne, Cummings, & Parks, 1995) and does not involve an exchange of resources (Organ, 1990). Lacking an exchange of resources, organizational citizenship is not likely to generate a sense of obligation on the part of either party. Thus, organizational citizenship behavior has small potential to generate social capital, but behavior associated with cadre status more likely reflects high levels of social capital upon which a leader can draw in order to meet critical or high priority objectives.

Attention should also be given to low-quality LMX in which any exchange is limited to the formal requirements of the job and customary organizational compensation. We have labeled such leader-member relationships as "non-cadre." Non-cadre behavior associated with low quality LMX results in less positive consequences for an organization than behaviors associated with high

quality exchanges (Linden, Sparrowe, & Wayne, 1997). Low quality LMX does not foster a sense of obligation to perform in ways beyond what is required by the formal employment contract (Settoon, Bennett, & Linden, 1996) and fails to generate the level of social capital necessary to realize unique contributions of subordinate knowledge, skill, and work related behavior. Thus, non-cadre relationships characterized by low quality LMX likely have small potential for generation of the social capital because these subordinates infrequently develop a sense of obligation to perform in ways beyond what is required of them in the formal employment agreement (Settoon et al., 1996). Lacking the presence of social capital, we argue that non-cadre status represents small potential for facilitating the generation of human capital at the firm level.

Social Capital and Human Capital

We acknowledge that the theory of social capital as related to leader-member relationships in organizational settings has not, to date, established that high-quality LMX generates social capital that facilitates development of human capital. However, from macro-perspective, human capital is an aggregate of each individual employee's knowledge, skills, and abilities (Ployhart, Weekley, & Baughman, 2006), and there is increasing evidence that a leader's ability to develop and maintain high quality exchanges with cadre-like subordinates with its social capital implications results in outcomes that maximizes this aggregation and are positive at the firm level. These outcomes include, but are not limited to, performance (Vecchio & Gobdel, 1984), job satisfaction (Graen, Novak, & Sommerkamp, 1982b), retention (Graen, Linedn, & Hoel, 1982a), career advancement (Wakabayashi, Grean, Graen, & Graen, 1988), employee commitment, ability to attract and retain more desirable top-level employees (Bulino & Turnley, 2003), and positive perceptions of organizational climate (Kozlowski & Doherty, 1989). Further, a review of the human capital disclosure literature by Abhayawansa and Abeysekewa (2008) concluded that the pool or stock of human capabilities does not create value alone, but human resource management practices, facilitative organizational systems, and a supportive culture must be in place to leverage the potential of individuals. So, it is logical to assert that that social capital emerging from high quality LMX may be one of the lubricants on the track to realizing human capital.

Anecdotal evidence supporting the above is found in Freiberg and Freiberg's (1996) research on Southwest Airlines. They found that the company's policy that employees come first and the focus on high quality relationships with all employees to be central to the creation of the culture of the company. This developed human capital that has enabled the company to remain profitable in the worst of times and to keep turnover at industry lows. The net result is that Southwest has developed a sustainable competitive advantage using essentially the process previously outlined.

Model Development

Figure #1 presents a model of the hypothesized relationship between the social capital believed to be inherent in high quality LMX and dispositions and attitudes that could serve as elementary human capital metrics. These are identified as: a willingness to endorse the organization, a general satisfaction with the organization, and intent to stay with the firm. We readily acknowledge that these variables are accurately classified as attitudes or dispositions rather than metrics of human capital, but these attitudes and dispositions are in concert with the previously discussed positive outcomes associated with high quality LMX and can stand as proxies for measures of human capital.

This study proceeded on the grounds that the social capital represented in varying levels of LMX predicts the intensity of these attitudes and dispositions. The dependent variables in the model constitute something greater than individual employee attitudes. Rather, the overlap of these three variables resulting from the social capital created by high quality LMX represents an inclination toward positive action on behalf of the firm that contributes to accumulation of human capital. That is, over time, a firm's solid reputation for attracting and keeping good employees whose behavior demonstrates a willingness to publicly endorse the employer, to express their general satisfaction with employment by the firm, and to remain with the firm even when courted by competitors

Figure 1
Theoretical Model of the Hypothesized Relationships in this Study

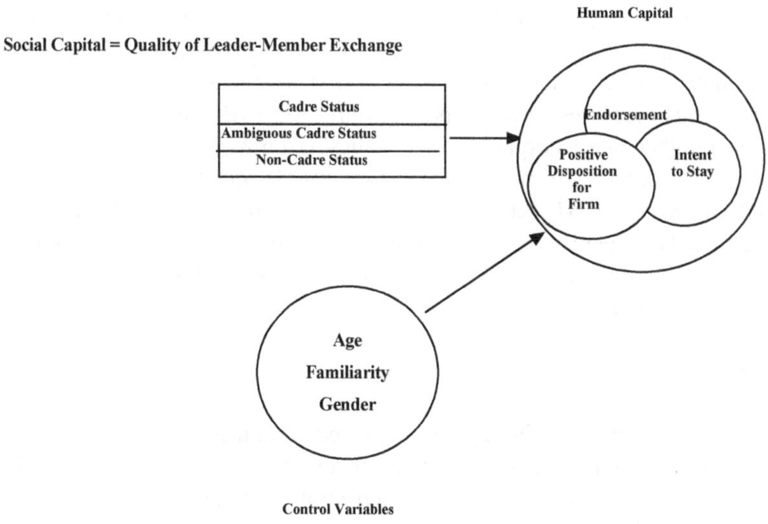

will act to draw further talent to that firm. While the metrics for translating this outcome into financial terms are not yet fully understood, the ability to attract and retain a rare pool of talented employees undoubtedly provides a firm with a sustainable competitive advantage, and retaining such rare talent acts like a magnet, drawing further talent to the firm (Jackson & Schuler, 2006).

Willingness to Endorse the Organization

High quality LMX relationships infused with relatively greater amounts of social capital should increase the probability that subordinates will publicly endorse their employer. Conversely, low quality LMX relationships lacking in such social capital should reduce the probability of such endorsement. Willingness of employees to publicly endorse their employer is a desirable behavior and has demonstrated a positive relationship with outcomes such as job satisfaction, potential to motivate, and organizational tenure (Van Dyne, Graham, & Dienesch, 1994). On the other hand, the presence of anti-company campaigns instituted by disgruntled employees has been observed as extremely harmful to the long-term survival of organizations (Konovsky & Folger, 1991). Therefore, employees willing to endorse their employer in public will generally have greater potential for contributing to that firm's human capital than employees unwilling to make such an endorsement.

Positive Disposition toward the Organization

Higher levels of social capital inherent in high quality LMX should be associated with a positive disposition toward one's employer. This disposition, characterized by an individual's positive feelings of identification with, attachment to, and involvement in the organization, is an indicator of the presence of human capital (Meyer & Allen, 1997). This disposition has been related to various measures of self-reported work effort (Bycio, Hackett, & Allen, 1995), adherence to organizational policy (Kim & Mauborgne, 1993), and objective measures of performance (DeCotiis & Summers, 1987; Konovsky & Cropanzano, 1991; Bashaw & Grant, 1994). Thus, employees maintaining high levels of positive disposition toward their employer have greater potential for contributing to a firm's human capital than employees with less of a positive disposition.

Intent to Stay with the Organization

The presence the social capital is expected to contribute to creation of human capital through the intent to stay with the organization. Cascio and Boudreau (2008) addressed the cost involved when employees voluntarily exit an organization. While there is a tendency to focus on costs incurred by an organization

in replacing departed employees (e.g., people' time, materials and equipment, cash outlays, etc.), an even greater cost may be found in the uncompensated performance differential between employees who leave and their replacements (Heneman & Judge, 2009). Cascio and Boudreau (2008) pointed out that the economic value of workers with firm-specific human capital is above their wage. It is true that employees with substantial amounts of firm-specific human capital can be replaced by workers receiving a lower wage. However, the gain achieved by reduced labor cost may be eliminated by the "uncompensated performance differential" reflected in the loss of firm-specific human capital. So, employees demonstrating greater intention to remain with their employer can be assumed as have greater potential for contributing to a firm's human capital than employees with less intention to remain.

Hypothesis: The social capital represented by the quality of dyadic exchange between leader and subordinate will account for a significant amount of the variance in measures appropriate to stand as proxies for human capital within organizational settings.

Method

Sample

The data used in this study were generated from a 360-degree feedback process conducted in a fast growing, small business unit of a large firm in the Midwest of the United States involved with electronic processing of financial data. The initial sample came from a population of 35 middle managers and 162 subordinates of these managers involved with the feedback process. The final sample used in this study consisted of 23 managers, and their 120 subordinates who submitted usable responses relevant to the questions posed in this study. Of the 23 managers in the sample, 10 were male and the average age was 41 years. Of the 120 subordinates in the sample, 61 were male and the average age was 37 years. The average length of employment with the firm was 1.6 years and the average length of time in which they had directly reported to the targeted manager was about 1 year.

Measures

Dependent Variables. The three dependent variables of the study are willingness to endorse the organization, positive disposition toward the organization, and intent to stay with the organization. These are described as follows.

Willingness to endorse the organization. Three direct and unambiguous items were used to measure the dependent variables in this study. A measure of the willingness of subordinates to publicly endorse the organization was obtained through response to a single item. The item asked the respondents to

indicate their level of agreement (1 = strongly disagree to 5 = strongly agree) with the statement "I am proud to tell others that I am a part of this organization."

Positive disposition toward the organization. A measure of subordinate disposition toward the organization was obtained through response to a single item. The item asked the respondents to indicate their agreement (1 = strongly disagree to 5 = strongly agree) with the statement "For me, this is the best of all possible organizations for which to work."

Intent to stay with the organization. A measure of subordinate intent to stay with the organization was obtained by asking respondents to indicate their agreement (1 = strongly disagree to 5 = strongly agree) with the statement "I think I will still be working here five years from now."

Independent variable: Quality of LMX. Seven items reported by Wayne, Shore, and Linden (1997) to measure Leader-Member Exchange were used to determine the quality of the leader-member exchange. This scale reflects the amounts of material resources, information, and support exchanged between a manager and direct reports. For example, subordinates were asked to respond to the statement "Regardless of how much power my manager has built into his/her own position, my manager would be personally inclined to use that power to help me solve problems in my work." Using a five-point scale with anchors of 1 being "strongly disagree" and 5 being "strongly agree," a high score is interpreted as a high quality interaction characterized by frequent reciprocal exchanges between the leader and the direct report, and a low score is interpreted as a low quality interaction depicted by less frequent exchange of resources between the two. This scale produced a Cronbach α of .93.

As suggested by Stark and Jeffries (2002), scores at or above the 75th percentile were categorized as indicative of the subordinate's cadre status in the exchange relationship (n = 29). Scores between the 25th and 75th percentile were categorized as ambiguous and representing neither cadre or non-cadre status (n = 57). Scores below the 25th percentile were categorized as non-cadre status (n = 32). Following the suggestion of Cohen, Cohen, West, and Aiken (2003), this variable was dummy coded for entry and analysis.

Control Variables. The control variables are age, familiarity, and gender. These are described as follows.

Age. Liden, Stilwell, and Ferris (1996) provided evidence that older subordinates are likely to bring to any evaluation of work place relationships more global experiences and greater understanding of what it takes to get work done in an organizational environment. Thus, they may be less inclined to assume an internal attribution for a leader's success or failure in establishing an exchange relationship than workers who are relatively younger and less aware of environmental constraints on the leader's behavior. From another perspective, Atwater and Yammarino (1997) suggested that perhaps individuals become less critical of themselves and others as they age and accumulate a work history. So, older subordinates may be more forgiving of a leader's failure to establish

an exchange relationship. These situations may result in an attitude toward the leader producing behavior that is consistent with that associated with generation of social capital. Thus, it is likely that they will be more willing to display desired role behaviors, consistent with the generation of human capital, even in the absence of a high quality LMX. This variable was self-reported as the age of the respondent at the time the survey was administered.

Familiarity. Work by Cascio and Valenzi (1997) and Ferris, Judge, Rowland, and Fitzgibbons (1994) suggested that familiarity developed over time and tenure will be positively related to perceptions of a supervisor. Atwater and Yammarino (1997) found that those with more years of experience or familiarity tend to perceive a leader in a more positive light than those with less years of experience or familiarity. Ferris et al. (1994) suggested that people move through a "toughness-leniency" progression where as they gain more experience and familiarity, they become more lenient in their perception of others. Such a positive perception of the leader may lead to behaviors that are consistent with those associated with the generation of social capital. This, in turn, may result in the subordinates engaging in extra role behavior that is associated with human capital. This variable was self-reported at the time the survey was administered as the number of years the subordinate had directly reported to his/her current supervisor.

Gender. Wayne, Liden, and Sparrowe (1994) advocated that gender may be important to attainment of a high quality LMX because gender is often a salient individual characteristic that influences the way individuals initially categorize others. Larwood and Blackmore (1978) found evidence that laboratory subjects were more likely to solicit the help of a same-sex individual than a person of the opposite sex for work on a challenging task. Duchon, Green, and Taber (1986) found that gender predicted subordinate status at the fourth week of a leader-member dyad's evolution, and Bauer and Green (1996) believed gender similarity to be a powerful predictor of LMX relationships. Following Cohen, et al. (2003), this self-reported variable was dummy coded for entry and analysis.

Analysis

Since this was a non-experimental study seeking to assess the differences between three groups (high LMX, low LMX, and ambiguous LMX) on three highly correlated dependent variables, a General Linear Multivariate Model (GLMV) was deemed appropriate (Tabachnick & Fidell, 2007; Harlow, 2005). A GLMV asks if the mean difference between groups on the combined dependent variables are larger than could be expected by chance. That is, using the control variables as covariates allowed a form of "what if" analysis by asking what would happen if all cases scored equally on the covariates so that the effect of the independent variables on the dependent variables over and beyond the covariates can be isolated (Tabachnick and Fidell 2007). By taking this approach, a more

powerful test of the relationship between the social capital assumed inherent in the subordinate's LMX relationship and indicators of human capital could be conducted than by conducting separate regressions on the DVs.

Prior to analysis, the measures of the independent variable and the dependent variables were examined for accuracy of the data and fit between their distributions and the assumptions of multivariate analysis. Although the measure of the quality of the LMX produced a kurtosis value in excess of 1.0, examination of the histogram for this measure suggested that scores on the measure conformed to accepted standards of normal distribution and no transformation was conducted. (Tabachnick & Fidell, 2007). While Box's M-test has been criticized as being a notoriously sensitive test of homogeneity (Tabachnick & Fidell, 2007), it demonstrated no reason for concern regarding differing covariance matrices across the three separate groups. An additional analysis using Levene's test gave no further concern regarding violation of the assumption of homogeneity. Missing values on the dependent and independent variables were replaced with the mean value for the specific variable as suggested by Harlow (2005). Table 1 presents the descriptive statistics and the correlation between the raw scores on the variables used in the study.

The high correlation between the dependent variables indicated that GLMV was appropriate for this study (Tabachnick & Fidell, 2007) and provides further support to the argument that they may be representative a latent variable that could stand as a measure of human capital. The lack of a significant correlation between the assumed confounding variables and the dependent variables indicated that it was not necessary to account for covariates in the equation. A test for regression of the hyperplanes produced a Wilk's Lamba of .81 [$F(18, 255) = 1{,}064, p < .388$] indicating the lack of a treatment by covariate effect (interaction) on the dependent variables.

Table 1
Descriptive Statistics and Correlations

	Variable	*N*	*Mean*	*SD*	1	2	3	4	5	6
1	Age	120	37	8.49						
2	Gender (Dummy coded)	120	1.49	.50	.02					
3	Familiarity	120	1.09	1.14	.09	.08				
4	Willingness to Endorse	120	4.11	.80	.09	.03	.04			
5	Intent to Stay	120	2.89	1.27	.12	.09	.03	.65***		
6	Disposition for Firm	120	3.21	1.15	-.02	.02	.03	.72***	.71***	
7	Quality of LMX (raw score)	120	4.03	.74	-.04	.19*	.03	.29**	.37***	.40***

* $p < .05$. ** $p < .01$. *** $p < .001$.

At the macro level, the value for Wilk's Lamba [F (78, 228) = 1.73, p <.001] demonstrated that the amount of variance in the linear combination of the dependent variables not explained by the independent variable was small and suggested that there were significant differences between at least two groups on the linear combination of the DVs. The value of Lamba indicated that approximately 37% (partial η^2) of the variance in the linear combination of the DVs could be explained by variance in subordinate response to the LMX measure. Thus, sufficient support appears to exist for acceptance of the hypothesis.

A common follow-up to a significant finding in a GLMV is to conduct separate analysis of variance for each DV (Harlow, 2005). We conducted an F-test of the effect of the quality of the LMX on linearly independent pair-wise comparisons of the DVs. Intent to stay [F (26,78) = 1.83, p < .03] and a Disposition for the firm [F (26,78)=1.87, p <.018] appeared to be influenced by the quality of the LMX, but the F-value for a Willingness to endorse the employer did not demonstrate significance at p < .05. A lack of fit test failed to reject the hypothesis that the data did not adequately fit the model. Tables 2, 3, and 4 report the results of a post-hoc test of the groupings of the quality

Table 2
Tukey's Honest Significant Difference Post-Hoc Analysis (One-Way ANOVA) of Quality of LMX Grouping by Willingness to Endorse the Organization

Group	*N*	*Mean*
High Quality LMX	29	4.36*
Ambiguous LMX	57	4.18
Low Quality LMX	32	3.75

Note: * Mean is significantly different from low-quality LMX grouping at p < .05.

Table 3
Tukey's Honest Significant Difference Post-Hoc Analysis (One-Way ANOVA) of Quality of LMX Grouping by Intent to Stay with the Organization

Group	*N*	*Mean*
High Quality LMX	29	3.32*
Ambiguous LMX	57	3.15*
Low Quality LMX	32	2.06

Note: * Mean is significantly different from low-quality LMX grouping at p < .05.

Table 4
Tukey's Honest Significant Difference Post-Hoc Analysis (One-Way ANOVA) of Quality of LMX Grouping by Disposition toward the Organization

Group	*N*	*Mean*
High Quality LMX	29	3.57*
Ambiguous LMX	57	3.46*
Low Quality LMX	32	2.47

Note: * Mean is significantly different from low-quality LMX grouping at p < .05.

of LMX on each individual dependent variable. Should these measures gain acceptance as proxy metrics for human capital, then results of these post-hoc tests further suggests that the social capital associated with high quality LMX will predict beyond random chance variation in these measures.

Discussion

Implications for Scholars

Based on the findings of the study, there appears support for the assertion that the creation of the social capital is inherent in LMX. That is, the creation of social capital is associated with obligations arising from feelings of gratitude, respect, and friendship experienced by both parties in the exchange relationship. These mutual obligations may be a motivator in the relationship because they foster development of the relationship. So, the respective investments made due to mutual obligations create joint ownership and build assets in the relationship, creating an incentive for both leader and member to avoid acting in ways that detract from the relationship's value. Indeed, work by Uhl-Bien et al. (2000) has suggested that to create relationships capable of creating the social capital necessary for enhanced firm performance, the LMX relationship must be of a relatively high quality. Specifically, the social capital believed inherent in high quality LMX should be characterized by people possessing complementary skills and equally committed to a common purpose, goals, and approach to working for which they hold themselves mutually accountable (Katzenbach & Smith, 1993). The net result of generating social capital in this way may well be to advance the creation of human capital at the unit level, or even the firm level.

The results of this study support much of what has been hypothesized about the relationship between generation of social capital and human capital. Differing levels of perceived LMX are associated with the variance common to an employee's intent to stay with his/her employer and a positive disposition toward the employment relationship. We assert that this variance represents a form of human capital that can be organized to achieve levels of rarity, inimitability, and non-substitutability that endow the firm strategic advantages over competitors (David, 2008; Hitt, Ireland, & Hoskisson, 2009). Thus, the social capital represented by the quality of LMX may indeed serve as an indicator of a firm's human capital. The results also suggest that there is value in obtaining an indication of the level of social capital within an organization that has implications for the successful implementation of a firm's business strategy. This supports Uhl-Bien et al.'s (2000) argument that a strategic initiative of HR architecture should be the integration of selection, training, development, and compensation practices designed to systematically promote effective relationship development within a strong relationship-based culture, hence greater firm performance through enhanced human capital.

Implications for Managers

The implications for strategic human resource management are clear. The development of human capital is generally accepted as source of competitive advantage (Barney, 1995; Becker & Gerhart, 1996) and the presence of social capital is likely a predictor of the potential for generation of human capital. Leveraging the human resources of a firm through active pursuit of high quality LMX has the potential to contribute to creation of greater amounts of human capital thus providing a sustainable competitive advantage for the organization. We suggest that it would be beneficial to train leaders to focus on specific behaviors and act in such a manner as to increase the potential for securing cadre-like behaviors from a greater number of their subordinates. In accomplishing such an objective, social capital at the dyadic level will likely be enhanced to the level of the larger good. That is, by creating high quality LMX one can foster high quality exchanges across co-workers as demonstrated by Sherony and Green (2002) thus increasing the potential for realizing greater levels of human capital across entire organizations.

Directions for Further Research

There needs to be further study, both theoretical and applied, to refine the operationalization of social capital, generate metrics for its measurement, and establish more complex theoretical models testing mediators and moderators in the relationship with human capital. As such, high quality LMX may prove to be only one of many predictors of social capital.

More germane to this study, future research would be beneficial to develop the line of inquiry pursued in this study. Specifically, we expected to find a relationship between the control variables; age, familiarity, and gender with the indicators of human capital, yet none was found. Regardless, there may be value in controlling for these variables in future studies. The mean tenure was 1.85 years. So it may be that members were not there long enough for familiarity to have a significant effect. In an organization with a higher mean tenure, this may not be the case. Gender of the participants was nearly an even split. We did not control for same gender pairs in LMX relationships, and this may be a more meaningful control variable in future studies. Regarding age, while it was significantly correlated with the quality of LMX, in this study it did not generate an interaction that would suggest it capable of influencing the generation of human capital.

Limitations of the Study

First, this study inherits all the weaknesses of surveys and self-reported measures. Second, because this study was cross-sectional in nature, the relation-

ships may be subject to temporal change. Third, we readily acknowledge that the theory underlying this study focuses on intangibles. However, we would also counter that as Cascio and Bourdreau (2008) advocated, intangible does not necessarily mean immeasurable. Fourth, we acknowledge the limitations of using three single items to study the relationships advanced in this study, and we further acknowledge that the three individual items may indeed measure a single latent variable. But we confidently assert that should the variance shared by these three measures constitute a single latent variable it would not negate the potential of such variance to represent a unique form of human capital.

Further, we acknowledge that this was not an experimental study and it is impossible to attribute causality to the significant findings because we did not manipulate the independent variables or control for confounding variables in an experimental manner. Indeed, there is certainly room in our model to further consider the influence of moderating variables.

That being said, the study has strengths as well. The data were collected in a field setting in an organization under live work conditions. There was a good distribution of ages and good representation of both genders. Also, because the average tenure was less than two years, it was very unlikely that any of the responses were biased by familiarity resulting in more positive perceptions of the supervisor (Ferris et al., 1994). However, caution is urged in extending the interpretation of the results of this study beyond the population from which the sample was taken.

References

Abhayawansa, S., & Abeysekera, I. (2008). An explanation of human capital disclosure from the resource-based perspective. *Human Resource Costing & Accounting, 12* (1), 51–64.

Adler, P. S., & Kwon, S. (2002). Social capital: prospects for a new concept. *Academy of Management Review, 27*, 17–40.

Atwater, L. E., & Yammarino, F. J. (1997). Self-other rating agreement: A review and model. *Research in Personnel and Human Resources Management, 15*, 121–174.

Babcock, P. (2007). *"Relational capital" becomes the newest differentiator of competitiveness.* Retrieved on July 28, 2008 at http://www.shrm.org/ema.new_published/CMS_023390.asp.

Barney, J. B. (1995). Looking inside for competitive advantage. *Academy of Management Executive, 9* (4), 49–61

Bashaw, E. R., & Grant, S. E. (1994). Exploring the distinctive nature of work commitments: Their relationships with personal characteristics, job performance, and propensity to leave. *Journal of Personal Selling and Sales Management, 14* (2), 41–56.

Bauer, T. N., & Green, S.G. (1996). Development of leader-member exchange: A longitudinal test. *Academy of Management Journal, 39*, 1538–1567.

Becker, B., & Gerhart B. (1996). The impact of human resource management on organizational performance. *Academy of Management Journal, 39*, 779–801.

Bolino, M. C., Turnley, W. H., & Bloodgood, J. M. (2002). Citizenship behavior and the creation of social capital in organizations. *Academy of Management Review, 27*, 505–522.

Bolino, M. C., & Turnley, W. H. (2003). Going the extra mile: Cultivating and managing employee citizenship behavior. *Academy of Management Executive, 17*, 60–71.

Brush, C. G., Greene, P. G., & Hart, M. M. (2001). From the initial idea to unique advantage: The entrepreneurial challenge of constructing a resource base. *Academy of Management Executive, 15*, 64–78.

Bycio, P., Hackett, R. D., & Allen, J. S. (1995). Further assessments of Bass's (1985) conceptualization of transactional and transformational leadership. *Journal of Applied Psychology, 80*, 468–478.

Cascio, W. F., & Boudreau, J. W. (2008). *Investing in people.* Saddle River, NJ: Person Education.

Cascio, W., & Valenzi, E. (1997). Behaviorally anchored rating scores: Effects of education and job experience on raters and ratees. *Journal of Applied Psychology, 62*, 278–282.

Cohen, J., Cohen, P., West, S. G., & Aiken, L. S. (2003). *Applied multiple regression/correlation analysis for the behavioral sciences.* Mahwah, NJ: Erlbaum.

Cook, J. D., Hepworth, S. J., Wall, T. D., & Warr, P. B. (1981). *The experience of work.* London: Academic Press.

David, F. (2008). *Strategic management: Concepts and cases.* Upper Saddle River, NJ: Pearson Education.

DeCotiis, T. A., & Summers, T. P. (1987). A path analysis of a model of the antecedents and consequences of organizational commitment. *Human Relations, 40*, 445–470.

Dess, G. D., & Shaw, J. D. (2001), Voluntary turnover, social capital and organizational performance. *Academy of Management Review, 26*, 446–456.

Duchon, D., Green, S., & Taber, T. D. (1986). Vertical dyad linkage: A longitudinal assessment of antecedents, measures, and consequences. *Journal of Applied Psychology, 71*, 56–60.

Ferris, G., Judge, T., Roland, K., & Fitzgibbons (1994). Subordinate influence and the performance evaluation process. *Organizational Behavior and Human Decision Processes, 58*, 101–135.

Freiberg, K., & Freiberg, J. (1996). *Nuts! Southwest Airlines' crazy recipe for business and personal success.* Austin, TX: Bard Press.

Gerstner, C. R., & Day, D. D. (1997). Meta-analytic review of leader-member exchange theory: Correlates and construct issues. *Journal of Applied Psychology, 82*, 827–844.

Graen, G. (1976). Role-making process within complex organizations. In M. D. Dunnette (Ed.), *Handbook of industrial and organizational psychology* (pp. 1202–1245). Chicago, IL: Rand McNally.

Graen, C. B. (2003). Interpersonal workplace theory at the crossroads: LMX and transformational theory as special cases of role making in working organizations. In G. B. Graen (Ed.), *Dealing with diversity, LMX leadership: The series* (Vol. 1, pp. 145–182). Greenwich, CT: Information Age.

Graen, G. B., Liden, R. C., & Hoel, W. (1982a). The role of leadership in the employee withdrawal process. *Journal of Applied Psychology, 67*, 868–892.

Graen, G. B., Novak, M. A., & Sommerkamp, P. (1982b). The effects of leader-member exchange and job design on productivity and satisfaction: Testing a dual attachment model. *Organizational Behavior and Human Performance, 30*, 109–131.

Graen, G. B., & Scandura, T. (1987). Toward a psychology of dyadic organizing. *Research in Organizational Behavior, 9*, 175–208.

Graen, G. B., & Ulh-Bien, M. (1995). Relationship-based approach to leadership : Development of leader-member exchange (LMX) theory of leadership over 25 years. *Leadership Quarterly, 6*, 219–247.

Harris, K. J., & Kacmar, K. M. (2006). Too much of a good thing: The curvilinear effect of leader-member exchange on stress, *Journal of Social Psychology, 146*, 65–84.

Harlow, L. L. (2005). *The essence of multivariate thinking,* Mahwah, NJ: Erlbaum.

Heneman III, H. G., & Judge, T. A. (2009). *Staffing organizations,* Middleton, WI: McGraw-Hill.

Hitt, M. A., & Hoskisson, R. E. (2009). *Strategic management: Competitiveness and globalization.* Mason, OH: South-Western Cengage.

Illgen, D. R., & Hollenbeck, J. R. (1991). The structure of work: Job design and roles. In M. D. Dunnette & L. M. Hough (Eds.) *Handbook of industrial and organizational psychology* (pp. 165–208). Palo Alto, CA: Consulting Psychologist Press.

Jackson, S. E., & Schuler, R. S. (2006). *Managing human resource through strategic partnerships.* Mason, OH: Thompson-Southwestern.

Katzenbach, J. R., & Smith, D. K. (1993). *The wisdom of teams: Creating high performance organizations*. Boston, MA: Harvard Business School Press.

Kim, W. C., & Mauborgne, R. A. (1993). Procedural justice, attitudes, and subsidiary top management compliance with multinationals' corporate strategic decisions. *Academy of Management Journal, 36*, 502–528.

Konovsky, M. A., & Cropanzano, R. (1991). Perceived fairness of employee drug testing as a predictor of employee attitudes and job performance. *Journal of Applied Psychology,76*, 698–707.

Konovsky, M., & Folger, R. (1991). The effects of procedures, social accounts, and benefits level on victims' reactions to layoffs. *Journal of Applied Social Psychology, 21*, 630–650.

Kostova, T., & Roth, K. (2003). Social capital in multinational corporations and a micro-macro model of it formation. *Academy of Management Review, 28*, 297–231.

Kozlowski, S. W., & Doherty, M. L. (1989). Integration of climate and leadership: Examination of neglected issues. *Journal of Applied Psychology, 74*, 546–553.

Larwood, L., & Blackmore, J. (1978). Sex discrimination in managerial selection: Testing predictions of the vertical dyad linkage model. *Sex Roles, 4*, 359–367.

Linden, R. C., Sparrowe, R. T., & Wayne, S. J. (1997). Leader-member exchange theory: The past and potential for the future. *Research in Personnel and Human Resources Management, 15*, 47–119.

Liden, R. C., Stilwell, D., & Ferris, G. R. (1996). The effects of supervisor and subordinate age on objective performance and subjective performance ratings. *Human Relations, 49*, 327–342.

Major, D. A., Kozlowski, S. W., Chao, G. T., & Gardner, P.O, (1992, May). *Newcomer expectations and early socialization outcomes: The moderating effects of role development factors*. Paper presented at the Society for Industrial and Organizational Psychology Conference, Montreal.

Maslyn, J. M., & Uhi-Bien, M, (2001). Leader-Member exchange and its dimensions: Effects of self-effort and other's effort on relationship quality. *Journal of Applied Psychology 86*, 697–708.

Meyer, J. P., & Allen, N. J. (1997).*Commitment in the workplace: Theory, research, and application.* Thousand Oaks, CA: Sage.

Nahapiet, J., & Ghoshal, S. (1998). Social capital, intellectual capital, and the organizational advantage. *Academy of Management Review, 23*, 242–266.

Organ, D. W. (1990). The motivational basis of organizational citizenship behavior. *Research in Organizational Behavior, 12*, 43–72.

Ployhart, R. E., Weekley, J. A., & Baughman, K. (2006). The structure and function of human capital emergence: A multilevel examination of the attraction-selection-attrition model. *Academy of Management Journal, 49*, 661–677.
Portes, A. (1998). Social capital: Its origins and applications in modern sociology. *Annual Review of Sociology, 24,* 1–24.
Robison, L. J., Schmid, A. A., & Siles, M. E. (2002). Is social capital really capital? *Review of Social Economy, 15*, 1–22.
Rosseau, D. M., & Schalk, R. (2000). *Psychological contracts in employment: Cross-national perspectives.* Thousand Oaks, CA: Sage.
Schyns, B. (2006). Are group consensus in Leader-Member Exchange (LMX) and shared work values related to organizational outcomes? *Small Group Research, 37*, 20–35.
Schyns, B., Paul, T., Mohr, G., & Blank, H. (2005). Comparing antecedents and consequences of leader–member exchange in a German working context to findings in the US. *European Journal of Work and Organizational Psychology, 14* (1), 1–22.
Settoon, R. P., Bennett, N., & Linden, R. C. (1996). Social exchange in organizations: Perceived organizational support, leader-member exchange, and employee reciprocity. *Journal of Applied Psychology, 81*, 219–227.
Shaw, J. D., Duffy, M. K., Johnson, J. L., & Lockhart, D. E. (2005). Turnover, social capital losses, and performance. *Academy of Management Journal, 48*, 594–606.
Sherony, K. M., & Green, S. G. (2002). Coworker exchange: Relationships between coworkers, leader-member exchange, and work attitudes. *Journal of Applied Psychology, 97*, 542–548.
Stark, E. E., & Jeffries, F. (2002, March). *Predictors of high quality leader-member exchanges: Implications for generation of social and human capital.* A paper presented to the annual conference of the Western Academy of Management, Santa Fe, NM.
Subramaniam, M., & Youndt, M. A. (2005). The influence of intellectual capital on the types of innovative capabilities. *Academy of Management Journal, 48*, 450–463.
Tabachnick, B. G., & Fidell, L. S. (2007). *Using multivariate statistics.* Boston, MA: Person Education.
Tjosvold, D. (1989). Interdependence and power between managers and employees: A case study of the leader relationship. *Journal of Management, 15*, 49–62.
Uhl-Bien, M., Graen, G. B., & Scandura, T. A. (2000). Implications of leader-member exchange (LMX) for strategic human resource management systems: Relationships as social capital for competitive advantage. *Research In Personnel and Human Resources Management, 18,* 137–186._
Van Dyne, L., Cummings, L. L., & Parks, J. M. (1995). Extra-role behaviors: In pursuit of construct and definitional clarity (a bridge over muddied waters). *Research in Organizational Behavior, 17,* 215–230.
Van Dyne, L., Graham, J. W., & Dienesch, R. M. (1994). Organizational citizenship behavior: Construct redefinition, measurement, and validation. *Academy of Management Journal, 37*, 765–802.
Vecchio, R. P., & Gobdel, B. C. (1984). The vertical dyad linkage model of leadership: Problems and prospects. *Organizational Behavior and Human Performance, 34*, 5–20.
Wakabayashi, M., Graen, G., Graen, M., & Graen, M. (1988). Japanese management process: Mobility into middle management. *Journal of Applied Psychology, 73*, 217–227.
Wayne, S. J., Liden, R. C., & Sparrowe, R. T. (1994). Developing leader-member exchanges. *American Behavioral Scientist, 37*, 697–715.

Wayne, S. J., Shore, L. M., & Linden, R. C. (1997). Perceived organizational support and leader-member exchange: A social exchange perspective. *Academy of Management Journal, 40*, 82–111.

Wayne, S. J., Linden, R. C., & Sparrowe, R. T. (1994). Developing leader-member exchanges. *American Behavioral Scientist, 37*, 697–715.

Yukl, G. A. (1998). *Leadership in organizations.* Englewood Cliffs, NJ: Prentice Hall.

Current Topics in Management, Vol. 15, 2011, pp. 137-152

RELATIONSHIP BETWEEN THE BIG-FIVE PERSONALITY AND THE FINANCIAL PERFORMANCE OF FUND MANAGERS

Selin Metin Camgoz, Mehmet Baha Karan, and Azize Ergeneli

Behavioral finance has made impressive progress through careful investigation of markets and individual investors' behaviors. Researchers in the field of behavioral finance argued that individuals' thoughts, perceptions and fears are displayed in their behavioral actions and judgments and, financially speaking, in their investment choices regarding their risk preferences (Daniel, Hirshleifer, & Teoh, 2002; De Bondt, 1998; Kahneman & Riepe, 1998). Gandevani (2002) pointed out that an investor's psychology was important to his or her ability to both select and implement trading methods. In other words, extensive research in behavioral finance and investment psychology propounded that investors' faulty decisions were blamed for their poor performance (Gandevani, 2002). As such, Kostalany (1977) asserted that market reactions were heavily based on psychology rather than objective facts (cf. Tigges, Riegert, Jonitz, Brengelmann, & Engel, 2000). This viewpoint clarified the importance of psychological research in the financial market field. Thus, if investors with specific psychographic profiles were more likely to exhibit specific investment outcomes, then practitioners could attempt to recognize the relevant tendencies before investment decisions were made.

The current study mainly addressed whether or precisely which personality traits would distinguish successful versus unsuccessful financial performance of fund managers. We measured the personality traits of fund managers by the Big-Five and observed their investment outcomes in the real market. Our methodology, which involves directly measuring personality traits and correlating them with real-economic behavior in terms of Sharpe indexes, could be useful

in shedding light on the impact of psychological variables in various economic situations. Given some evidence that personality characteristics might affect financial performance, one begins to speculate about implications for selecting, evaluating and training employees in financial organizations.

Moreover, in the vast literature on financial markets, relatively little attention has been paid to the role of professional investors, while overwhelmingly focusing on individual investors and undergraduate students. Thus, this study is distinguished from previous research by gathering data from professional investors and bringing together various insights from different disciplines of psychology and finance.

Big-Five Personality and Its Relationship with Financial Performance

Digman (1990) described personality as central and stable individual differences in the tendency to behave in certain ways (Digman, 1990). Similarly, Allport (1961), the pioneer of personality psychology, defined personality as "the dynamic organization within the individual of the psychophysical systems that determine his characteristics, behavior and thought" (p. 28). Within the last few decades the consensus has emerged that the most salient aspects of an individual's personality could be described with a five factor model (FFM), commonly referred to as the "Big-Five"(Goldberg, 1990). The Big-Five personality consisted of 5 basic dimensions namely Agreeableness (A), Conscientiousness (C), Extraversion (E), Neuroticism (N) and Openness to Experience (O) (McCrae & John, 1992). These traits represent personality at the broadest level of abstraction and each dimension has included a large number of distinct, more specific personality characteristics (Costa & McCrae, 1995; John, 1990). The Big-Five personality dimensions have been studied extensively for their plausible effects on organizational and individual outcomes such as job performance, academic performance and well being as well as on productivity (Barrick & Mount, 1991; Salgado, 1998). The five dimensions of personality are as follows.

Agreeableness–Hostility

Agreeableness is accepted to relate an individual's interpersonal style and strategies to act in accordance with other people's interests. This dimension concerns the degree of likeableness, courtesy, good-naturedness, cooperation, thoughtfulness, forgiveness, altruism, trustworthiness, helpfulness and trust that an individual has. It also denotes the degree to which people believe that others they deal with have good intentions. Fenton-O'Creevy, Nicholson, Soane, and Willman (2007) asserted that organizations have a preference for a low agreeableness dimension because of the tendency of competition in the business environment.

Conscientiousness–Undirectedness

Conscientiousness measures the degree to which an individual is oriented toward duty, responsibility, and dependability. It covers impulse control and goal directed behavior. It includes the individual's preferences for following rules and schedules, and the extent to which individuals are hardworking, organized, self-disciplined, achievement oriented and dependable as opposed to lazy and unreliable. Salgado (1997) identified conscientiousness as a strong predictor of occupational success and his research showed that conscientiousness was positively correlated with job proficiency, training proficiency and high academic achievement (Salgado, 1997).

Extraversion–Introversion

Extraversion is marked by pronounced engagement with the external world. It relates to the individual's level of sociability and agency. It includes the traits of warmth, excitement seeking, persistence, industriousness, dependability, thoroughness, and responsibility. Extroverted people tend to be enthusiastic, action-oriented individuals, who like to talk and assert themselves. In other words, activity and energy level traits, sociability and emotional expressiveness are heavily emphasized. Introverts, on the other hand, tend to be quiet, low-key, deliberate, and less dependent on the social world and simply need less stimulation than an extravert (Costa & McCrae, 1995). Zuckerman (1994) indicated that extraversion had a strong genetic underpinning of thrill-seekers. Nyhus and Pons (2005) stated that the effect of extraversion on earnings might be more ambiguous than other factors and may depend on the occupation under consideration.

Neuroticism–Emotional Stability

Neuroticism is the tendency toward negative emotional experience, and it addresses the degree to which the individual shows anger, anxiety, or depression rather than calmness, self-confidence, and coolness. Digman (1990) pointed out that individuals with on neuroticism looked out for danger and suffered more due to their own anxiety, fear, and imagination. High neuroticism scores could also be seen as a liability in many risk environments (Fenton-O'Creevy et al., 2007). Emotional stability is at the other extreme of the neuroticism continuum. Barrick and Mount (1991) and Salgado (1997) reported that emotional stability had a positive effect on job performance across different occupations.

Openness to Experience–Conservatism

Openness to experience relates to intellectual curiosity as well as willingness to try different activities or consider unconventional ideas. It includes the

breadth, complexity, and depth of an individual's life (McCrae & Costa, 1997). Individuals with a high degree of openness to experience are generally creative and will attempt different or novel approaches in their field. At the other extreme there are people with a high tolerance for uncertainty and a demand for change. Therefore, this dimension is accepted as a tendency toward sensation seeking and risk-taking (McCrae & Costa, 1997).

Personality characteristics are believed to play a critical role in financial matters. There has been considerable research applying psychological theory to a broad range of investment topics including saving, earning, consumption and risk taking. However, most of the studies focused on the relationships between specific personality traits and risk taking behaviors in different domains. In earlier studies, McInish (1980, 1982) investigated the association between the riskiness of investment opportunities and locus of control as a personality trait. Based on a student sample, McInish (1980) found that externals favored less risky portfolios; however, in a later study with actual investors, McInish (1982) reported that externals tended to choose more risky portfolios. Later, Zuckerman and Kuhlman's (2000) study revealed that risk taking in the areas of smoking, drinking, drugs, sex, driving and gambling was related to the scales for impulsive sensation seeking, aggression and sociability but not for neuroticism. Similarly, in their findings, Nicholson, Fenton-O'Creevy, Soane, and Willman (2002) noted that risk propensity is strongly rooted in personality and sensation seeking (a sub-scale of extraversion), which is highly correlated with risk taking in all domains. Additionally, risk propensity was greater for subjects with higher extraversion and openness to experience scores and less for subjects with higher neuroticism, agreeableness and conscientiousness scores. Last but not least, Kowert and Hermann (1997) pointed out that individuals with low ratings in the conscientiousness dimension are more risk inclined and individuals with high scores in the openness to experience trait are more open to action and risk taking. Likewise, individuals who scored high on the excitement seeking facet of the extraversion scale were characterized as intentional risk takers.

While there is a plethora of research demonstrating the relationship between personality traits and risky behavior, little systematic research (Biais, Hilton, Mazurier, & Pouget, 2001, 2005; Lo, Repin, & Steenbarger, 2005) has been conducted on the relationship between the personalities of investors and their financial outcomes. Oberlechner (2004) examined which characteristics and individual decision making factors are important for a successful foreign exchange trader. His findings, based on 291 professional foreign exchange traders in European banks, reported that quick reaction time, discipline, experience, concentration and stress are the most important characteristics of successful traders, ranked in a list of 23 items. He added that emotional stability is considered a crucial feature for a successful foreign exchange trader. Biais et al. (2001) conducted an experimental study with 67 university students for relating psychological traits and cognitive biases to trading performance in-

dicators. They simulated an experimental financial market where the average number of orders per replication and the orders that result in losses are taken as financial performance. The results suggested that impulsive subjects placed more orders and overconfident subjects were more likely to place loss-making orders. Later, Biais et al. (2005) examined the effects of overconfidence and self-monitoring on the trading performance of subjects in an experimental asset market and concluded that male subjects with high self-monitors achieve superior trading performance. The study of Witteloostuijn and Muehlfeld (2008) with 34 economics students suggested that different personality traits (regret disposition, self-monitoring, sensation seeking and Type A/B behavior) affect distinct components of trading behavior in that Type-B behavior is associated with lower trading frequency. Moreover, Grinblatt and Keloharju (2006) studied the links between trading activity, overconfidence, and sensation seeking. Their findings revealed that sensation seeking was related to higher trading frequency for Finnish equity trading data.

Similarly, Lo et al. (2005) explored the possible links between psychological factors and trading performance, operationalized as account size, in a sample of 80 anonymous day-traders. The correlation analysis revealed a small negative correlation between trading performance and the personality dimensions of agreeableness, neuroticism, conscientiousness and openness to experience, while exhibiting a positive correlation between extraversion and trading performance. However, none of these correlations were significant.

A study using the Big-Five to assess the relationship between the personality traits and trading performance of professionals was conducted by Fenton-O'Creevy et al. (2007). The authors collected quantitative and qualitative data from traders and trader managers at four large investment banks in London to explore the relationships among their psychological profiles, roles, performance and behavior. The authors utilized total remuneration as well as managerial ratings of performance (using four criteria: profit contribution, analytical ability, risk management and interpersonal skills) as proxy for trader performance. In their sample of 64 traders, the findings revealed that the higher performing traders were those emotionally stable introverts who were open to experience. Still another study revealed that conscientiousness and openness to experience as personality traits are associated with the successful market timing performance of fund managers while neuroticism was negatively related to both selectivity and the market timing performance of fund managers (Camgoz, 2009).

In the majority of the aforementioned studies, the performance measures were based on the trading outcomes in experimental markets in which subjects were asked to participate in hypothetical scenarios. Unlike the previous studies, the current study evaluated the financial performance of fund managers by estimating the portfolio performance of managed equity mutual funds in terms of the Sharpe index, which is defined as a measure of the excess return

(or risk premium) per unit of risk in an investment asset or trading strategy (Sharpe, 1966).

The current study was based on the assumption that investors had underlying risk propensities as part of their personalities (Nicholson et al., 2002; Kowert & Hermann, 1997; Zuckerman & Kuhlman, 2000). Hence, the arguments presented by the hypotheses are based on the logic that higher performing investors would be the ones possessing personality traits in which risk propensity is high. Our orientation to risk, on the other hand, was dependent upon the relationship between risk and return, indicating that higher rates of return would involve taking increased risks, as indicated in Modern Portfolio Theory. Therefore, we hypothesized that fund managers with high scores in extraversion, openness to experience and conscientiousness would exhibit higher financial performance whereas managers with high scores in neuroticism and agreeableness would likely exhibit lower financial performance.

Method

Sample and Procedure

This study, as a part of a larger study, has been carried out to estimate the financial performance of professional investors, namely fund managers who actively manage mutual funds in different investment companies and banks in Turkey. Professional investors are the major actors in financial markets since they are well placed to exploit market imperfections by accessing privileged information or critical mass.

Mutual funds, on the other hand, are defined as the collection of assets which have been established with the money to be collected from the public in return for participation certificates with the purpose of managing portfolios of capital market instruments, gold and precious metal on the account of the holders of these certificates based on the principle of risk distribution and fiduciary ownership (www.cmb.gov.tr). The assets in mutual funds are managed by the manager (corporate body) appointed by the founder with respect to the portfolio management contract (www.cmb.gov.tr).

There are two different types of mutual funds: equity mutual funds (Type A) and fixed income mutual funds (Type B) in Turkey. Equity mutual funds are the mutual funds maintaining at least 25% or more Turkish equity weighting in their portfolio on a monthly average basis for 12 months. Mutual funds that have no such obligations are classified as fixed income funds and they comprise mainly fixed income debt instruments: bonds, treasury bills, and other fixed income debt instruments. There are a total of 256 mutual funds operating in Turkey, of which 114 are equity mutual funds and 142 are fixed income mutual funds.

The population of this study included all the mutual fund managers; however, the target population was limited to equity mutual fund managers. The

reason for restricting the sample to equity mutual fund managers only was that equity funds consist of more than 25% equity and thus allow more volatility compared to fixed income funds. Although there are 114 equity funds, these funds are managed by only 72 fund managers working in 51 different investment companies and banks.

The sampling methodology of this study employed a purposive sampling strategy in which subjects were selected because of their characteristics (Patton, 1990). Equity mutual fund managers were initially contacted via telephone and were assured that the data was highly personal, confidential and could not be obtained through any institutional source. Then, an Internet-based survey questionnaire was e-mailed to equity fund managers. Of those receiving emails, 65 completed and returned the online survey. However, the research sample was restricted depending on 2 criteria. First, only those managers who indicated that they were responsible for investment allocation decisions of equity mutual funds in their investment company were included. Second, the sample was limited to those who indicated that they had been managing the same mutual fund continuously for at least 2 consecutive years at the time of the survey. This resulted in a sample size of 60 professional equity mutual fund managers representing 83% of the whole population, a reasonably high ratio, which increases the generalizability of the study findings. 85% of the participants were male, 61.7% were married and the mean age was 35.8. The ratio of men to women in the sample is parallel to the notion that trading environments are not perceived as female friendly (Fenton-O'Creevy et al., 2007) and that men are disproportionately represented in the finance sector (Barber & Odean, 2001).

Measurement

The measurement instrument was composed of 2 parts.

The Big-Five Personality Instrument. This study used the 44-item Big-Five Inventory (BFI) developed by John, Donahue, and Kentle (1991) to assess the personality typologies of professional fund managers. The BFI with 44 items was constructed to allow an efficient and flexible assessment of five dimensions when there is no need for a more differentiated measurement of individual facets (Benet-Martinez & John, 1998). These five dimensions were agreeableness, conscientiousness, extraversion, neuroticism and openness to experience. Some examples of the sets of items in the questionnaire were as follows: "likes to cooperate with others/is generally trusting/is helpful and unselfish with others" for *agreeableness*; "perseveres until the task is finished; does a thorough job" for *conscientiousness*; "is outgoing/talkative/is full of energy" for *extraversion*; "gets nervous easily/worries a lot" for *neuroticism*; *and* "is original, comes up with new ideas; has an active imagination" for the *openness to experience* dimension of BFI. Participants rated each BFI item on a 5-point scale ranging from 1 (disagree strongly) to 5 (agree strongly). The

Turkish translation and adaptation of the instrument was conducted by Sümer, Lajunen, and Özkan (2005) using the standard translation and back translation procedure. The internal reliability coefficients for each of the BFI subscales were all in reasonable intervals ranging from .75 to .81 (see Table 1).

Fund Type and Demographics. The participants were asked to identify the type and the specific names of the equity mutual funds that they have been managing for at least two consecutive years in addition to some demographic questions such as gender, age and marital status.

Analysis and Results

Composition of the Dependent Variable

The financial performance of fund managers was calculated by the Sharpe index, which corresponds to the weekly portfolio performance funds for two consecutive years spanning a period when markets were experiencing sustained growth. We initially studied the weekly returns for 69 open-end equity mutual funds with a total of 113 observations. The Sharpe index is formulated as follows:

$$S_i = (R_p - R_f) / \sigma_p$$

Where:

S_i = Sharpe performance index

R_p = Portfolio's actual weekly return during a specified time period. The daily prices of all 69 funds were obtained from Capital Markets Board (CMB) statistics and weekly returns were calculated thereupon.

R_f = Weekly risk-free rate of return during the same period (rate of Treasury Bills)

σ_p = Portfolio's standard deviation (Systematic risk)

After Sharpe indexes were calculated for each of the 69 particular funds, the funds were ranked according to scores in descending order. Although the number of equity fund managers was 60, some managers were responsible for the management of multiple funds, which makes the total number of equity funds 69. However, for those managers, fund performance was assigned only to one mutual fund that had the highest Sharpe index throughout the investing weeks.

Data Screening, Descriptive Statistics, and Intercorrelations among Variables

Prior to analysis, the data were screened for missing values and outliers. The variables of interest were scanned for normality using the indexes of kurtosis and skewness. None of the variables other than age required substantial trans-

formation to achieve acceptable levels of parametricity. Box-plots detected one outlier case in age variable; however, as sample size is limited, that case was not excluded from the analysis.

The statistical analysis started with designating the descriptive statistics as well as zero-order correlations concerning the study variables.

The results seen in Table 1 display some evidence that fund managers scored quite low in the neuroticism dimension and relatively high in the openness to experience, agreeableness, and conscientiousness and extraversion dimensions. These patterns might suggest a certain personality type for fund managers. However, a sample size of 60 may make such a conclusion unwarranted. We concentrated on the variance inflation factor (VIF) to detect multicollinearity. As the VIF scores for agreeableness and conscientiousness were found to be greater than 5, we excluded the agreeableness dimension from the proceeding analyses to eliminate redundancy (Tabachnick & Fidell, 2001).

A visual inspection of the scatter plots as additional analyses indicated that some relationships were not satisfactorily described by a straight line. An examination of the non-significant correlations also supported the view that linearity cannot be assumed and some relationships may be better described by non-linear functions. Therefore, the hypotheses were tested with logistic regression.

Testing the Hypotheses

Sharpe performance scores were divided into subgroups in order to determine successful and unsuccessful performances. The funds were classified into quar-

Table 1
Intercorrelations and Cronbach Reliabilities of Major Variables

Variable	*M*	*SD*	1	2	3	4	5	6	7	8	9
1. Marital status			1.00								
2. Gender			.256	1.00							
3 Age	35.58	4.7	–.354**	–.112	1.00						
4. Extraversion	3.56	.7	–.091	.023	.165	1.00	**.75**				
5 Agreeableness	3.64	.5	.173	.062	.005	.205	1.00	**.81**			
6. Conscientiousness	3.56	.5	.224	.046	.038	.180	.755**	1.00	**.78**		
7. Neuroticism	2.77	.8	–.075	–.233	.069	–.345**	–.336**	–.248	1.00	**.78**	
8. Openness to experience	3.74	.7	–.201	.027	.121	.443**	.157	.087	–.332*	1.00	**.76**
9. Sharpe index	–1.169	8.3	–.027	–.027	.–247	.092	–.100	–.139	–.215	.140	1.00

Notes: $N = 60$. reliability coefficients are in boldface along the diagonal.
$*p < .05$. $**p < .01$.

tiles according to the Sharpe index scores to explore the break-even points in relation to study variables. The decision to divide the sample into four, instead of five, six or ten performance subgroups was only a matter of preference (see Lewellen, Lease, & Schlarbaum, 1979). A quick examination of the Sharpe index quartiles allowed us to notice a deviation/break-even point between the mean scores of the first quartile and the other quartiles. An analysis of variance (ANOVA) was conducted and a significant F-value suggested that the mean values of the quartile groups differed significantly [(F (3, 59) = 84.85)]. Additionally, the Post-hoc comparison of the Scheffe test reported a significant difference between the first quartile and all the other quartiles.

We composed a new Sharpe index in dummy coding. The dummy variable took the value of "1" for the Sharpe performance indexes of mutual funds ranking in the top quartile (the best performing 25%) and took the value of "0" for the Sharpe performance indexes of mutual funds ranking in other quartiles (average to poor performing 75%). This newly composed Sharpe index served as the main outcome variable such that the first group was represented by "high financial performance" whereas the second group was represented by "average to poor financial performance."

The relevant hypotheses were tested with logistic regression analysis. This is the preferred method for binary dependent variables, as in our case, since it does not face strict multivariate assumptions like OLS models (Tabachnick & Fidell, 2001). Hierarchical logistic regression analysis was performed to assess the prediction of the financial performance of 2 categories (high performance versus average to poor performance) on the basis of independent variables. Demographic variables (age, gender and marital status) as control variables were first entered as a block. Next, the Big-Five personality factors as main effect variables were entered as the second block.

The initial examination of the logistic regression results yielded inordinately large parameter estimates for the gender variable, signaling a problem with too many empty cells or with outcome groups perfectly predicted by any variable. The examination of the cross tabulation revealed that the outcome group (high performance) was perfectly predicted by gender (men). Therefore, gender was omitted and analysis was conducted with the remaining variables (Tabachnick & Fidell, 2001). The comparison of each model's significance, including different variables, was based on goodness of fit tests, Hosmer-Lemeshow and traditional chi-square tests. The Hosmer and Lemeshow test was considered more robust than the traditional chi-square test, particularly if continuous covariates are in the model or the sample size is small (Garson, 2010).

Table 2 displays the goodness of fit tests, regression coefficients, Wald statistics, odd ratios, and significance levels. When financial performance was regressed on demographic variables alone (age and marital status), the model against a constant model was statistically reliable [χ^2 (2, N =60) = 9.91, $p <$ .05; Nagelkerke R^2 = .99]. Hosmer and Lemeshow was insignificant, indicating

Table 2
Logistic Regression Estimations Predicting High Financial Performance

Predictors	B	*SE*	Wald	*p*-value	Exp (B)
Block 1: Control variables					
Intercept	−3.09	3.20	.93	.34	.05
Age	−.20	.10	4.23*	.04	.82
Marital Status	−.05	.67	.01	.94	.95
χ^2	9.91*				
Hosmer-Lemeshow test	3.66				
Goodness of fit tests					
Cox & Snell R^2	.08				
Nagelkerke R^2	.10				
-2 Log Likelihood	64.18				
Block 2: Main effects					
Conscientiousness	.92	.460	3.953*	.47	2.498
Extraversion	.87	.452	3.691*	.55	2.378
Neuroticism	−.57	.449	1.59	.207	.568
Openness to experience	−.20	.400	.251	.616	.818
χ^2	12.68*				
Hosmer-Lemeshow test	7.53				
Goodness of fit tests					
Cox & Snell R^2	.23				
Nagelkerke R^2	.35				
-2 Log Likelihood	51.50				

Notes: This table provides results of the sequential binomial logistic regression. The dependent variable is a dummy variable which takes the value of unity for the Sharpe performance indexes of mutual funds ranking in the top quartile (the best performing 25% percentile) and takes the value of "0" for the Sharpe performance indexes of mutual funds ranking in the other quartiles.
* $p < .05$

that the model adequately fit the data. According to Wald's criterion, age was found to be significant ($z = 4.23$, $p < .05$). After controlling for demographics, the second block of the logistic regression model was statistically reliable, indicating significant improvement with the addition of personality variables [$\chi^2(6, N = 60) = 15.91$, $p < .05$; with a non-significant Hosmer and Lemeshow test and an increased estimate of Nagelkerke $R^2 = .34$]. Among the personality factors, conscientiousness ($z = 3.95$, $p < .05$) and extraversion ($z = 3.69$ $p < .10$) reliably predicted financial performance outcomes.

We based our interpretation of the results on the odd-ratios. Thus, an examination of the Exp(B) ratios of the significant variables revealed that the odds of exhibiting high financial performance were associated with an increase in conscientiousness and extraversion scores. Put differently, a one unit increase in conscientiousness score was associated with an approximate increase by a factor of 2.5 in the odds of exhibiting high financial performance. Similarly,

when extraversion increased one unit, the odds of exhibiting high financial performance increased by a factor of 2.4 when other factors were controlled. However, the odds of exhibiting high financial performance decreased with age. As such, a one unit increase in age is associated with a decrease of 17% in exhibiting high financial performance.

Discussion

The aim of the present study was the identification of Big-Five personality traits that might play a role in promoting or inhibiting the financial performance of professional fund managers. Using a self-administered personality questionnaire, we gathered data from 60 fund managers and observed their financial behavior in the real market by estimating their financial performance in terms of the Sharpe index.

Bivariate estimations yielded interesting results in predicting the odds of high financial performance. Our findings were consistent with the notion that the fund managers' personality traits and demographics played a role in distinguishing high financial performance from average to poor financial performance. In particular, the results suggested that among the personality traits, high extraversion and high conscientiousness increased the likelihood of exhibiting high financial performance after controlling for the effects of demographics. A high extraversion score meant that the individual seeks out activity, dominance and stimulation of highly dynamic action environments. Earlier research also showed that risk-taking was strongly rooted in extraversion and risk propensity was higher for individuals with higher extraversion scores (Kowert & Hermann, 1997; Nicholson et al., 2002). As our orientation to risk argued that larger rates of returns were required to take greater risks, those findings confirmed our expectations that higher performing traders were the ones whose underlying risk propensity exists as part of their personalities. This finding was also consistent with Grinblatt and Keloharju's (2006) result in which sensation seeking was found to be related with higher trading frequency. Additionally, this particular result overrides the finding of Lo et al. (2005), which exhibited a positive but insignificant correlation between the extraversion trait and financial performance.

The positive association between conscientiousness and high financial performance highlighted the importance of conscientiousness in the finance sector as well. A high conscientiousness score meant that individuals exhibited high levels of self-control, discipline and self-determination, while a low conscientiousness score denoted behaving spontaneously, taking shortcuts to save effort and preferring a careless route. The conscientious fund managers' persistence and self-discipline might motivate them to continue doing tasks until they have been accomplished. Previous meta-analytic studies have shown that conscientiousness is regarded as a strong predictor of occupational success and

work performance across jobs and criteria (Barrick and Mount, 1991; Salgado, 1997). This finding was also consistent with Salgado and Rumbo's (1997) study in which conscientiousness was found to be a valid predictor of the job performance of financial service managers. Those results also converged with the findings of Camgoz (2009), in which conscientiousness is found to be related to the successful market timing performance of fund managers operationalized as Treynor and Mazuy indexes. In terms of practical implications, this finding supported the argument of Dunn, Mount, Barrick and Ones (1995), emphasizing that cognitive ability and conscientiousness are the most important perceived attributes related to applicants' hireability.

Additional findings suggested that certain commonly used demographics might be used to explain the effectiveness of financial performance. Specifically, the findings might indicate that the probability of exhibiting high financial performance decreases as age increases. Although investors acquire skill with experience, trading was not considered a suitable game beyond the age of 35 or 40 due to the pace and stress of the trading environment (Fenton-O'Creevy et al., 2007). Another explanation for why younger fund managers are more likely to have greater performance measures might be that younger individuals have stronger goal orientation. This finding is also consistent with Barber and Odean's (2001) study, in which the authors analyze the common stock investment of individuals. Concerning age, their findings revealed that young investors' average monthly turnover declines as age increases. Similarly, Chevallier and Ellison's (1999) study provided that younger fund managers outperform older ones. They pointed out that younger managers need to work harder because they not only have to advance in their careers, but are also more likely to be fired for their low performance.

Implications for Management

In terms of practical implications, top managers of the investment companies need to be aware of the fact that employees' personality characteristics display themselves in their financial actions. The identification of the promoting or inhibiting factors of high financial performance is of high practical relevance both for individuals who want to increase their welfare and for policy makers who have special responsibilities toward their clients. This type of knowledge is valuable for managers in positioning or promoting employees to key positions within the organization. Moreover, the findings of this research have certain implications for the practice of personnel selection. The results of the study suggested that personality traits are valid predictors of financial performance. Thus, the results provided support for the relevance of the five-factor model in predicting job performance. Therefore, it might be reasonable to include the Big-Five in personnel selection batteries for the "personality-job fit" purpose as indicated by Holland (1997). According to Holland, people who choose to work

in an environment similar to their personality are more likely to be successful and satisfied. Therefore, as fund management is highly prestigious job with a high salary that attracts young people without considering their adaptability in this particular job; this inventory might be useful for not only newcomers but also for current managers to evaluate themselves for their career plans.

Directions for Future Research

Further research is needed to enhance the understanding of the relationships between personality factors and financial performance. Replications with a larger number of participants would be valuable. Ideally, future studies might be replicated with a more heterogeneous and extended sample including investors who are actively managing their own portfolios in addition to professional investors. This may allow a comparison concerning the effects of personality traits on the financial performance of both professional and non-professional investors in which knowledge about fiscal issues varies. Future replications might also include situational or environmental variables like market events that may interfere or override personality variables. In this sense, it would be worthwhile to include the moderating effects of market microstructure on the relationship between personality and financial performance (Cheng, 2007).

Strengths and Limitations

Although the sample size was not very big, the participants of the study comprised 83% of the equity fund managers currently operating in Turkey. Given that this was a reasonably high ratio, our empirical results could be relevant for equity fund managers in financial institutions operating in countries similar to Turkey. The strength of the study was that the independent and the dependent variables were collected via different methods that will overcome the problem of common method variance. This study also exhibited several limitations, pointing toward future follow-up studies. Due to our purposively selected small sample of professional fund managers, we were quite limited in the extent to which we could use more complex statistical methods or larger batteries of variables for investigating our research questions.

References

Allport, G. (1961). *Pattern and growth in personality.* London: Holt, Reinhart and Winston.

Barber, B., & Odean, T. (2001). Boys will be boys: Gender, overconfidence, and common stock investment. *Quarterly Journal of Economics, 116*, 261–292.

Barrick, M. R., & Mount, M. K. (1991). The Big-Five personality dimensions and job performance: A meta-analysis. *Personnel Psychology 44*, 1–26.

Benet-Martinez, V., & John, O.P. (1998). Los Cinco Grandes across cultures and ethnic groups: Multitrait-multimethod analyses of the Big-Five in Spanish and English. *Journal of Personality and Social Psychology 75,* 729–750.

Biais, B., Hilton, D., Mazurier, K., & Pouget, S. (2001). Psychological traits and trading strategies. *CSEF Working Papers 39.* Centre for Studies in Economics and Finance, London.

Biais, B., D. Hilton, Mazurier, K., & Pouget, S. (2005). Judgmental overconfidence, self-monitoring, and trading performance in an experimental financial market. *Review of Economic Studies, 72,* 287–312.

Cheng, P. Y. (2007). The trader interaction effect on the impact of overconfidence on trading performance: An empirical study. *Journal of Behavioral Finance, 8,* 59–69.

Chevalier, J., & *Ellison*, G. (*1999)*. Are some mutual fund managers better than others? Cross-sectional patterns in behavior and performance. *Journal of Finance 54,* 875–899.

Costa, P., & McCrae, R. R. (1995). Domains and facets: Hierarchical personality assessment using the Revised NEO Personality Inventory. *Journal of Personality Assessment 64,* 21–50.

Daniel, K. D., Hirshleifer, D., & Teoh, S. H. (2002). Investor psychology in capital markets: Evidence and policy implications. *Journal of Monetary Economics, 49,* 139–209.

De Bondt, W. F. (1998). *The psychology of under and overreaction in world equity markets.* IIR Seminar on Behavioral Finance: The Psychology of Investment Decision Making, London.

Digman, J. M. (1990). Higher-order factors of the Big-Five. *Journal of Personality and Social Psychology, 73,* 1246–1256.

Dunn. W. S., Mount, M. K., Barrick, M. R., & Ones, D. S. (1995). Relative importance of personality and general mental ability in managers' judgment of applicant qualifications. *Journal of Applied Psychology, 80,* 500–509.

Fenton-O'Creevy, M., Nicholson, N., Soane, E., & Willman, P. (2007). *Traders, managing risks and decisions in financial markets.* Oxford: Oxford University Press.

Gandevani, N. (2002). *How to become a successful trader: The trading personality profile: Your key to maximizing your profit with any system.* New York: Writer's Club Press.

Garson, G. D. (2010). *Logistic regression.* In Statnotes: Topics in multivariate analysis. Retrieved May 10, 2010 from, http://faculty.chass.ncsu.edu/garson/pa765/statnote.htm.

Goldberg, L.R. (1993). The structure of phenotypic personality traits. *American Psychologist 48,* 26–34.

Grinblatt, M., & Keloharju, M. (2006). *Sensation seeking, overconfidence, and trading activity.* NBER Working Paper No. W12223, Cambridge, MA. Available at SSRN: http://ssrn.com/abstract=902575.

Holland, J. (1997). *Making vocational choices: A theory of vocational personalities and work environments.* Florida: Psychological Assessment Resources.

John, O. P. (1990). The "Big-Five" factor taxonomy: Dimensions of personality in the natural language and in questionnaires. In *L. A Pervin, &* O. P. John (Eds.), *Handbook of personality: Theory and research* (pp. 66–100). New York: Guilford.

John, O. P., Donahue, E. M., & Kentle, R. (1991). *The 'Big-Five' Inventory: Versions 4a and 54. Technical report, Institute of Personality and Social Psychology.* Berkeley: University of California.

Kahneman, D., & Riepe, M.W. (1998). Aspects of investor psychology. *Journal of Portfolio Management, 24,* 52–67.

Kowert, P. A., & Hermann, M. G. (1997). Who takes risks? Daring and caution in foreign policy making. *Journal of Conflict Resolution, 41,* 611–637.
Lewellen, W. G., Lease, R. C., & Schlarbaum, G. G. (1979). Investment performance and investor behavior. *Journal of Financial and Quantitative Analysis 14* (1), 29–57.
Lo, A. W., & Repin D. V., & Steenbarger, B. N. (2005). Fear and greed in financial markets: A clinical study of day-traders. *American Economic Review, 95*, 352–359.
McCrae, R. R., & Costa, P. T. (1997). Conceptions and correlates of openness to experience. In R. Hogan, J. A. Johnson, & S. R. Briggs (Eds.), *Handbook of personality psychology* (pp. 826–847). San Diego CA: Academic Press.
McCrae, R. R., & John, O. P. (1992). An introduction to the Five-Factor Model and its applications. *Journal of Personality, 60,* 175–215.
McInish, T. H. (1980). A game-simulation of stock market behavior: An extension. *Simulations and Games, 11*, 477–484.
McInish, T. H. (1982). Individual investors and risk-taking. *Journal of Economic Psychology, 2,* 125–136.
Metin Camgoz, S. (2009). Kişilik özelliklerinin A-tipi fon yöneticilerinin seçicilik ve zamanlama becerileri üzerine etkileri. *Journal of Iktisat Isletme ve Finans*, *24* (3), 109–141.
Nicholson, N., Fenton-O'Creevy, M., Soane, E., & Willman, P. (2002). *Risk propensity and personality*. Working Paper, London Business School, UK.
Nyhus, E. K., & Pons, E. (2005). The Effects of Personality on Earnings. *Journal of Economic Psychology, 26,* 363–384.
Oberlechner, T. (2004). Perceptions of successful traders by foreign exchange professionals. *Journal of Behavioral Finance, 5,* 23–31.
Patton, M. Q. (1990). *Qualitative evaluation and research methods* (2nd ed.). Newbury Park: Sage.
Salgado, J. F. (1997). The five factor model of personality and job performance in the European community. *Journal of Applied Psychology, 82,* 30–43.
Salgado, J. F. (1998). Big-Five personality dimensions and job performance in army and civil occupations: A European perspective. *Human Performance, 11*, 271–288.
Salgado, J. F., & Rumbo, A. (1997). Personality and job performance in financial services managers. *International Journal of Selection and Assessment, 5,* 91–100.
Sharpe, W. F. (1966). Mutual fund performance. *Journal of Business, 39*, 119–138.
Sümer, N., Lajunen, T., & Özkan, T. (2005). Big-Five personality traits as the distal predictors of road accident involvement. In G. Underwood (Ed.), *Traffic and transport psychology* (pp. 216–227). Elsevier Science.
Tabachnick, B. G., & Fidell, L. S. (2001). Using multivariate statistics (4th ed.). Needham Heights, MA: Allyn and Bacon.
Tigges, P., Riegert, A., Jonitz, L., Brengelmann, J., & Engel, R. R. (2000). Risk behaviour of east and West Germans in handling personal finances. *Journal of Psychology and Financial Markets, 1*, 127–134.
Zuckerman, M., & Kuhlman, M. D. (2000). Personality and risk-taking: Common biosocial factors. *Journal of Personality, 68*, 999–1029.
Zuckerman, M. (1994). *Behavioral expressions and biosocial bases of sensation seeking*. New York: Cambridge University Press.
Witteloostuijn, A. V., & Muehlfeld K. (2008). Trader personality and trading performance. A framework and financial market experiment, *Tjalling C. Koopmans Institute Discussion Paper* 08–28, Utrecht University (Retrieved February 2, 2009, from http://www.koopmansinstitute.uu.nl.).
www.cmb.gov.tr retrieved January 10, 2008.

PART III

ISSUES IN ENTREPRENEURSHIP AND SMALL BUSINESS

Current Topics in Management, Vol. 15, 2011, pp. 155-174

MODIFYING PHELAN'S MODEL: A CONCEPTUAL FRAMEWORK LINKING ENTREPRENEURS TO INTERNATIONAL NEW VENTURE COMPETITIVENESS

Florinel-Frank Cotae

The chapter seeks to provide and create a theoretical framework for understanding entrepreneurs, entrepreneurial activities and international new ventures (INVs). Defining and designing a conceptual model that would be able to address the factors influencing a manager and entrepreneur entry into international market have not been studied and identified in a detailed matter. The extant research has largely focused on either measurements of the effect of internationalization related liabilities—smallness, foreignness and newness—observations of particular industry related case studies and onto defining new theoretical frontiers for the field of internationalization as it relates to entrepreneurial activities in the pursuit of international new ventures creation. We argue here that these efforts, for the purposes of defining a conceptual model relating to INV creation, should to be subordinated to the human factor considerations—the entrepreneur as the origination point for the discussion. At the center of such a conceptual framework we searched for a model that had as a center point the entrepreneur in the context of international new venture creation. The closest match was provided by the conceptual model advanced by Phelan, Dalgic, and Sethi (2006) as the authors enunciated just such related subject matter. The authors point to an entrepreneur's personal traits of astuteness and competence as the key variables for explaining INV and entrepreneurial networks.

The chapter acknowledges the contribution made by the conceptual framework defined by Phelan et al. (2006) and it focuses on substantiating, accepting, questioning or refuting—on the basis of field studies or of extant theoretical knowledge in the field of entrepreneurship—of the supported findings. The chapter sustains that entrepreneurs, entrepreneurship, entrepreneurial activities,

as they apply to the success of international new ventures are not necessarily a function of social competence and astuteness (Phelan et al., 2006) per se, but are rather affected by a multitude of factors, each possibly representing a different facet of the complex process of globalization.

The chapter is organized into several subsections, each addressing a different facet of the argument directed at the Phelan's model. First, the social attributes supported by the model are placed in the context of internationalization, embeddedness and tacit theories. Second, external considerations/factors such as behavior, legal environment, subsidies and goal commitment are highlighted as contributing components to a INVs existence and competitive advantage vis-à-vis the costs of internationalization. The third section looks at refuting the claim that INVs exist primarily due to small domestic markets or strong immigrant communities and points out certain geographical particularities with regards to undertaking entrepreneurial activities in China, USA and France. The concluding segment presents the findings alongside a new schematic conceptual framework; framework considered better supported by extant research and section by section issued statements.

Phelan vs. Embeddedness, Internationalization, and Tacit Theories

The fragment takes a look at the model advanced by Phelan et al. (2006) in comparison to the social network paradigm proposed by Fraser and Huddleston (2009), internationalization theory (Beamish, Morisson, Inkpen, & Rosenzweig, 2003) and the role of tacit and codification opportunity elements supported by Matthews, Schenkel, and Smith (2009). The rationale is to accept, enrich and/or question the model's point of view by applying the new findings and verifying or issuing a corresponding proposition.

Social Competence and Astuteness

Phelan et al. (2006) supports the idea that the entrepreneur is the key for the success of international new ventures (INV). The entrepreneur is the driving force and by becoming socially astute and social competent will develop the necessary entrepreneurial networks capable of assuring success for new INVs. While the conclusions are presented in systematic and logical manner the fact that they are not supported by actual studies and given other contrarian points of view originating from the extant research allows for the findings to be subjected to review, discussion and argument.

First and to assure an appropriate background qualification, the terminologies of social astuteness and competence need to be presented and defined so as to allow for adequate comparison and analysis.

Social astuteness is defined as "the ability to influence the expectations of potential and existing stakeholders so they will commit resources to a busi-

ness network on favorable terms" (Phelan et al., 2006, p. 3). A socially astute person is an effective negotiator, aware of other's motives, and diplomatic in presenting issues to others (Phelan, 2006). The authors go further with their model and quote research by Phelan and Alder (2005) which has shown that socially astute people perform significantly better on resource picking tasks and social astuteness as a concept points to a high degree of correlation with other traditional entrepreneurial variables: risk taking, openness to experience, and propensity for innovation (Phelan et al., 2006; Phelan & Adler, 2005).

Phelan et al. (2006) define *social competence* as an entrepreneur's "ability to form and maintain relationships" (p. 4) by building a core of skills and capabilities that include impression management, social perceptiveness, social adaptability, and persuasiveness (Fligstein, 1997; Baron and Markman, 2000; Baron and Markman, 2003; Phelan et al., 2006). While social astuteness can be considered an aspect of social competence, "not all socially competent people have developed the ability to manage expectations" (Phelan et al., 2006, p. 5).

While Phelan et al. (2006) findings point out that the area that would define the mechanism that underwrites the development of a network, as prescribed by the social competence ability, has been largely understudied, they nevertheless propose that a directly proportional relationship exists between the possession of social competence and the strength of social networks and social capital. The authors further their theoretical concepts and claims by further elongating them into defining *international social competence* as "the ability to form and maintain relationships across national borders" (Phelan et al., 2006, p. 10). The success of INV is subordinated to an individual's competence and skill vis-à-vis cross-cultural components such as language skill and cultural empathy (Karra & Phillips, 2004; Phelan et al., 2006).

Internationalization

Looking at internationalization as a process; process of intrinsic importance to INVs; the fragment will highlight the born global presentation of INVs' success from a different angle—that of a three stage sigmoid—one well published and researched for several decades now. Sigmoid which seems to have limited, or no relation with the language skills and cultural empathy elements, supported by Phelan's international competence definition, and a lot more to do with pure economic realities.

Internationalization is defined as the "process by which firms increase their awareness of the influence of international activities on their future, and establish and conduct transactions with other firms from other countries" (Beamish et al., 2003, p. 27). Although, most related literature seems to either reconcile or promote internationalization as the appropriate direction for warranting a SME/MNE's superior performance attainment (Contractor, 2007; Riahi-Belkaoui,

1998; Sullivan, 1994; Tallman & Li, 1996), there are voices doubting the linear and equating relationship between a business entities's degree of globalization and its level of performance (Hennart, 1982, 2007; Johanson & Vahlne, 1990). Other voices are merely questioning the process (Glaum & Osterle, 2007; Lopez, Duarte, & Garcia-Canal, 2007) as the absolute promise for increased performance levels; process which is generally seen as not existing devoid but rather as a result of interactions between entrepreneurial decisions, business environment, operational efficiencies and organizational learning/adaptability capabilities—a common trait for entrepreneurial companies.

A multi-stage and s-curve hypothesis is advanced as the model for the multinational degree of international expansion (DOI) and performance relationship (P) (Beamish & Lu, 2004). There are three distinct stages of internationalization in the life of a firm, best exemplified by the General Sigmoid model (Johanson & Vahlne, 1977; Lu & Beamish 2004; Thomas & Eden, 2004), as shown in Figure 1: Stage I–early internationalization, Stage II–later internationalization, and Stage III–excessive internationalization. At the first stage a global endeavor is expected to incur costs as it sets up shop in a foreign place (Thomas & Eden, 2004), yet these costs are expected to be recovered during the second stage as the firm's performance reaches superior or often forecasted results. The third stage has been the matter of debate as globals eventually reach a point where increasing the degree of internationalization becomes a counterproductive activity (Beamish et al., 2003) as the firm gradually reaches a level of operational resource saturation (Cotae, 2009), so to speak. The saturation point is where the core operational capabilities of a firm are no longer adequate for servicing the needs stemming from operating a large number of global vendors, subsidiaries, retail channels, customers and associates (Cotae, 2010).

Figure 1
Internationalization Sigmoid (Beamish et al., 2003)

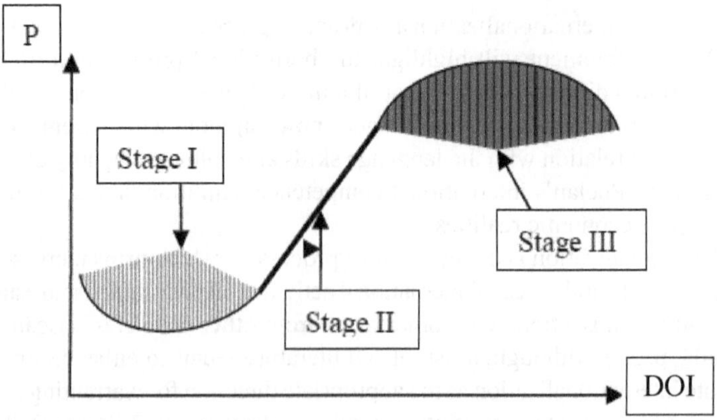

Note: P = Performance, DOI = Degree of Internationalization

Furthermore, during the third stage the cost or maintaining a global operation and/or growing internationally renders the internationalization strategy as inefficient and usually requires efforts outside a firm's realm of operational logistics/realities (Cotae, 2010). Results, productivity and profits are expected to decline. Simply put the firm finds itself overleveraged and overextended. Current research has not yet produced a model or factor by virtue of which this stage on internationalization can be predicted or its effects ameliorated, postponed, or diminished. It is therefore suggested as necessary for a SME to continuously attempt to assess and forecast its operational environment, degree of operational knowledge and core abilities before pursuing higher degree of globalization (Cotae, 2009).

The first argument is raised by internationalization as a process that cannot be exclusively mitigated by an entrepreneur or leader's social skills. No practical research has pointed out any ameliorating circumstances arisen from social astuteness or social competence as applied to the effect of excessive internationalization. No entrepreneur, regardless or social skills, is seen as having the competence or negotiating techniques to counter the negative predicaments described above. Therefore, it is primarily the *economic limitations* of INVs—i.e., limited resources, increased costs, operational saturation—that affect their performance and are influenced to a lesser degree by an individual's social skills. As such the following proposition is advanced:

> *Proposition* 1. The performance of an international new venture is affected by the stage of internationalization in which the endeavor operates as defined by economic limitations.

Embeddedness

Frazier and Huddleston (2009) study of 119 US retailers support the idea that for a SME to be successful an entrepreneur needs to be attentive to local networking and have market research skills. All other competences, such as market competence, the byproduct of networking, is seen as primordial only when related to performance but "not in creating and sustaining competitive advantage capabilities" (Fraizier & Huddleston, 2009, p. 11) as it occupies a subordinate place to social capital accumulated through localized network relationships. Relationships seen as, if employed as part of a consistent operational strategy, to lead "a high degree of marketing scanning abilities" (Frazier & Huddleston, 2009, p. 14).

Market scanning and market knowledge are estimated as critical in aligning a SME's strategy (Frazier & Huddleston, 2009) with its customers' needs and wants (Darroch & McNaughton, 2004). Tapping into local information networks may be one way that small firms can capitalize on their embeddedness in the market, giving them the ability to assess and respond to market demand more quickly and effectively than large-scale stores/companies (Clow & Cole, 2004).

Frazier and Huddleston's study draws on the *embeddedness* argument (Granovetter, 1985; Frazier & Huddleston, 2009), which maintains that market exchanges are affected by the values and norms of the social networks in which it takes place. Embeddedness suggests that individuals are motivated beyond simple economic goals to pursue the improvement of business relationships and the concept of market embeddedness is advanced. *Market embeddedness* is seen to reflect the extent to which "individuals are socially connected to the marketing environment in which they operate" (Cooke, Clifton, & Oleaga, 2005, p. 18) business endeavors. Market embeddedness is therefore found useful in explaining: differences in access to local market information (Frazier & Huddleston, 2009) as managers of small firms create and execute competitive strategies (Lee & Trim, 2006), and as a perspective in examining the customer-retailer exchange process in smaller communities/markets (Miller & Kean, 1997; Subramanian, 1993).

Embedded relationships are therefore characterized by high levels of trust, amity and support, and are seen to produce benefits (Frazier & Huddleston, 2009) by "providing access to more valuable information than can be attained by arms length relationships" (Burt, 2004, p. 14). Embedded relationships are seen to be created through repeated social interactions and are generated anywhere there are "individuals interacting in dense, lateral networks involving voluntary engagement, trust, and mutual benefit" (Frazier & Huddleston, 2009, p. 15); Uzzi (1996) found that small firm embeddedness in social networks influenced information and resource exchange, which in turn "affected economies of time, integrative agreements, resource allocation efficiency, and adaptation" (Frazier & Huddleston, 2009, p. 16).

To summarize the findings, a firm's ability to accumulate a certain degree of social capital through embeddedness is seen as instrumental in achieving not only a certain market presence, but also in reaching pertinent local market information and in establishing business networks; all significant in mitigating competitive advantage related challenges. Embeddedness is seen to mitigate some of the advantages that large firms have in favor of their smaller entrepreneurial counterparts by allowing the latter to capitalize and adapt based on unique local market information; information not readily available to large corporations. Frazier and Huddleston (2009) seem to certainly give Phelan et al. (2006) theoretical argument a certain degree of legitimacy as their social competence entrepreneur related label seems to fit, even though it is explained in a general form and does not take the detailed form advanced by the embeddedness argument. In keeping with this the following proposition is advance:

> *Proposition* 2. Social capital accumulated through market and relationships embeddedness is seen to affect a firm's ability to achieve competitive advantage when compared to larger firms.

Tacitness and Codification

An entrepreneur and INV's success have often been linked to the first's ability to recognize and capitalize upon new or available opportunities, be they in domestic or international markets. The segment looks at the process of recognizing opportunities and reconciles it with Phelan's argument. Smith, Mattheus, and Schenkel (2009) have advanced that differences in how entrepreneurs identify and capitalize on present and future opportunities are explained by tacitness and codification.

The identification of opportunities is seen as significant as it is generally considered the first step in the developing an entrepreneurial process and attitude (Baron & Shane, 2005). Such identification was first advanced as based on an individual's personal traits and lately was enriched so as to include cognitive decision making (Busenitz & Barney, 1997) and pattern matching (Baron & Ensley, 2006).

Therefore the two recognized roles for identifying entrepreneurial opportunities are: tacitness and codification. *Tacitness* is seen as a form of knowledge that is unique to each entrepreneur as it is personal, practical, context specific, acquired on the job and describes an individual's know-how about a process (Kogut & Zander, 1992; Smith, Mattheus, & Schenkel, 2009). Due to its uniqueness tacit knowledge is difficult to copy or imitate and as such is generally regarded as a positive influence in securing a certain level of competitive advantage for the entrepreneur and a particular business venture. From the concept of tacitness the study conducted by Smith et al. (2009) moves towards defining tacit opportunities as a situation during which an entrepreneur seeks to realize profits by exploiting market inefficiencies in a less-than-saturated market (Smith et al., 2009), the overall process is individual-unique and as such it cannot be easily articulated, copied or communicated. The focus is placed on significant innovations and improvements of goods, products, services and organization models. The result is as identified through an entrepreneur securing a certain degree of market competitiveness that is mainly unique, at least in the short-run.

Codification is seen as an entrepreneurial skill of articulating information so as "specific knowledge is transmitted through formal language" (Johnson, Lorentz, & Lundvall, 2002, p. 9). A codified opportunity is defined, just as above, as a situation during which an entrepreneur—while seeking profits—is exploiting market inefficiencies through focusing on imitation and moderate improvement of goods, products, services and organizational models (Smith et al., 2009). The path is not unique or uniquely formulated and can be transmitted and copied by competitors or other industry players. The difference between the two is the degree of tacitness that is to be employed by an entrepreneur as the more unique an individual is in the pursuit of an opportunity, the better the chances of achieving a degree of market competitiveness. Phelan's model

(2006) does not recognize the uniqueness or the opportunity recognition concepts, instead opting for an argument that pointed to general skills, skills that as all codified information can be easily matched and copied. Mitigating the costs of foreignness/newness/smallness, for example, for an INV will not be sustainable against larger business endeavors unless the entrepreneur develops a unique approach to profit seeking, opportunity recognition and realization. Given these considerations the following proposition is stated:

> *Proposition* 3: Entrepreneurial success in achieving profits and market competitiveness depends on the tacitness with which opportunities are recognized and pursued.

External Factors: Behavior, Legal and Goal Commitment

The fragment aims at supporting the argument that establishing entrepreneurial networks, while important, is not the absolute answer—as supported by Phelan et al. (2006)—that would assure entrepreneurial success and that other external factors such as: behavior, local legal conditions, differences in goal commitment need to receive equal consideration. A point can be made that establishing networks for an international new venture is in itself a skill and an accomplishment particular to entrepreneurs and representative of the entrepreneurial activity. Establishing networks is in itself dependent on the above list of factors—list by no means exhaustive—each with a different implication and possible repercussion upon the overall success of an INV.

Behavior

Brandl and Bullinger (2009) have exposed entrepreneurship as a reality of life in modern Western societies and the entrepreneurial behavior as a legitimate concept and activity (Zibler, 2006) that has become economically institutionalized (Brandl & Bullinger, 2009). The entrepreneurial behavior is seen as been supported and encouraged through positive valuation by Western societies, fact which is seen to give entrepreneurs/individuals from such societies a certain competitive advantage as they are given access to certain economic mechanisms and educational experiences passed on over the years (Brandl & Bullinger, 2009; Munir & Phillips, 2005).

Adopting an entrepreneurial behavior is cultivated in individuals through a certain degree or economic freedom granted by the Western educational, economic and legal systems. The societal wide merriment of individual entrepreneurial behavior is seen as characteristics of these societies as they emphasize modern ideals of cultural individualism, free market elements, change and economic wealth (Brandl & Bullinger, 2009). The above are supported by reality as societies that did not officially support in the past entrepreneurial behavior—those of the Communist Eastern bloc (China and North Korea)—realized

modest economic results and grew economically only when they allowed and implemented free market policies in which entrepreneurship was encouraged, recognized and accepted.

International new ventures led by entrepreneurs from Western societies tend to have the benefit of the behavior and knowledge accumulated in such societies, both capable of delivering a certain measure of competitive advantage that mitigates the liabilities of going global detailed above. Is should be mentioned that this competitive advantage could be short-term, as members of other societies are expected to bridge the knowledge and behavioral differences. The above behavioral related considerations are not factored in Phelan's conceptual model as it supports an approach based on an individual's having had studied in an other than domestic market as a contributing factor in pursuing an INV, how this applies to national and cultural support/attitude of entrepreneurial activities is unclear. In keeping with these considerations another proposition is formulated:

> *Proposition* 4: Entrepreneurial behavior, having institutional status in some societies, can assist an entrepreneur in securing a certain level of competitive advantage.

Legal Conditions

Entrepreneurial networks and entrepreneurs alike are subject to the legal conditions present in each international market they enter. These conditions can substantially affect the outcome of an entrepreneurial activity, the ability to realize profits and/or the overall attractiveness that would convince an entrepreneur to enter a particular market. A federal survey published in the *International Herald Tribune* (2009/2010) revealed that three-quarters of the entrepreneur-participants—a 2002 sample—felt that their ability to expand operations internationally was seriously hindered by the US stricter business regulations, especially when applied to SMEs. The rationale why the US legal environment is utilized is because in itself the world's largest economy is an appropriate and relevant indicator of entrepreneurial feedback and general direction.

Restrictions, such as those levied on executive compensations and the Sarbanes-Oxley Act of 2002, have made entrepreneurs less likely to seek or invest in new international ventures and expansion (Miller, 2009) as the legal cost to mitigating these new legal requirements have increased. Therefore and individual did not pursue an INV not due to any cost associated with going international, but rather due to new cost generated by domestic legislation. An individual's social competence and astuteness cannot mitigate an ever-changing legal environment that in turn can reduce the resources available for pursuing an INV. To this point the following proposition is issued:

> *Proposition* 5: New and changing legal domestic conditions affect an entrepreneur's propensity to seek growth and expansion through new international ventures.

Subsidies

The success of a new international venture is generally agreed upon as being the result of an entrepreneur's skills and opportunity recognition. The segment does not refute this but it diverges into also explaining entrepreneurial success and the establishment of networks for the purpose of international new ventures as being affected by the availability of subsidies (Clouser, Etzkowitz, Li, & Papagiannidis, 2009) as a government form or support/intervention. Subsidies are direct assistance offered entrepreneurs in the form of tax advantages, access to incubators, business networks and information, direct payments from governments/private sponsors and access to synergies.

Clouser et al. (2009) present the case of subsidies as a matter of economic development policy in the UK and several other European Union country-members. Subsidized assistance is directed at increasing the degree of international competitive advantage for new entrepreneurs pursuing new international ventures. The case of subsidies comes to further complicate the ability for an entrepreneur to compete in a foreign market as if such individual does not have access to subsidy form the home country it will have to find a response to subsidized competitors entering the same market at what appears a significant advantage. This further complicates and entrepreneur's newness, smallness and foreignness costs as they affect some more the SME owners sees as able to better mitigate them. In keeping with the subsidies availability the following propositions are advanced:

> *Proposition* 6: The availability of subsidies could increase entrepreneurial INV competitive advantage, as they address better the global expansion costs.

> *Proposition* 7: Entrepreneurs entering new markets might need to mitigate the competitive advantages of their subsidized counterparts.

Goal Commitment

The segment points out to an often ignored phase in opting for pursuing a new venture: *goal commitment* gestation (De Clercq, Diochon, Gasee, & Menzies, 2008). During this phase individual deciding to become entrepreneurs develop a series of attitudes with regards to starting up a new venture or expanding into new markets. Once a positive decision is made, the next step is to understand the commitment they will be willing to follow-up with so as to see the goal of developing an international new venture, for example, to fruition.

This goal commitment and the ensuing effort acceptance vary from individual to individual and are highly dependent of how entrepreneurs perceive the success of desired outcomes (De Clercq et al., 2008); outcomes which need to be both feasible and desirable (De Clercq et al., 2008; De Clercq & Arenius, 2006).

Feasibility refers to the probability that a goal will be attained and desirability points to the anticipated satisfaction with the expected results, consequence of goal attainment. In other words, the effort to achieve a goal needs to be acceptable and it needs to provide enough benefits to make it valuable. These considerations have no commonalities with social competence and astuteness reflected in Phelan's model. Simply said, an individual can be skilled but if is not committed, or does not see as worthwhile the goal of pursuing an INV, then the skill and social capital related concerns appear as mute and uneven considerations. Pursuing an INV is therefore centered not on the ability to necessarily establish entrepreneurial networks, at least during this phase, but in its inception on the level of commitment the entrepreneur is ready to commit given the set goals and expected benefits. The corresponding proposition is submitted bellow:

> *Proposition* 8: The goal commitment for establishing an INV is affected by feasibility and desirability of expected outcomes—taking place during goal commitment phase.

Geographic Considerations

Phelan et al. (2006) theoretical argument points out a general framework in which entrepreneurial networks and INVs, especially, exist in countries with small domestic market and strong immigrant communities (Knight et al., 2001; Phelan et al., 2006). The segment attempts to focus on the claim and just as above seek to accept, enrich and/or reject the findings, while establishing the components for building of a new semantic and schematic argument.

The point for the fragment is to establish that INV exist/succeed differently from a geographic standpoint, as each country or area might present particularities that significantly affect the expected an INV's outcome. For an appropriate geographical valuation several continents—Asia, North America—are focused upon. The countries represented in the argument are: China, US, and France.

China

As the world's most populous and faster growing economy is therefore without hesitation that it would be chosen as basis for a new theoretical framework. To begin with, China is neither a country with a small market—a consumer base of 1.33 billion makes any further size related argument uneven—nor does it have a strong immigrant community, therefore providing a basis for a contrarian argument to Phelan's et al. (2006) model.

The study conducted by Naude and Rossow (2009) included data from 3,948 Chinese firms. The study found that 62% of these firms started exporting activities within 3 years of their inception. The pursuit of INVs was seen as a result

of challenging or adverse domestic conditions (Naude & Rossow, 2009). To reality was that entrepreneurs were encouraged, through government's related initiatives—i.e., lower taxation, exporting tariffs—to pursue internationalization, be that through exporting or establishing of INVs. The lack of domestic infrastructure in comparison to the international one also made a difference in the entrepreneurial decision to pursue global expansion.

A significant percentage of the firms studied—81% of ones that started exporting activities or INVs—pointed out that by pursuing INVs they mediated the lack of technological knowledge they faced by pursuing domestic ventures and economic opportunities. Entering into INVs alongside a foreign partner was seen to give a local entrepreneur access to technological information too costly or otherwise unavailable.

The size and potential of domestic markets were not seen as important under the duress of an external forces present in their domestic environment: government economic policy, lack of domestic infrastructure and unavailable technological knowledge. All these factors were seen to be mediated through the pursuit of INVs (Naude & Rossow, 2009). A point can be made here that Chinese entrepreneurs found internationalization related costs/liabilities preferable when compared to the domestic ones. Given these reflections following proposition is advanced:

> *Proposition* 9: Entrepreneurs pursue INVs under the pressure of domestically external factors such as: governmental economic policy, infrastructure and access to technological information.

United States

The world's largest economy points to pure business considerations for entrepreneurs in establishing networks so as to success in the pursuing internationalization through INVs. Brown and Butler (1995) after conducting a field study of 30 SME wineries in Western and Northeastern US pointed out that in the industry entrepreneurs displayed a great degree of "maturity" (Brown & Butler, 1995, p. 19) in that they pursued joint INVs based on networks in collaboration with domestic competitors. This was seen as mediating the high costs of doing business in a foreign market—newness, smallness, and foreignness. The competition in the domestic market was not affected by the partnership with competitors secured for entering the international arena. Each entrepreneur contributed, besides inventory, to the INVs directly proportional with the value of product to be retailed.

Building or capturing international market share was therefore pursued though inter-organizational networks with local competitors-where synergies, information, resources were equally accessed- as a modality to mediate the strategic advantages that large multinational wineries had internationally. Given the above, entrepreneurial maturity—that is the ability to put aside domestic

considerations and pursue competitors as partners for INV—appears to generate the following proposition:

> *Proposition 10:* Entrepreneurial maturity and competitors as partners could mediate the costs of pursuing internationalization.

France

Bossin, Branchet, Emin, and Herbert (2008) conducted a study of 340 students from France, majority of which had had completed advance coursework in entrepreneurship studies. Their findings were than compared with the results from those of student counterparts from USA—270 students surveyed. In their opinion the probability for an individual to become an entrepreneur and pursue INVs depended largely on their opinion of the personal economic value/reward that such a choice was estimated to bring, their perception as to what acceptable risks were and their proximity to family members that were entrepreneurs themselves.

The findings elongate the sections related to goal commitment and behavior as it points out, in an advanced form, that the individual's perception of entrepreneurship and the required effort perception would be the foundation for INVs success an ability to reach/pursue a certain degree of competitiveness (Bossin et al., 2008). The difference is that individual's attitude vis-à-vis entrepreneurship is seen as the prerequisite for internationalization and entrepreneurial activity.

In the above mentioned study Bossin et al (2008) pointed out that French students, in absence of having examples of relatives as entrepreneurs—only 40.8% of them knew one—and inclined towards risk adversity, were less likely to consider becoming entrepreneurs as a career choice and perceived INVs as effort intensive and devoid of significant positive returns. By comparison U.S. students, 83.8% of which had or knew relatives that were entrepreneurs, perceived self-employment as preferable to working for a corporation and considered risk as of medium importance when pursuing INVs. The size of domestic markets or strength of immigrant communities was again not the factor, but rather individual attitudes were the key; attitudes shared differently, even by individuals in two closely related Western economies.

The attitude that one has towards entrepreneurship as a process is geographically dispersed and affects differently individual behavior needed in pursuing INVs and building the networks necessary for its success. The proposition is therefore:

> *Proposition* 11: Individual attitude towards entrepreneurship and the overall benefits versus efforts of pursuing INVs can vary from country to country.

The consideration presented above paint a complex environment that allows for a substantially changed model to emerge; a model that questions the social

competence and astuteness as factors capable to mediate the risks associated with SMEs going global, and in doing so a new framework emerges. Nevertheless, Phelan et al. (2006) do the field of entrepreneurship a great favor as they initiate a continuous dialogue regarding the ability for SMEs to achieve competitiveness internationality as INVs and to modalities so as to mitigate the costs associated with such pursuits. Moreover, Phelan's model findings with regards to social capital as it applied to personal skill, market and relationship embeddedness were accepted as factors in explaining some aspects or achieving INV competitive advantage. The model is seen to apply to embeddedness considerations as a skilled individual would recognize and utilize market and local information for competitive advantage and successful market scanning.

As seen in the Figure 2 below and by following the propositions stated above, an entrepreneur's tacit recognition of opportunities, degree of local embeddedness. and pursuit of internationalization are all seen to positively affect an INVs competitive position with the caveat of excessive internationalization as an exception; exception occurring when internal capabilities would not match the required efforts/resources for undertaking of a successful INV. The external factors pertaining to behavior, goal commitment and subsidies are all seen to positively affect a INVs ability to become or stay competitive as they could mitigate the costs/liabilities associated with global expansion. National attitudes towards entrepreneurial activities as well as availability of subsidies are considered to both be positives, as an individual having benefited from years of passed on knowledge or receiving government/private support would be better enabled to mitigate the costs of going global.

Difficult or restrictive legal environments, as well as a low level of commitment, are assessed as negatives in the life of an INV. Rightly so, as the costs associated with expanding into new markets are affected if domestic regulations increase and/or if the entrepreneur lacks the necessary commitment, motivation or does not see a positive outcome when compared to the effort required to pursue an INV or an entrepreneurial activity in general.

Geographical considerations are in themselves complex as in each economy and country entrepreneurs pursue INVs from a variety of reasons, be they domestic influenced, due to having ascertained a certain entrepreneurial maturity or attitude. In the case of China individuals had to adapt their business endeavors so as to export their products due to domestic deficiencies represented by government regulations, inadequate local infrastructure and lack of access to technological advancements or technology in general. All geographic considerations are seen to provide a positive environment for establishing competitive INVs, yet one could assess that in China's case pursuing internationalization occurs at a cost as an entrepreneurs is unable to capitalize on local opportunities.

The attitude part paints an equally complex picture as pursuing entrepreneurship—as a precursor to INV and networks—is perceived as a choice that has a different degree of acceptance from one society/country to another. As

Figure 2
Modified Conceptual Framework

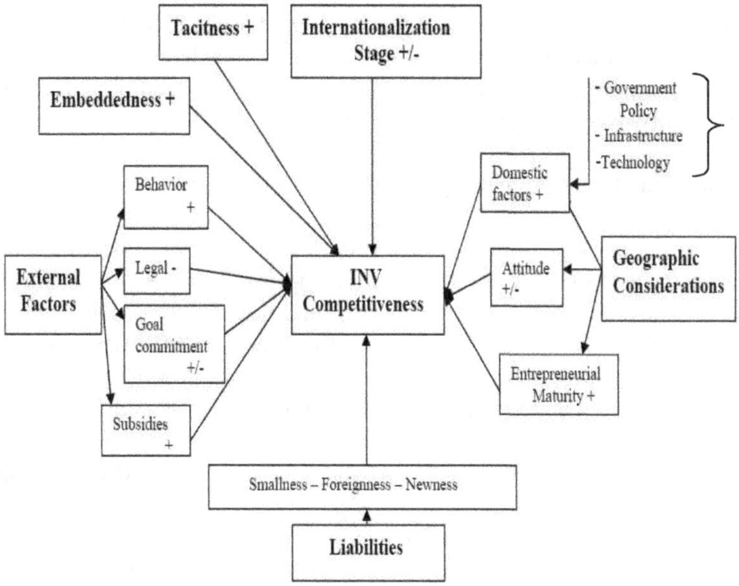

Note: INV = International new ventures

such, attitude could have either a positive or negative connotation with regards to INVs. A case could be made that is should only be recognized as a positive as an individual that does not decide to become an entrepreneur will therefore not affect the competitiveness of a non-existent INV.

Discussion

The field of entrepreneurship is ever-changing and as such any conceptual framework will be subject to continuous review. The framework presented here is not comprehensive by any means as each point made could be enlarged and further refined so as to better represent existing and upcoming realities. This article cannot neither underestimate, nor ignore the findings generated by extant research, yet it does attempt to address and start a dialogue regarding the void of research leading to a model capable of defining the factors affecting international new ventures (INVs), the corresponding entrepreneurial networks and the involved entrepreneurs in general.

This study does not provide an ample model capable of fully presenting the complexities associated with the traits defining of the entrepreneurial behavior or INV success, as it provides only a framework for an understudy for

it. Further research is needed to mitigate the risks that SMEs encounter when pursuing globalization as the infrastructure, technology, opportunity costs/liabilities could be added to smallness, newness and foreignness. The study while attempting to present a variety of factors related to the complex relationship between entrepreneurs has only pointed the need for dialog; dialog that will need to continue so as to result in the creation of a general model to ample applicability over industries and geographical areas.

Implications for Managers

Entrepreneurship, international ventures and business networks have been the subject of extensive research, yet most of it has been focused either on theoretical concepts or on the overall interpretation of results harvested through observations. This article cannot neither underestimate, nor ignore some of the findings generated by the extant research, yet it does attempt to address and start a dialogue regarding the void of research leading to a model capable of defining the factors affecting international new ventures (INVs), the corresponding entrepreneurial networks and the involved entrepreneurs and managers in general.

This chapter and ensuing argumentation aims at issuing a commentary regarding some of the present findings as it builds the rationales for pursuing the foundation for a representative model. These rationales rely upon the perceived importance of enunciating a comprehensive conceptual framework linking the three related concepts—entrepreneurs, international ventures and the corresponding business networks—as being of significant importance to management professionals. Managers would therefore be enabled to: first, define and identify the variety of external factors needed to be understood and taken under considerations for professionals considering international markets entry and second, acquire the ability to model their mode and modality of entry according to a framework (or its role and components) that if implemented and understood would render the entrepreneur an outcome capable of assisting with a successful INV pursuit and realization.

Direction of Further Research

It will be recommended that the direction of further research would focus upon statistical testing of the propositions and factors presented and identified in this chapter as by doing so a higher degree of legitimacy would be applied to the conceptual framework. Organizing such measurements should not be inclusive of results of new research that would target results and measurement from a wide range of industries and economies. The expected research should continue on the path of further identifying external factors able to mediate the costs and liabilities of entering international markets as well as estimating the

implications of such factors upon entrepreneurs, INVs creation/pursuit and entrepreneurial networks functionality in this context.

Strengths and Limitations

The article's main strength is that it provides, just as mentioned above, the backdrop for a discussion and dialogue related to defining a model that identifies the factors affecting entrepreneurs entering international markets through international new ventures and assisted by business networks. The limitation for the chapter's findings is that it provides only a background for an understudy studying born globals, SMEs and INVs in general. It does not provide measurements to substantiate the actual effect of each factor upon mitigating the liabilities of foreignness, newness and smallness.

References

Baron, R. A. & Ensley, M. (2006). Opportunity recognition as the detection of meaningful patterns: Evidence from comparisons of novice and experienced entrepreneurs. *Management Science, 52*, 1331–1344.

Baron, R. A., & Markman, G. D. (2000). Beyond social capital: How social skills can enhance entrepreneurs' success. *Academy of Management Executive, 14*, 106–116.

Baron, R. A., & Markman, G. D. (2003). Beyond social capital: The role of entrepreneurs' social competence in their financial success. *Journal of Business Venturing, 18*, 41–60.

Baron, R. A., & Shane, S. (2005). *Entrepreneurship: A process perspective*. Mason, OH: South-Western.

Beamish, P. W., Morrison, A. J., Inkpen, A. C., & Rosenzwig, P. M. (2003). The internationalization process. *International management: Text and cases* (pp. 3–16). New York: McGraw-Hill/Irwin.

Boissin, J.-P., Branchet, B., Emin, S., & Herbert J. I. (2009). Students and Entrepreneurship: A Comparative Study of France and the United States. *Journal of Small Business and Entrepreneurship, 22*, 119–139.

Brandl, J., & Bullinger, B. (2009). Reflections on the societal conditions for the pervasiveness or entrepreneurial behavior in Western Societies. *Journal of Management Inquire, 18*, 159–171.

Brawn, B. & Buttler, J. E. (1995). Competitors as allies: A study of entrepreneurial networks in the US wine industry. *Journal of Small Business Management*; 33 (2), 57, 1–26.

Burt, R. S. (2004). Structural Holes and Good Ideas. *The American Journal of Sociology, 110*, 349–99.

Busenitz, L. & Barney, J. (1997). Differences between entrepreneurs and managers in large organizations: Biases and heuristics in strategic decision-making. *Journal of Business Venturing, 12*, 9–30.

Clouser, M., Etzkowitz, H., Li, F., & Papagiannidis, S. (2009). Entrepreneurs and Opportunity Recognition. *Journal of International Entrepreneurship, 7*, 215–235.

Clow, K. E., & Cole, H. S. (2004). Small retailers' road to success: The customer value concept. *Services Marketing Quarterly 26* (2), 69–81.

Cooke, P., N. Clifton & M. Oleaga. (2005). Social capital, firm embeddedness and regional development. *Regional Studies,* 39, 1065–1071.

Contractor, F. (2007). Is international business good for companies?: The evolutionary or multi-stage theory on internationalization vs. the transaction cost perspective. *Management International Review, 47*, 453–475.

Cotae, F. F. (2010). Internationalization: Learning curve and transfer costs. *Journal of American Academy of Business, 15*, 80–206.

Cotae, F. F. (2009). Leadership and the internationalization Sigmoid. *International Leadership Journal, 2*, 129–136.

Darroch, J., & McNaughton, R. (2004). Examining the link between knowledge management practices and types of innovation. *Journal of Intellectual Capital 3*, 210–22.

Davenport, T. H., DeLong, D. W., & Beers, M. C. (1998). Successful knowledge management projects. *Sloan Management Review, 39* (2), 43–57.

De Clercq, D., Diochon, M., Gasse, Y., & Menzies (2009). Explaining nascent entrepreneurs goal commitment: An exploratory study. *Journal of Small Business and Entrepreneurship, 22*, 146–175.

De Clercq, D., & Arenius, P. (2006). The role of knowledge in business start-up activity. *International Small Business Journal, 24*, 339–58.

Frazier, B. J., & Huddleston, P. (2009). The role of market embeddedness in market scanning and marketing competence. *Journal of Small Business and Entrepreneurship, 22* (2), 1–24.

Fligstein, N. (1997). Social skill and institutional theory. *American Behavioral Scientist, 40*, 397–405.

Glaum, M., & Oesterle, M-J. (2007). 40 Years of research on internationalization and firm performance: More questions than answers? *Management International Review, 47*, 307–317.

Granovetter, M. (1985). Economic Action and Social Structure: The Problem of Embeddedness. *American Journal of Sociology, 91*, 481–510.

Guarriello, M. L. (1996). The management of leadership. *Hospital Material Management Quarterly, 17* (3), 17–21.

Hennart, J-F. (2007). The theoretical rationale for a multinationality-performance relationship. *Management International Review, 47*, 423–452.

Hennart, J-F. (2001). Theories of the multinational enterprise. In A. Rugman & T. Brewer (Eds.), *The oxford handbook of international business* (pp. 127–145). Oxford: Oxford University Press.

Johanson, J., & Vahlne, J.-E. (1977). The internationalization process of the firm: A model of knowledge development and increasing foreign commitments. *Journal of International Business Studies, 8*, 23–32.

Johanson, J., & Vahlne, J-E. (1990), The mechanism of internationalization. *International Marketing Review, 7* (4), 1–24.

Johnson, B., Lorentz, E., & Lundvall, B. (2002). Why all this fuss about codified and tacit knowledge? *Industrial and Corporate Change, 11*, 245–262.

Karra, N., & Phillips, N. (2004, December 18). Entrepreneurship goes global. *Ivey Business Journal Online*, p. A1.

Kogut, B., & Zander, U. (1992). Knowledge of the firm, Combinative capabilities and their replication of technology, *Organizations Science, 3*, 383–397.

Lee, Y., & Trim, P. R. (2006). Retail marketing strategy: The role of marketing intelligence, relationship marketing and trust. *Marketing Intelligence & Planning, 24*, 730–745.

Lopez-Duarte, C., & Garcia-Canal, E. (2007). Stock market reaction to foreign direct investments: Interaction between entry mode and FDI attributes. *Management International Review, 47*, 393–422.

Lu, J. W., & Beamish, P. W. (2004). International diversification and firm performance: The S-curve hypothesis. *Academy of Management Journal, 47*, 598–609.

Miller, C. C. (2009/2010, July 20). For start-ups less appeal in going public: Stricter Us regulations are driving entrepreneurs from market: A federal study. *International Herald Tribune,* p. 17.

Miller, N., & Kean, R. (1997). Reciprocal exchange in rural communities: Consumers' inducement to in-shop. *Psychology & Marketing 14*, 637–61.

Munir, K. A., & Phillips, N. (2005). The birth of the Kodak moment: Institutional entrepreneurship and the adoption of new technologies. *Organization Studies, 26*, 1665–1687.

Naude, W., & Rossouw, S. (2009). Early international entrepreneurship in China: extent and determinant. *Journal of International Entrepreneurship 16*, 1–48.

Phelan, S. E., Dalgic, T., & Sethi, D. (2006). The development of entrepreneurial networks: A necessary condition for international new ventures. *Strategic Management Review, 1* (1), 1–21.

Phelan, S. E., & Alder, S. (2005, August). *An experimental study of entrepreneurial exploitation.* Paper presented at the annual meeting of the Academy of Management, Honolulu, HI.

Phelan, S. E., & Lewin, P. (2000). Arriving at a strategic theory of the firm. *International Journal of Management Reviews, 2*, 305–323.

Smith, B. R., Matthews, C. H., & Schenkel, M. T. (2009). Differences in entrepreneurial opportunities: The role and tacitness and codification. *Journal of Small Business Management, 47* (1), 37–48.

Riahi-Belkaoui, A. (1998). The effects of the degree of internationalization on firm performance. *International Business Review, 7*, 315–321.

Subramanian, A. (1993). Investigating the role of market embeddedness in consumer outshopping behavior. Unpublished doctoral dissertation, University of Nebraska, Lincoln.

Uzzi, B. (1996). The sources and consequences of embeddedness for the economic performance of organizations: The network effect. *American Sociological Review, 61*, 674–98.

Zilber, T. (2006). The work of the symbolic in institutional processes. *Academy of Management Journal, 49*, 281–303.

Current Topics in Management, Vol. 15, 2011, pp. 175-186

BSL PRINTING COMPANY: A CASE STUDY

Joseph P. Lakatos, Donald R. Soucy, and Stephen J. Bukowy

The BSL Printing Company has been in business since 1976, printing folding cartons primarily for the textile industry. The company is a major employer in the small town of Oakville, which is located in the southeastern United States. The town's population is 2,536 residents. In 1976, the company struggled to get started in business, but thanks to the support from a number of other regional companies, BSL managed to stay afloat. Jack Sprague, BSL's CEO and chairman, recalled pleading with Peter Lint, the CEO and founder of Advent Textile, for his first order. Advent began its operations in 1972 and operates 20 miles away (although in the same county) from BSL in a town of 4,000.

Over the years, Jack, Peter, and their families became very close friends. They attended the same church and their children went to the same school. In fact, Jack and his wife, Laurie, are the godparents to the Lint's third child. Meanwhile, Advent continued to be a loyal and significant customer of BSL, whose sales reached $17.6 million in 2008.

BSL's Client Problem

On a Friday afternoon in mid-2008, a loud commotion erupted outside Jack's office. "Mary what's that racket going on out there?" Jack barked over the intercom to his administrative assistant. "Just Harry and Jim carrying on an argument," replied Mary. Harry was Harry Stahl, the vice president of marketing and Jim was Jim Care, the recently hired general manager of operations. "Well, send them in here and I'll see if I can find out what the problem is now."

"Okay, you two what are you arguing about now?" "I'll tell you what the problem is," said Jim, "Harry wants to make a sale well below acceptable margins." Jack turned to Harry and said, "Well, what about it Harry?" "It's true,

but it's for some printed cartons for Advent Textile." "But the expected profit margin is less than 3%," chimed in Jim. Jack asked Harry why he would even bring such a proposal to him, since the VP knew that this margin was totally unacceptable. Harry replied "if we don't quote the price in this manner, we will not get the sales order." Harry went on to say, "The Advent Textile Company has just filed for bankruptcy under Chapter 11."

Harry thought Jack would want to help his old friend, Peter Lint. "Jack, how many times have you told me what a great relationship you had with Peter?" "Didn't Advent help BSL when it needed it? Shouldn't we help them now?" Harry further explained "if we do not help Advent by reducing our price to them, then Advent would be doomed. Without support from some of its key suppliers, Advent would be unable to secure the business that it desperately needs while attempting to restructure under Chapter 11 protection."

In this type of industry, set-up costs are very high. For instance, it might take an employee eight (8) hours to set up a printing press. The set up costs remain the same regardless of order size. Therefore, as order size increases, the price per unit decreases. For example, the total cost to produce 10,000 cartons might not be much greater than the total cost to produce 100,000 cartons, thus the per unit cost will be much less for the 100,000 carton order due to higher set up costs. Given this fact, BSL, as well as others in the industry, gave discounts for larger volumes. For BSL, these volume discounts were as follows:

Quantity ordered	Price reduction
1 – 99,000	0 %
100,000 – 499,000	10 %
500,000 +	15 %

Therefore, customers were always trying to reduce the total cost per carton by ordering larger quantities than they really needed to gain the volume discount price. In the past, BSL tried to accommodate the customer by permitting this practice. BSL's policy for preferred customers was to produce the entire order, make a partial shipment in accordance with the customer's shipping request and store the remainder of the order in BSL's warehouse, until the customer requested the remainder of the order for shipment.

In researching Advent's order history, Jack noticed that Advent had been paying its bills slower and slower. If BSL had analyzed its accounts receivables on a regular basis, it might have noticed the trend and approached Advent about the situation sooner. Advent's cash flow apparently deteriorated slowly over the years and eventually forced Advent into filing for bankruptcy protection while it tries to reorganize. In further analyzing Advent's ordering history, Jack noticed that Advent placed about five orders each month. Each order was for a different printed carton. Some cartons might have been ordered every month, but others were different from month to month. On the average these orders

were for 100,000 pieces. It appeared that Advent was taking advantage of BSL's preferred customer policy.

Jim Care noted that all 15 of BSL's preferred customers were taking advantage of the quantity discounts offered. However, he further noted that BSL had a major problem with most of the other preferred customers. "We have 10 million cartons sitting in our warehouse right now," said Jim. "So, what's wrong with that?" questioned Jack. "I've only been here for a few months, so I don't know how long this problem has been going on." "What problem are you talking about Jim" asked Jack. "Your preferred customers order enough to get the 15% discount and only take a small fraction of the amount and we store the rest." "That's right, we've been doing that for years, good customer service and convenience" said Harry. "It would be if BLS got paid for its work," said Jim. "What are you getting at Jim," asked Jack. "Jack, your clients place large discounted orders but only take about 10–25% of the order. They only pay for what they take for delivery, the rest we hold. Therefore, while they are getting the benefit of the discounts, we are not getting the benefit of faster cash flow. In fact, cash flow is impeded because they take their sweet old time taking delivery of the balance of the order if ever. We have spent large amounts of money preparing the order but are left with receivables and printed cartons to hold for these people. In the meantime of course, we have to pay our suppliers for the inks and the cardboards."

Company Meeting

Jack called a meeting with Laurie Sprague, who was the treasurer/secretary, Harry, Jim, and Ben McDole, the CFO. Jack summarized the situation for the entire group and solicited input. Ben quickly opened the discussion. Ben stated, "I have only been with the company a little over two years, so I do not fully know all of the past relationships with critical clients nor am I fully aware of the personal relationships that might exist between you and Advent's owners. As your CFO, I must recommend that BSL not agree to this order proposal to Advent. I remind all of you that Advent currently has not been paying its bills in a timely manner. In fact, our account receivable amount from Advent is at $253,850 and Advent is taking over 60 days to pay its bills. As CFO I find these facts distressing and do not want BSL to expose itself to more potential bad debts." Laurie replied, "I understand your concern Ben, but we must think what will happen if we do not support Advent and they cease to continue. What will happen to its employees who will not be employed or are not receiving unemployment compensation? Won't this lead to higher taxes on those companies that are still operational? Also, how will the loss of $2,000,000 in sales affect our company? Will BSL suffer the same consequences? Ben, you know that Oakville will suffer greatly if BSL ceases business and the County will be in dire straits if both Advent and BSL go out of business."

Harry pointed out that Advent can make money on this order if everything goes right. Ben rebutted, pointing out that he was unsure if BSL could consider this order as revenue, since there was so much speculation about whether Advent would be able to pay for the order. Ben further thought that while the auditors might not allow this to count as revenue, the IRS might still classify the order as revenue and BSL may have to pay taxes on it.

Laurie mentioned the long lasting relationship between the two companies and between the two families. She could not think of letting the Lints down by not supporting them in their moment of tribulation. In addition, she stated that she could not visualize what would happen to the two communities. Jack knew that Advent had been a very good client over the years; in fact Advent was very supportive of BSL in the beginning when BSL, itself needed all of the orders possible to stay afloat. Advent sourced all its printed cartons with BSL and assisted BSL to increase its client list. In the beginning, Advent was BSL's # 1 customer, but is now listed in the top 10% on BSL's preferred client list. Advent orders represented about 10% of BSL's yearly sales budget of about $17,000,000. Jack certainly felt the loyalty strings tugging at his sense of honor making a decision most difficult. Jack thanked everyone for his or her participation and candor in the matter. He told everyone that he wanted to sleep on the situation before he made a decision concerning the order. That night, Jack mentally reviewed the situation and tried to find a feasible solution for both parties.

BSL Printing
Teaching Note

Problems Faced by BSL

BSL Printing Company faced significant affects on its operations and financial condition from the pending bankruptcy filing of Advent Textiles, a major and longstanding customer. BSL's CEO sought to develop and implement a strategic plan that balanced the associated benefits and risks of the various stakeholders. Readers are encouraged to apply the following management theories to the CEO's decision making process: (1) "Leadership Styles" (Goleman, Boyatzis, & McKee, 2002), (2) "The Leadership Continuum Model" (Tannenbaum & Schmidt, 1973), (3) "Results Based Leadership" (Ulrich, Zenger, & Smallwood, 1999), and (4) "The 7 Habits of Highly Effective People" (Covey's, 1989). In addition, readers will find that by incorporating applicable ethical theories, discussed herein, into the analysis of BSL's strategic alternatives, a sounder business decision will be reached.

BSL's Strategic Alternatives

There are three alternatives that BSL's CEO may consider undertaking: (1) BSL Printing could cease doing business with Advent Textiles immediately. This

Table 1
BSL Printing Company's Balance Sheet for Three Years

	2006	2007	2008
ASSETS			
Cash	$ 480,000	600,000	800,000
Accounts Receivable	2,500,000	2,200,000	1,800,000
Inventory	2,000,000	2,200,000	1,300,000
Building	1,500,000	1,500,000	1,500,000
Accumulated Depreciation	(1,200,000)	(1,275,000)	(1,350,000)
Equipment	10,000,000	10,000,000	3,000,000
Accumulated Depreciation	(8,000,000)	(9,000,000)	(400,000)
Total Assets	7,280,000	6,225,000	6,650,000
LIABILITIES			
Accounts Payable	1,500,000	1,200,000	1,050,000
Interest Payable	86,100	86,100	86,100
Loan Payable	1,325,000	1,325,000	1,325,000
Total Liabilities	2,911,100	2,611,100	2,461,100
Owner's Equity	4,368,900	3,613,900	4,188,900

alternative would most probably lead to the demise of Advent Textiles since it would not be able to continue to do business without the support of BSL. (2) BSL Printing could continue doing business with Advent Textiles with no contractual changes. This could allow Advent to stay in business while preserving its supply chain for printed cartons. On the other hand, BSL would run the risk of incurring more uncollectible accounts receivable, thereby draining its cash position. (3) BSL Printing could continue doing business with Advent Textiles utilizing a modified or new contract. This could assist Advent in its efforts to work itself out of its financial dilemma. The costs and benefits of each alternative are examined below from the points of view of BSL and Advent.

What Are the Costs/Benefits of Each Alternative?

For alternative A, the potential *costs* for BSL Printing are that the sales could drop immediately leading to a reduction of operating costs, including labor, while jeopardizing other customer relationships. BSL could lose local societal support and receive a bad reputation from the local workforce. For Advent Textiles, current orders would be at risk due to lack of raw materials leading

Table 2
BSL Printing Company's Income Statement

	2006	2007	2008
Sales	$16,910,000	17,330,000	17,600,000
Sales Discounts	1,753,000	1,846,000	1,992,000
Net Sales	15,157,000	15,484,000	15,608,000
Direct labor	1,183,700	1,410,000	1,534,100
Direct Material	9,469,600	9,954,800	9,992,800
Gross Profit	4,503,700	4,119,200	4,081,100
Operating Expenses:			
Waste Costs	1,325,700	1,358,700	1,382,200
Indirect material	94,700	97,050	98,730
Variable OH	227,270	232,920	236,950
Write-offs-Abnormal Scrap	550,000	431,000	396,000
Dep-Equipment	448,060	409,310	355,310
Dep-Building	84,375	84,375	84,375
Property Tax	24,000	24,300	24,600
Utilities	19,500	21,000	22,500
Insurance	7,500	7,650	7,800
Commissions	303,140	309,680	313,560
Salaries	634,044	667,800	701,190
Bad Debt	37,893	38,710	39,195
Total Operating Expenses	3,756,182	3,682,495	3,662,410
EBIT	747,518	436,705	418,690
Interest	86,100	86,100	86,100
EBT	661,418	350,605	332,590
Taxes	263,003	140,242	133,036
Net Income	398,415	210,363	209,554

to the need to develop a new supplier chain. Lack of raw materials would lead to layoffs and create a sense of doubt on the part of Advent's customers, which could then risk future business and possibly bankruptcy. Under alternative B, BSL would experience obsolete finished goods inventories leading to more bad debt and greater negative cash flow. Employee morale could suffer along with productivity. Meanwhile, Advent might relax, thinking it's out of trouble, and not continue to improve its financial situation maintaining high account payables. If alternative C was selected, BSL would need to negotiate a new contract with Advent and develop a system to maintain control over the receivables plan set forth in the new contract. Advent would have to order smaller quantities more frequently, thus increasing its procurement costs by not getting the volume discount price.

The possible *benefits* of alternative A for BSL Printing are that the negative cash flow it has been experiencing would cease. Advent Textiles, however, would receive no benefits under alternative A. With alternative B, BSL would retain customer goodwill while Advent continued its operations, avoiding supply chain disruptions and a near term Chapter 7 bankruptcy filing. Under alternative C, BSL would allow Advent to pay down its debt reducing its own bad debt accounts. Advent would have a better chance of remaining a viable customer and maintain its supply chain network. Advent and BSL would be able to maintain its experienced workforce, and retain its customer and community goodwill.

What Are the Societal Costs/Benefits of These Alternatives?

If BSL or Advent or both go out of business, society may pay the following *cost:* pay more unemployment compensation; receive less tax monies; experience an increase in the costs associated with higher crime rates and the demand for social programs given the higher level of unemployment. The possible psychological costs for society include individual and collective loss of self-esteem and deterioration of community morale, trust, and hope.

If both companies remain in business the benefits to society are numerous, including stable or higher tax revenues; lower demand for social programs; the infusion of capital in the form of wages and money spent; revenue increases for local businesses due to greater infusion of money into the local economy; and the attraction of new businesses to the community. The psychological benefits to society include improvement of individual and collective self esteem, morale, trust, and hope, and a decrease in crime levels due to better employment.

Theories of Leadership Style

The following are theories of leadership style that may be applied to our case study. The first, "Leadership Styles", was developed by Goleman, Boyatzis, and McKee (2002). In this theory, six emotional styles of leadership are offered: (1) the *visionary* leader is one who moves people towards a shared vision, telling them where to go but not how to get there, and provides clear direction when change is needed; (2) the *coaching* leader connects "wants" to organizational goals, holding long conversations that reach beyond the workplace with the intent of helping staff tie their strengths and weaknesses to their career aspirations and actions; (3) the *affiliative* leader takes on a collaborative style, seeking to create people connections and harmony within the organization; (4) the *democratic* leader acts to value inputs and commitment via participation, listening to both the bad and the good news; (5) the *pace-setting* leader builds challenge and exciting goals for people, expecting excellence and often exemplifying it themselves; and (5) the *commanding* leader soothes fears and

gives clear directions by his or her powerful stance, commanding and expecting full compliance (agreement is not needed). The commanding leader needs emotional self-control for success and can seem cold and distance.

Readers are challenged to ascertain the leadership style that would best enable BSL to optimally resolve its problem. Jack Sprague demonstrates aspects of each of these styles. Jack demonstrated characteristics of a *visionary* and *democratic* leader by providing clear direction with the plan he developed (see Epilogue) after seeking input from others in the organization. One could reasonably assert that Jack also acted as a *commanding* leader by soothing the concerns of Advent and the bankruptcy court with the details of his plan. Readers should gleam from this case study that a leader can take on characteristics from more than one style of leadership.

In the second theory, "The Leadership Continuum Model," Tannebaum and Schmidt depict leadership styles ranging from autocratic to democratic, leaving a range of choices for involvement by the various stakeholders. The Model suggests that autocratic leaders are more likely to make their own decisions and not engage their subordinates, whereas a democratic leader gives subordinates a greater degree of delegation in decision making. Prior to the financial concerns with Advent, Jack took on a democratic style with his subordinates. However, according to MacGregor's Theory X versus Theory Y, the Theory X (autocratic) should be used when the situation has a critical time constraint with implementation needed immediately. Given the need to implement a plan in a timely fashion, Jack ultimately decides to be more autocratic than democratic in effecting the solution (see Epilogue). It should be recognized that Jack does not act fully autocratic, since he did seek input from his subordinates.

Under the third theory, "Results Based Leadership" by Ulrich, Zenger, and Smallwood (1999), the optimal solution for BSL needs to be: (1) *balanced*: results balance the major dimensions of the total organization. In BSL's situation, the organization includes all stakeholders, customers, suppliers, employees, and communities; (2) *strategic*: results link strongly to the strategy of the firm's and its competitive position; (3) *lasting*: results meet both short – and not sacrifice the long-term goals; and (4) *selfless*: results support the whole enterprise (organization) and transcend the manager's personal gain. Jack learned that one must achieve both results and positive attributes to demonstrate leadership. He knew that the BSL's bottom line was important but was not everything, thereby falling under the premise of Ulrich et al. (1999) "sustainable shareholder value comes from assets not accounted for on an organization's balance sheet. The assets include a company's reputation, its ability to attract talent, and its ability to react quickly to new opportunities in the marketplace" (p. 37).

Based on the facts depicted in the case study and epilogue, the reader would ascertain that Jack's actions also fall within our last theory, Stephen Covey's "The 7 Habits of Highly Effective People", as follows: (1) in *being productive*, Jack was efficient in seeking input and reaching a solution; (2) by *beginning with*

the end in mind, Jack sought an outcome that was positive for all stakeholders; (3) by *putting things first,* Jack discussed possible solutions with the appropriate parties prior to implementation; (4) by *thinking win–win,* Jack wanted all parties to remain whole and prosper; (5) by *seeking first to understand, then to be understood,* Jack moved quickly after he understood the root cause problem, possible solutions, and potential side effects, and communicated the details of his solution to all participants; (6) by *synergizing,* Jack mobilized all parties to participate in the implementation of the solution; and (7) by *sharpening the saw,* Jack knew that he had to balance and provide renewal of resources, energy, and health to create a sustainable long-term effective strategy.

As can be ascertained from the Case Study and Epilogue, Jack instituted a series of attributes under the aforementioned leadership theories to come up with an effective solution. However, by incorporating the following ethical theories into the analysis of business problems, sounder decisions are undoubtedly reached.

Ethical Approaches to Business Decisions

There are several approaches to ethics. Familiarity with these approaches can support a manager's thought process in at least two ways when facing business dilemmas. First, the models for analysis can spark creative thinking as they brainstorm ways of handling the dilemma. Second, ethical approaches offer a means of explaining one's decisions to others. In the case of BSL, knowing the theoretical basis for ethical decision making would help Jack better understand his stance and in turn, help him better articulate it to stakeholders.

Free Market Ethics

Under this theory, Milton Friedman argues that in a free market society the only social responsibility of business is to engage its resources in activities designed to increase its profits so long as it stays within the rules of the game and does not engage in deception or fraud. Friedman argues that it is wrong for managers to use corporate resources to deal with problems in society at large. The only stakeholders' interests that should be considered are those of shareholders. Initially alternative A, in which BSL ceases to do business with Advent, would seem to satisfy proponents of free market ethics by focusing on BSL's shareholders. However, this would not provide a "win–win" situation under Covey's theory. On the other hand, one could argue that Alternative C could maximize BSL shareholder value if implemented effectively as shown by the actions depicted in the Epilogue.

While Alternative A may be the right thing to do for the shareholders of BSL *(free market ethics),* the question would be posed under *utilitarian and deontological approaches*, discussed below, as to whether it is the right thing

to do for the employees and other stakeholders? *Virtue ethics* and the *ethics of care* viewpoints require more consideration. As noted below, both approaches would lead BSL's CEO to adhere to the moral obligation to do right by Advent in light of the long standing relationships of the two companies and the people within them. This would lead to the implementation of Alternative C.

Utilitarianism

Under the ethical principle of utilitarianism, proposed by John Stuart Mill, the right way to behave in a given situation is to choose the alternative that is likely to produce the greatest overall good. It asks us to compare the harms and benefits of an action not just for the decider, but for all persons who will be affected by the decision.

Deontology

In contrast to the utilitarian concern with maximizing social welfare, deontological ethics is marked by steadfastness to universal principles, such as respect for life, fairness, telling the truth, keeping promises, etc., no matter what the consequences. Under this approach, it is believed that each person has the right to be treated with respect as the equal of very other, and that each person has the corresponding duty to treat everyone else with respect as an equal. If we apply this approach to this case, one should ask: Would I want to live in a world where a company would not assist another company through a time of financial strife particularly when they have had a long standing relationship?

Virtue Ethics

Virtue ethics focuses on what human beings are capable of being—on how they can cultivate the habits of good character that will naturally lead them to their fullest potential. Ethics, then, is not a matter of teasing out the correct choice given a series of dilemmas; rather, it is a lifelong conditioning process. In harmonious relationship with their communities, people thrive, reaching the fullest unfolding of their potential, learning the habits that allow them to excel at everything they are capable of doing.

Virtue ethics does raise some questions such as what does it mean to define moral character in term of one's community? Cultures vary as do the communities in which people are raised. Thus, moral character cannot be defined universally. Moreover, what do we mean by community in the business context? Where is the community touchstone in the BSL scenario? A company can define its community through its corporate culture, which encompasses business principles or virtues.

Ethic of Care

The ethical approaches examined so far assume that a decision about the right thing to do is ultimately a private decision, made by an individual in isolation. Whether using their intellectual abilities or responding to trained habit, people act as autonomous beings in this process. Differently, the "ethic of care" approach assumes that people are deeply connected to one another in webs of relationships, and that ethical decisions cannot be made outside the context of those relationships. This view suggests that ethics is a matter of nurturing and reinforcing the ties we have with one another.

Operating under Chapter 11 Bankruptcy

Many readers might not be familiar with the differences between a Chapter 11 or Chapter 7 bankruptcy filing. When they hear the word "bankruptcy" they assume the end of a company. A Chapter 11 reorganization is one that allows a company to continue operations, unlike a Chapter 7 filing, which liquidates the company. In both cases, a petition is filed to initiate the proceedings. This can be voluntarily filed by the company or involuntarily forced by the creditors.

A Chapter 11 reorganization can be avoided if creditors are willing to negotiate a debt-adjustment agreement, also known as a "workout." If an agreement such as this cannot be reached a petition is filed, and the company receives an automatic stay that suspends all actions by creditors against the company. When a company is involved in a Chapter 11 reorganization, they are referred to as a debtor-in-possession. This allows the company to continue to operate the business despite claims against the assets. A reorganization plan is submitted that designates the classes of claims and specifies the treatment of each class. The plan also must outline how all of the actions will take place and how the company will rehabilitate as a result. When a reorganization plan receives approval from a bankruptcy court, the creditors must accept the plan. A plan will not be confirmed, however, unless creditors will receive as much as they would under a Chapter 7 filing. As noted in the Epilogue, BSL's CEO developed a plan that was accepted by the bankruptcy court.

In a Chapter 7 filing, a trustee is appointed to oversee liquidation. The company must file an inventory of property and debts/claims. The company's assets are liquidated and the debts/claims of the entity are settled. There are different types of creditor parties in a bankruptcy case that include fully secured, partially secured, unsecured with priority, and unsecured without priority. A statement of affairs is filed to approximate the estimated amounts available to each class of claims. After distribution to creditors, remaining debts are discharged. There are some claims that are not dischargeable. As a result of the efforts of BCL's CEO, a Chapter 7 filing by Advent was averted.

Epilogue

After giving the matter much thought, Jack came to the realization that he wanted to help Advent get through its current dilemma. He wanted to help Advent avoid a Chapter 7 bankruptcy, but at the same time he did not want to jeopardize his own company's financial well being. Jack developed a plan that permitted him to sell printed cartons to Advent and at the same time reduce the A/R balance. As part of his plan, BSL would accept future orders from Advent for the full list price for the quantity requested. Advent would pay the full list price for the cartons and the difference between full list price and discounted volume based price would be applied toward the retirement of Advent's outstanding debt. In this way, Advent would receive the cartons it needed for its product shipments and BSL would begin to retire Advent's debt.

For example:

- Advent orders 560,000 cartons
- Full price is $167 per thousand
- Order value = $93,520; Order volume discount, less 15% = $14,028
- Advent would pay the total price of $93,520 for the order and the $14,028 would be applied to its outstanding debt, thus reducing the debt from $253,850 to $239,832.

When Jack proposed this payment strategy to Peter and ultimately, the bankruptcy court, both agreed to the strategy and requested that the plan be implemented immediately. Over the next 15 months, Advent was able to weather its financial storm. It developed a plan to reduce its costs, improve its productivity, improve its product quality and expand it customer base in the international markets. At the end of the 15 months, Advent earned a modest profit, and was prepared to exit from Chapter 11 bankruptcy. At the same time, Advent not only eliminated its outstanding debt with BSL, it began paying its bills within 30 days.

References

Covey, S. (1990). *The seven habits of highly effective people: Powerful lessons in personal challenge*. Tampa, FL: Free Press.

Goleman, D., Boyatzis, R., & McKee, A. (2002). *Primal leadership: Realizing the power of emotional intelligence.* Cambridge, MA: Harvard Business Press.

Halbert, S., & Ingulli, R. (2006). *Law & ethics in the business environment* (6th ed.). Newark, NJ: Prentice Hall.

Tannenbaum, R., & Schmidt, W. (1973). How to choose a leadership pattern. *Harvard Business Review, 51* (3), 162–180.

Ulrich, D., Zenger, J., & Smallwood, M. (1999). *Results based leadership.* Cambridge, MA: Harvard Business Press.

PART IV

ETHICS, LEARNING, AND CHANGE

Current Topics in Management, **Vol. 15, 2011, pp. 187-198**

ETHICS, RHETORIC, AND THE SELF AS AN EXPANDING WEB OF CONVERSATIONS

Can M. Alpaslan, Sandy E. Green, and Ian I. Mitroff

This main purpose of this chapter is to invite scholars to study how language and rhetoric shape the self and constructs the interests the self seeks. The main contribution of this chapter is a re-conceptualization of the self as an ever-expanding web of conversations. We draw from a variety of foundational studies to theorize that the self and its interests are at least partially constructed and shaped by conversations the self has with others.

Ethics, Rhetoric, and the Self

Within the field of economics and management, the conventional view of morality and ethics often suggests a model of *restrained egoism*: "It is egoistic because it is an ethic based on the active pursuit of one's self interest. It is restrained because self-interest is subservient to the rules of business practice" (Beauchamp & Bowie, 1979, p. 11). Restrained egoism rests on the assumptions that human beings are motivated by self-interest, and the pursuit of self-interest is a moral good in itself (Rand, 1943) or a means to the moral good because the pursuit of self-interests benefits society (Friedman, 1970; Smith, 1776). The notion of self-interest is often invoked by researchers to explain human behavior (Frank, 2004; Sen, 1977, 1993). For example, in transaction cost economics, individuals seek self-interest with guile (Williamson, 1985). Similarly, in agency theory, individuals are assumed to pursue their self-interest, and under certain conditions, engage in opportunism and shirking, as well as deception, coercion, and fraud (Boatright, 1999; Dees, 1982; Jensen & Meckling, 1976).

Within the fields of management and economics, the self is often viewed as unitary and aware of its interests (Seabright & Kurke, 1997; Taylor, 1989).

The self is individuated in advance, and has no "constitutive attachments" to any community (Burkitt, 1991; Sandel, 1998). That is, the self is prior to its ends, stakes, or interests (Rawls, 1999; Sandel, 1998), and self-interest is often assumed to be self-evident, whether the self pursues it or not (Johnson, 1993; Lakoff & Johnson, 1999). Moreover, the self's moral reasoning consists of assessments of situations in order to determine what principles apply and what actions ought to be taken (Anderson, 1997; Johnson, 1993; Jones, 1991). Thus, to be moral is to stick with one's principles, and not allow outside forces to corrupt one's "core or essential self" (Goodstein, 2000, p. 809; May, 1996, p. 12).

Some philosophers, sociologists, and economists, however, suggest that these conceptualizations of the self, its interests, and moral reasoning are flawed. Specifically, these conceptualizations fail to address the dynamic, multifaceted, constructed, and evolving nature of the self (Cooley, 1902; Flanagan, 1991; Kegan, 1982; Lakoff & Johnson, 1999; Mead, 1934; Peirce, 1931; Sandel, 1998; Solomon, 1992; Thaler, 2000). Furthermore, these scholars argue that, because the self and morality are inextricably intertwined (Mead, 1982; Taylor, 1989), the conventional view of the self as unitary and disengaged distorts and obfuscates our understanding of morality (Johnson, 1993). According to these scholars, the self is created and constructed by society (Burkitt, 1991; Quinn, 1996; Sandel, 1998; Taylor, 1989). The self is always a member of a community, and exists in a moral horizon shaped by the values, stories, and guidelines of the community (Sandel, 1998, p. 62; Taylor, 1989). It is not prior to its ends or interests; rather, it is constituted in part by them (Sandel, 1998) and the language of the community (Burkitt, 1991; Peirce, 1992; Quinn, 1996). Put differently, the self is a product of conversation or symbolic exchange (Booth, 1974; Mead, 1934), and is created "in the process of sharing intentions, values, and meanings" (Booth, 1974, pp. 134–135; Taylor, 1985, pp. 9–10). It emerges and changes as a result of ongoing action and reflection (Johnson, 1993, p. 148), an interaction between the "I" and the "me" (Mead, 1934), or revised self-understandings (Sandel, 1998, p. 172). Within this framework, the self's moral reasoning is conceptualized as more than an outcome, it is also an "unfolding conversation with one's self and others" (Churchman, 1983; Pauchant & Mitroff, 1992, p. 189). Thus, during moments of moral choice or deliberation, the boundary between the self and the other is not clear and stable (Booth, 1974); it is negotiated. In short, the self is not always a disengaged, instrumentally rational, and impervious core of commitments or preferences as described by most economists; rather, the self is an expanding and evolving web of commitments, constitutive attachments, or conversations (see May, 1996; Quinn, 1996; Sandel, 1998; Taylor, 1989).

If these scholars are right, if the self is not always stable and unitary as described in economics and game theory, but rather is a dynamic, multifaceted, and evolving product of symbolic exchange, identifying constantly with its

expanding web of commitments and constitutive attachments to community, then there may be important implications for understanding the self's moral goal, reasoning, and behavior.

The Goal of Moral Reasoning and the Expanding Self

Moral reasoning in contemporary ethics is mostly deductive: A general moral principle is applied to a specific situation, and a conclusion is derived, telling what one ought to do (Velasquez, 1994). Accordingly, most discussions of ethics focus on establishing the most fundamental moral principle (Velasquez, 1994). Several scholars and philosophers, however, have rejected the idea of a *summum bonum*, the highest good from which others are derived, or a final hierarchy of all goods and moral principles. As James says, an ethical philosophy cannot be created in advance or made final because moral experiences cannot be captured by a *summum bonum* (James, 1967). Thus, the grand theories of ethics such as deontology and utilitarianism are theoretically incomplete (Dewey, 1976), oblivious to the roles individuals play in business context, and inaccessible to managers (Solomon, 1992).

A view of the self as an expanding web resonates with the ideas of James, Dewey, and Solomon. The self that expands over time by including or identifying with a greater number of others implies that a moral philosophy cannot be finalized prior to experience. For the self cannot understand the highest good, but depending on its ability to expand its consciousness and conscientiousness, commits to different moral principles or ideals at different times to capture only part of the good (James, 1967). Trying to excel or do its best (Solomon, 1994), the virtuous self opens itself to increasingly varied moral experiences, voices, or conversations (James, 1967). Within this framework, the goal of moral reasoning is neither the pursuit of a fundamental principle, nor the application of a fundamental principle to business context (Solomon, 1994); the only moral goal is growth or the constant expansion of the self or consciousness (Dewey, 1976). And the guarantor of moral conduct in ethical dilemmas is "good judgment" or *phronesis:* the ability to acknowledge and value the particularity of a great variety of conflicting perspectives and principles (Solomon, 1994, p. 59). Thus, within this perspective, business itself becomes another perspective, commitment, or conversation but a powerful one among many others that constitute the self (Solomon, 1994, p. 9).

Rhetoric Theory and the Expanding Self

In order to study the self as an evolving web of conversations, we suggest scholars utilize rhetorical theory. The link between rhetoric and ethics has been stressed both by the sophists and by philosophers such as Socrates, Plato, and Aristotle (Herrick, 2001; Plato, 1998). Although the term rhetoric, which is

defined as "discourse calculated to influence an audience toward some end" (Gill & Whedbee, 1997, p. 157), has negative connotations, scholars of rhetoric agree that its methods and purposes are inextricably linked to ethics and morality. Aristotle argued that every act of communication aims for the good of someone or something, and thus is a rhetorical act with ethical consequences (Aristotle, 1991; Porter, 1993). Modern rhetoricians have defined rhetoric as "the art of reasoning together about shared concerns" (Booth, 1988, p. 105). Rhetoric influences the way we make judgments, and making moral judgments is a main component of ethical decision making and behavior (Aristotle, 1991; Rest, 1986; Solomon, 1994). We suggest that conversations shape the self and what the self comes to perceive and label as acceptable or unacceptable behavior. Specifically, the rhetoric of these conversations persuade the self to make a moral judgment that a particular action, whether in the past, present, or future, is ethical or unethical (Aristotle, 1991; Nienkamp, 2001).

If human beings are constructed and shaped in symbolic exchange, then rhetoric is inextricably linked with thoughts and ways of thinking (Booth, 1974; Enos, 1996; Maanen, 1995; McCloskey, 1998; O'Neill, 1997; Perelman & Olbrechts-Tyteca, 1969; Taylor, 1985). The rhetorical construction of the self begins with children's conversations with parents about various topics such as norms and values (Azmitia & Perlmutter, 1989). Children reenact these external conversations in private speech or internal conversations (Diaz & Berk, 1992). Later, these conversations are internalized, becoming a part of the conscience to guide the self (Diaz & Berk, 1992; Freud, 1933). That is, conversations that create and shape the self appear at the social or interpersonal level, and then are internalized at the psychological or personal level (Vygotsky, 1978). In a sense, the self's conversations are constructed and shaped by what the self and others have said before and their ways of saying (Bakhtin, 1986). This internalization process, which also resonates with Mead's idea of thinking as a conversation between the self and the generalized other (Mead, 1934), continues into adulthood (Fry, 1992; John-Steiner, 1992; Vygotsky, 1962). Triggered by social experiences, deep conversations with others facilitate role or perspective taking, stimulate broader viewpoints or different voices, and motivate the self to engage in more sophisticated internal conversations about moral problems (Crain, 2000; Kohlberg, Kauffman, Scharf, & Hickey, 1975). From a rhetorical perspective the self judges actions, attitudes, and decisions, whether one's own or those of others, as moral or immoral often by engaging in self-talk, that is, by having internal conversations among its constituent voices (Nienkamp, 2001). In short, the self is constructed by conversations that take place first externally, occurring among an expanding group of others, and then internally, occurring among internal voices within an individual's psyche (Mead, 1982; Nienkamp, 2001; Vygotsky, 1978).

As different and persuasive external conversations are internalized, the self begins to realize a larger self or web of commitments. The greater the variety and

persuasiveness of external conversations internalized, i.e., the greater the extent and depth of moral issues and justifications discussed in these conversations, the more conscious or aware the self becomes of its web of commitments, and hence the greater the variety of perspectives or roles the self may take to judge behaviors and decisions as moral or immoral. In a sense, the self becomes more aware or conscious of its embeddedness in multiple relational contexts (Emirbayer & Mische, 1998; Mead, 1932). The more aware or inclusive self is more attuned to differing moral perspectives, and thus may more easily empathize with others. As the self's ability to empathize increases so too does its ability to grasp the *kairos* of a situation, that is, "to speak, act, or decide appropriately to the time and situation" (Nienkamp, 2001, pp. 38–39).

Discussion

Conceptualizing the self as constructed and shaped by conversations, and conceptualizing organizations as a set of managerial conversations (cf., Ford, 1999) allow us to use rhetorical theory to study and operationalize the effects of managerial conversations on the self's moral reasoning and ethical/unethical decision making. These conversations create and shape "conceptual schemes" (Werhane, 1998) or "scripts", which enable understanding of ethical situations and provide a guide to ethical behavior and decision making within organizations (Gioia & Poole, 1984). Many scholars argue that organizations or managerial scripts may induce unethical behavior (Jones & Ryan, 1997; Misangyi, Weaver, & Elms, 2008; Trevino, Butterfield, & McCabe, 1998; Victor & Cullen, 1988; Werhane, 1998). According to Werhane, most of the unethical behavior in organizations result from managerial scripts that fail to trigger moral imagination (Werhane, 1998). For example, in his account of the Ford Pinto case, Gioia argues that managerial scripts in Ford failed to include ethical dimensions (Gioia, 1992), and emotions were a weak part of these scripts (Gioia, 1992), making it more difficult for Ford managers' to recognize the moral issue surrounding the Ford Pinto case. Other scholars have pointed out that organizations and managers may collectively and sometimes inadvertently endorse unethical behavior (Brief, Buttram, & Dukerich, 2001), rationalizing and normalizing their acts and decisions, and through the use of euphemistic language, turning, for example, bribes into "auditioning fees", "fringe benefits" (Anand, Ashforth, & Joshi, 2004, pp. 40–47; Ashforth, 2001; Ashforth & Kreiner, 2002), or "administrative gratuities" (Jones & Ryan, 1998, p. 439).

Direction For Future Research

Rhetorical theory may offer several analytical frameworks for understanding the role of language in moral reasoning. Managerial conversations that persuade the self to engage in ethical or unethical conduct can be analyzed in terms of

their content (what is communicated) and style (how it is communicated). For example, scholars may analyze managerial conversations in terms of their (a) use of persuasive appeals such as pathos (appealing to emotions and feelings), logos (appealing to the instrumental mind), ethos (appealing to the speaker's moral character and reputation); (b) virtues of style (correctness, clarity, evidence, propriety, ornateness); (c) oratorical style such as judicial (accuse/defend), deliberative (exhort/dissuade), epideictic (praise/blame); (d) use of figures of speech and thought; (e) use of tropes such as metaphor and irony. We believe there are systematic rhetorical differences between managerial conversations that persuade managers to behave ethically and those that fail to do so, between managerial conversations that took place in Enron before it collapsed and those in Johnson & Johnson before and after its Tylenol crisis.

Managerial conversations can be measured empirically in several places such as letters to shareholders, public speeches, annual reports, internal memos, special reports on specific issues, corporate announcements, board meeting minutes, or electronic communications such as electronic mail. Computer-aided text analysis software and scientifically validated dictionaries such as the Harvard IV–4 dictionary may be used to operationalize managerial conversations.

Limitations

There are two basic limitations of the main ideas expressed in this chapter. First, the self is exposed to a great number and variety of conversations. Thus, the conceptualization of the self as an expanding web of conversations may be too complex and dynamic and may not lend itself easily to scientific analysis. Second, although rhetorical theory can help scholars analyze conversations or texts, text/content analysis techniques may not dig deep enough to help scholars analyze rich meanings and interpretations that are hidden below the surface. In other words, these techniques may not help scholars read in between the lines.

Managerial Implications

Understanding the role of language and conversations in ethical decision making and moral reasoning is important particularly in the light of arguments that economic theories can be self-fulfilling, creating that which they predict (Ferraro, Pfeffer, & Sutton, 2005), and the evidence suggesting that exposure to the self-interest model makes individuals less cooperative (Frank, 2004; Frank, Gilovich, & Regan, 1993). We believe that an awareness of the effects of language and conversations on moral reasoning will enable managers and organizations to manage ethical conduct better, and educators to teach ethics in a more effective way. Through conversations and stories as diverse as those in religious texts, in ancient Greek myths, human beings have used rhetoric and language to share ethical codes and shape moral reasoning.

An Invitation

We call for management researchers to study in more detail the rhetoric of managerial conversations, to uncover the role of language and rhetoric in shaping the self and in constructing the interests the self seeks. We call for management researchers to make more explicit the role and power of language in moral reasoning, and to study the link between language and ethics in order to advance our understanding of ethical practice and decision making.

References

Anand, W., Ashforth, B. E., & Joshi, M. (2004). Business as usual: The acceptance and perception of corruption in organizations. *Academy of Management Executive, 18* (2), 39–53.

Anderson, J. (1997). What cognitive science tells us about ethics and the teaching of ethics. *Journal of Business Ethics, 16*, 279–292.

Aristotle. (1991). *The art of rhetoric*. New York: Penguin Books.

Ashforth, B. E. (2001). *Role transitions in organizational life: An identity-based perspective*. Mahwah, NJ: Erlbaum.

Ashforth, B. E., & Kreiner, G. E. (2002). Normalizing emotion: Making the extraordinary seem ordinary. *Human Resource Management Review, 12*, 215–235.

Azmitia, & Perlmutter. (1989). Social influences on young children's cognition: State of the art and future directions. In H. W. Reese (Ed.), *Advances in child development and behavior* (Vol. 22, pp. 89–145). New York: Academic Press.

Bakhtin, M. (1986). *Speech genres and other late essays* (V. W. McGee, trans.). Austin, TX: University of Texas Press.

Beauchamp, T. L., & Bowie, N. E. (Eds.). (1979). *Ethical theory and business*. Englewood Cliffs, NJ: Prentice-Hall.

Boatright, J. R. (1999). *Ethics in finance*. Malden, MA: Blackwell.

Booth, W. (1974). *Modern dogma and the rhetoric of assent*. Chicago: University of Chicago Press.

Booth, W. (1988). *The vocation of a teacher: Rhetorical occasions, 1967–1988*. Chicago: University of Chicago Press.

Brief, A., Buttram, R. T., & Dukerich, J. M. (2001). Collective corruption in the corporate world: Toward a process model. In M. E. Turner (Ed.), *Groups at work: Theory and research* (pp. 471–499). Mahwah, NJ: Erlbaum.

Burkitt, I. (1991). *Social selves: Theories of the social formation of personality*. London: Sage.

Churchman, C. W. (1983). *Thought and wisdom*. Seaside, CA: Intersystems Press.

Cooley, C. H. (1902). *Human nature and the social order*. New York: Scribners.

Crain, W. (2000). *Theories of development: Concepts and applications* (4th ed.). Upper Saddle River, NJ: Prentice Hall.

Dees, J. G. (1982). Principals, agents, and ethics. In N. E. Bowie & R. E. Freeman (Eds.), *Ethics and agency theory* (pp. 25–58). New York: Oxford University Press.

Dewey, J. (1976). *The middle works of John Dewey, 1899–1924* (Vol. 15). Carbondale: Southern Illinois University Press.

Diaz, R. M., & Berk, L. E. (1992). *Private speech: From social interaction to self-regulation*. Hillsdale, NJ: Erlbaum.

Emirbayer, M., & Mische, A. (1998). What is agency? *American Journal of Sociology, 103*, 962–1023.

Enos, T. (1996). *Encyclopedia of rhetoric and composition: Communication from ancient times to the information age*. New York: Garland.
Ferraro, F., Pfeffer, J., & Sutton, R. I. (2005). Economics language and assumptions: How theories can become self-fulfilling. *Academy of Management Review, 30*, 8–24.
Flanagan, O. J. (1991). *Varieties of moral personality: Ethics and psychological realism*. Cambridge, MA: Harvard University Press.
Ford, J. D. (1999). Organizational change as shifting conversations. *Journal of Organizational Change Management, 12*, 480–490.
Frank, R. H. (2004). *What price the moral high ground? Ethical dilemmas in competitive environments*. Princeton, NJ: Princeton University Press.
Frank, R. H., Gilovich, T., & Regan, D. T. (1993). Does studying economics inhibit cooperation? *Journal of Economic Perspectives, 7*, 159–171.
Freud, S. (1933). *New introductory lectures on psychoanalysis* (J. Strachey, trans.). New York: Norton.
Friedman, M. (1970, September 13). The social responsibility of business is to increase profits. *New York Times Magazine,* 33, pp. 122–126.
Fry, P. S. (1992). Assessment of private and inner speech of older adults in relations to depression. In R. M. Diaz & L. E. Berk (Eds.), *Private speech: From social interaction to self-regulation* (pp. 267–284). Hillsdale, NJ: Erlbaum.
Gill, A. M., & Whedbee, K. (1997). Rhetoric. In T. A. Van Dijk (Ed.), *Discourse as structure and process* (Vol. 1, pp. 157–184). Thousand Oaks, CA: Sage.
Gioia, D. A. (1992). Pinto fires and personal ethics: A script analysis of missed opportunities. *Journal of Business Ethics, 11*, 379–389.
Gioia, D. A., & Poole, P. P. (1984). Scripts in organizational behavior. *Academy of Management Review, 9*, 449–459.
Goodstein, J. D. (2000). Moral compromise and personal integrity: Exploring the ethical issues of deciding together in organizations. *Business Ethics Quarterly, 10*, 805–820.
Herrick, J. A. (2001). *The history and theory of rhetoric: An introduction* (2nd ed.). Boston: Allyn and Bacon.
James, W. (1967). *The writings of William James: A comprehensive edition*. New York: Random House.
Jensen, M. C., & Meckling, W. H. (1976). Theory of the firm: Managerial behavior, agency costs and ownership structure. *Journal of Financial Economics, 3*, 305–360.
John-Steiner, V. (1992). Private speech among adults. In R. M. Diaz & L. E. Berk (Eds.), *Private speech: From social interaction to self-regulation* (pp. 267–284). Hillsdale, NJ: Erlbaum.
Johnson, M. (1993). *Moral imagination: Implications of cognitive science for ethics*. Chicago: University of Chicago Press.
Jones, T. M. (1991). Ethical decision making by individuals in organizations: An issue-contingent model. *Academy of Management Review, 16*, 366–395.
Jones, T. M., & Ryan, L. V. (1998). The effect of organizational forces on individual morality: Judgment, moral approbation, and behavior. *Business Ethics Quarterly, 8*, 433–446.
Jones, T. M., & Ryan, V. L. (1997). The link between ethical judgment and action in organizations: A moral approbation approach. *Organization Science, 8*, 663–680.
Kegan, R. (1982). *The evolving self: Problem and process in human development*. Cambridge: Harvard University Press.
Kohlberg, L., Kauffman, K., Scharf, P., & Hickey, J. (1975). The just community approach to corrections: A theory. *Journal of Moral Education, 4*, 614–640.
Lakoff, G., & Johnson, M. (1999). *Philosophy in the flesh: The embodied mind and its challenge to Western thought*. New York: Basic Books.

Maanen, J. V. (1995). Fear and loathing in organization studies. *Organization Science, 6*, 687–692.
May, L. (1996). *The socially responsible self: Social theory and professional ethics*. Chicago: University of Chicago Press.
McCloskey, D. N. (1998). *The rhetoric of economics* (2nd ed.). Madison, WI: University of Wisconsin Press.
Mead, G. H. (1932). *The philosophy of the present*. Chicago: University of Chicago Press.
Mead, G. H. (1934). *Mind, self, and society*. Chicago: University of Chicago Press.
Mead, G. H. (1982). *The individual and the social self: Unpublished work of George Herbert Mead*. Chicago: University of Chicago Press.
Misangyi, V. F., Weaver, G. R., & Elms, H. (2008). Ending corruption: The interplay among institutional logics, resources, and institutional entrepreneurs. *Academy of Management Review, 33*, 750–770.
Nienkamp, J. (2001). *Internal rhetorics: Toward a history and theory of self-persuasion*. Carbondale, IL: Southern Illinois University Press.
O'Neill, J. (1997). Rhetoric, science, and philosophy. *Philosophy of the Social Sciences, 28*, 205–225.
Pauchant, T. C., & Mitroff, I. I. (1992). *Transforming the crisis-prone organization: preventing individual, organizational, and environmental tragedies*. San Francisco: Jossey-Bass.
Peirce, C. S. (1992). *The essential Peirce: Selected philosophical writings* (Vol. 11). Bloomington: Indiana University Press.
Peirce, C. S. (1931). *Collected papers of Charles Sanders Peirce* (Vol. 4). Cambridge: Harvard University Press.
Perelman, C., & Olbrechts-Tyteca, L. (1969). *The new rhetoric: A treatise on argumentation*. Notre Dame, IN: University of Notre Dame Press.
Plato. (1998). *Phaedrus* (J. H. Nichols, trans.). Ithaca, NY: Cornell University Press.
Porter, J. (1993). Developing a postmodern ethics of rhetoric and composition. In T. Enos & S. C. Brown (Eds.), *Defining the new rhetorics* (pp. 207–226). Newbury Park, CA: Sage.
Quinn, K. (1996). A rhetorical conception of practical rationality. *Journal of Economic Issues, 30*, 1127–1142.
Rand, A. (1943). *The fountainhead*. Indianapolis: Bobbs.
Rawls, J. (1999). *A theory of justice* (rev. ed.). Cambridge, MA: Belknap Press of Harvard University Press.
Rest, J. R. (1986). *Moral development: Advances in research and theory*. New York: Praeger.
Sandel, M. J. (1998). *Liberalism and the limits of justice* (2nd ed.). Cambridge, UK: Cambridge University Press.
Seabright, M. A., & Kurke, L. B. (1997). Organizational ontology and the moral status of the corporation. *Business Ethics Quarterly, 7*, 91–108.
Sen, A. K. (1977). Rational fools: A critique of the behavioral foundations of economic theory. *Philosophy and Public Affairs, 6*, 317–344.
Sen, A. K. (1993). Does business ethics make economic sense? *Business Ethics Quarterly, 3*, 45–54.
Smith, A. (1776). *An inquiry into the nature and causes of the wealth of nations*. Oxford: Oxford University Press.
Solomon, R. C. (1992). *Ethics and excellence*. New York: Oxford University Press.
Solomon, R. C. (1994). Business and the humanities: An Aristotelian approach to business ethics. In T. J. Donaldson & R. E. Freeman (Eds.), *Business as a humanity* (pp. 45–75). New York: Oxford University Press.

Taylor, C. (1985). *Philosophy and the human sciences*. Cambridge: Cambridge University Press.

Taylor, C. (1989). *Sources of the self: The making of the modern identity*. Cambridge, MA: Harvard University Press.

Thaler, R. H. (2000). From homo economicus to homo sapiens. *Journal of Economic Perspectives, 14*, 133–141.

Trevino, L. K., Butterfield, K. D., & McCabe, D. L. (1998). The ethical context in organizations: Influences on employee attitudes and behaviors. *Business Ethics Quarterly, 8*, 447–476.

Velasquez, M. G. (1994). Some lessons and nonlessons of casuist history. In T. J. Donaldson & R. E. Freeman (Eds.), *Business as a humanity* (pp. 184–195). New York: Oxford University Press.

Victor, B., & Cullen, J. (1988). The organizational bases of ethical work climates. *Administrative Science Quarterly, 33*, 101–125.

Vygotsky, L. S. (1962). *Thought and language* (E. Hanfmann & V. Gertrude, trans.). Cambridge, MA: MIT Press.

Vygotsky, L. S. (1978). Internalization of higher psychological functions. In M. Cole, V. John-Steiner, S. Scribner & E. Souberman (Eds.), *Mind in society: The development of higher psychological processes* (pp. 52–57). Cambridge, MA: Harvard University Press.

Werhane, P. H. (1998). Moral imagination and the search for ethical decision making in management. *Business Ethics Quarterly, 1*, 75–98.

Williamson, O. E. (1985). *The economic institutions of capitalism: Firms, markets, relational contracting*. New York: Free Press.

Current Topics in Management, Vol. 15, 2011, pp. 199-224

FLEXIBILITY, LEARNING, AND CONTROL: ENTRY MODE CHOICE UNDER UNCERTAINTY

Mujtaba Ahsan and Martina Musteen

There are a host of uncertainties that multinational enterprise (MNEs) managers must factor in when making entry mode decisions, some of which are learnable through firm actions while others remain unknown despite the MNEs actions. For example, demand uncertainty represents uncertainty that MNEs must consider when making entry mode decisions. Although this uncertainty exists at the time of making entry mode decision, it can subsequently be reduced by the firm's action such as market research, incremental product introductions and dealing with local channel members. On the other hand, political uncertainty is an example of uncertainty that is not learnable through MNEs actions.

A number of studies have investigated various forms of uncertainty arising in the local environments of host countries and their effect on entry strategies of MNEs (Miller, 1992). The predominant theoretical perspective used to examine the role of uncertainty on entry modes has been the transaction cost (TC) perspective (Brouthers & Hennart, 2007; Canabal & White, 2008). Its primary focus has been on the ways to minimize internal and external uncertainty arising from asset specificity and free-riding potential (Anderson & Gatignon, 1986; Gatignon & Anderson, 1988). While the TC perspective has provided invaluable insights into the entry mode choices of MNEs, one of the criticisms of this approach has been its lack of attention to opportunity costs (Brouthers, Brouthers, & Werner, 2008) and the dynamics associated with learning and knowledge development resulting from entering foreign markets (Meyer, Wright & Pruthi, 2009). Recently, scholars have turned to real options to explain entry mode choices and to overcome some of the weaknesses of the TC view (e.g., Brouthers et al., 2008; Fisch, 2008; Li & Rugman, 2007; Reuer & Tong, 2005;

Reuer & Tong, 2007; Tong, Reuer, & Peng, 2008). In this chapter, we draw on the real options perspective to develop a parsimonious theoretical framework that accounts for uncertainty arising in the local environment, firm capabilities and the effect of this uncertainty on the mode of entry. Specifically, our goal is to use real option reasoning to advance current theory and examine how uncertainty impacts MNEs' need for flexibility, control and learning in foreign markets and, in turn, the choice of entry mode.

By focusing on two broad types of uncertainty—exogenous and endogenous—we parsimoniously incorporate a host of uncertainties identified in previous literature (e.g., legal, political, demand, supplier, market, operating, behavioral, etc.) (Miller, 1992). We categorize uncertainties as either endogenous or exogenous where the former represents learnable uncertainties while the latter includes uncertainties that cannot be dispelled through firm's learning. The exo-endo distinction allows us to address the issue of uncertainty from the point of view of the MNEs and their capabilities (i.e., whether or not they have the capability to cope with the uncertainty). We argue that when the uncertainty is predominantly endogenous, firm managers will adopt entry modes that focus on learning (i.e., enhancing the ability of a firm to learn) while preserving certain degree of flexibility. However, when the uncertainty is predominantly exogenous, firm managers will develop entry mode strategy that provides most flexibility (i.e., entry mode strategies that limit irreversible commitments) while sacrificing development of new capabilities. However, we make a case that those relationships will be moderated by the attractiveness of the host market and the experience of MNEs. Specifically, greater market attractiveness and experience of MNEs is expected to increase the desire for more control.

This chapter makes two major contributions to the previous literature. First, in integrating the real options approach with the literature on learning and capability development, we put forward the notion that firm managers have the ability to learn to not only deal with present uncertainties but also to create future competitive advantages. Our chapter thus offers a more dynamic view of entry modes than the transaction cost (TC) perspective and pushes the research agenda on entry modes further. As Li (2007) noted in his recent review of real options theory and international strategy: "Real options theory presents ways to keep flexibility so as to strategically benefit from uncertainty, whereas transaction cost theory shows passive methods to control costs related to uncertainty" (p. 90). Second, our chapter also adds to the previous literature by conceptualizing entry modes in terms of three broad strategic objectives that they meet from the point of view of MNEs managers. Specifically, we advance the literature on entry modes by theorizing that depending on the type of uncertainty, local context and previous experience, MNEs will choose entry modes that provide either the most flexibility (i.e., reversibility of the international investment decision), shared learning and/or development of new capabilities (by way of dealing with local partners), or control over the international investment. Our chapter

is structured as follows: first, we provide a brief review of the literature on real options theory. Following a discussion of the different types of uncertainty relevant to the entry mode choices, we develop our propositions and present our theoretical framework. We conclude with discussion of the implications for theory and practice and directions for future research.

Theoretical Background

Research in strategic management has conceptualized real options as various investments such as equity joint ventures (Kogut, 1991), investments in emerging markets (Kogut & Kulatilaka, 1994a) and R&D projects (Ahsan, 2009; Folta, 1998). The reason for the increasing interest in real options theory is the practical concern that strategic decisions are often made under uncertainty (Dixit & Pindyck, 1994) and the theoretical appeal that real options theory has in capturing managers' flexibility in adapting their future actions to changing market or technological conditions (Brouthers et al., 2008). In its broadest interpretation, a real option is the right but not an obligation on the part of a firm to pursue or terminate a set of actions in the future (Mitchell & Hamilton, 1988). The primary advantage of holding a real option is that it offers flexibility to its holders by conferring them the ability to make deferred actions, i.e., an option to defer (McDonald & Siegel, 1986), or terminate the action, i.e., an option to abandon (Myers & Majd, 1990).

Real options must meet two criteria in order to be viable. First, the decision must be characterized by uncertainty and, second, the investment should not be easily reversible. That is, once the decision is made, it cannot be reversed without incurring cost. According to Dixit and Pindyck (1994), irreversibility arises from the fact that investments tend to be firm or industry-specific. In the case of the former, an investment has little or no value beyond the firm that carried it out. Marketing and R&D are examples of firm-specific investments. Similarly, purchasing commercial planes or thin slab steel mills are examples of industry-specific investment.

Under the conditions of uncertainty and irreversibility, holding an option represents the right to postpone the decision in order to resolve some of the uncertainty (Li & Rugman, 2007; McDonald & Siegel, 1986). In our case, this can be uncertainty surrounding MNEs host country environment. Once the decision to implement the strategy has been made (i.e., the option has been exercised by making an investment in another country, for example), the resources spent to implement the strategy cannot be easily recovered if the decision is revealed to be suboptimal.

In his recent review of real options theory in literature on international strategies, Li (2007) identified two streams of real options research: real options reasoning and real options modeling. The former deals with logical explanations of real option choices, with focus on managerial flexibility, and largely

highlights the importance of limiting upfront commitments and preserving the right to make future decisions in conditions shrouded by uncertainty. Studies grounded in this approach tend to consist of quantitative analyses of cross-sectional samples of entry modes made by actual companies. The latter approach centers on real-option models often combined with economic and game theory to explain the various strategies managers or firms should adopt to limit the downsides of uncertainty and take advantage of the new opportunities. Studies based on the modeling approach thus use simulation techniques as opposed to analysis of primary or secondary data based on entry mode choices of firms. There are several studies in both streams of research that address the role of uncertainty in the context of entry mode choices. Li and Rugman (2007), for example, used the modeling approach to generate propositions related to the location of foreign direct investment and type of investment under uncertainty. Based on the results of their simulation, they proposed that the potential to generate real options in non-home region prompts MNEs to build a subsidiary there. High option exercise cost, however, reduces the option value of investment outside of a home region. For example, a U.S. firm is more likely to build a subsidiary in Vietnam (i.e., non-home region) than in Mexico (i.e., home region) due to higher potential upsides in non-home regions. However, this decision is also influenced by the cost of operations; the high cost of operating in Vietnam than in Mexico due to greater adaptation issues will offset the potential upsides of locating a subsidiary in Vietnam; thereby, prompting the U.S. firm to build the subsidiary in the home region. This argument is consistent with previous studies that found that most MNEs operate in home regions (e.g., Rugman & Verbeke, 2004).

Perhaps the most relevant empirical study using the real options approach is that of Brouthers et al. (2008) who found that demand uncertainty increases the value growth options (i.e., JVs) while the length and diversity of previous international experience decreases such value and therefore calls for non-equity modes of entry or wholly owned subsidiaries. Reuer and Tong's (2005) study also used the real options approach to examine the determinants of firm's option to acquire equity in their international joint ventures (IJVs). They found that the likelihood that firms will have an explicit option to acquire such equity is highest for non-core IJVs (i.e., IJVs outside firm's primary business) in politically unstable countries with weak intellectual property regimes. In another study, Tong et al. (2008) found evidence that the value of MNEs growth options is enhanced when investments are made in non-core, minority-owned IJVs. In our study, we seek to extend the previous research by devising a three-dimensional theoretical framework that does not only distinguish between exogenous and endogenous uncertainty like some of the previous studies did (e.g., Li & Rugman, 2007) but also incorporates the role of local context and draws on a more fine-grained classification of entry mode choices. We focus on real options reasoning (not real option modeling). That

is, it is not our intention to model option-pricing solutions using well-specified parameters used in the real options modeling stream of literature (e.g., Chi & Seth, 2009; Fisch, 2008; Li & Rugman, 2007). Rather, we develop a model of strategic choice applicable to top managers' entry mode decisions involving uncertainty as arising from different political, cultural and competitive environments in foreign countries. The types of uncertainty that we consider in our framework are discussed next.

A Two Dimension Matrix of Uncertainty: Endogenous and Exogenous

A wide variety of definitions of uncertainty have been used in the literature. In general, uncertainty is described as a condition in which one cannot accurately predict the outcome of an event due to lack of information, and therefore cannot insure against it (Milliken, 1987; North, 1990) Simply put, uncertainty is the inability to assign a probability to future and predict the outcome of a decision (Miller & Shamsie, 1999). Uncertainty is often (but not always) distinguished from risk. While uncertainty refers to a situation where outcomes do not have known distribution, risk has been viewed as an uncertain realization that has known probability distribution (Adner & Levinthal, 2004; Knight, 1921). Under Knightian uncertainty, it is not possible for the MNEs managers to know *a priori* which outcome will occur, although it may be possible for them to estimate the probability of each outcome. Researchers have focused on many different uncertainties (Miller, 1992), such as exchange rate uncertainty (Campa, 1993), policy uncertainty (Delios & Henisz, 2003), demand uncertainty (Bollen, 1999), supplier uncertainty (Min & Galle, 1991), partner uncertainty (Chi & McGuire, 1996) and other environmental uncertainties, such as political, social and legal (Akhter & Robles, 2006; Kobrin, 1982).

Our chapter extends the previous literature in several respects. First, by distinguishing between only two types of uncertainty—exogenous and endogenous—our framework is more parsimonious and more suitable to the real options approach. Specifically, our theoretical perspective accounts for both competitive and supplier uncertainty as well as other types of uncertainty such as cultural, demand, policy, and political uncertainty. Second, our work highlights the importance of strategic flexibility and capability development and learning, which can help firms not only deal with present uncertainties, but also create future competitive advantage. Such learning occurs by means of successive investments (i.e., options).

The distinction between endogenous and exogenous uncertainty is well established in previous literature (Chi, 2000; Dixit & Pindyck, 1994; Folta, 1998; Li & Tong, 2007). The difference between the two forms of uncertainty depends on the MNEs ability to influence the uncertainty. Endogenous uncertainty relates to the internal function of the firm and refers to the uncertainty surrounding the physical difficulty of completing an investment. This uncertainty can be

reduced by the firm's actions and it is dependent upon firms' know-how (Chi, 2000; Folta, 1998). Roberts and Weitzman (1981) state that under conditions of endogenous uncertainty, firms undertaking sequential development of a project would benefit as each stage reveals new information that can be used to make a subsequent decision, i.e., at the end of each stage more and more information is generated and learning can occur incrementally (Folta, 1998). The learning that results from such actions is often firm-specific in nature and represents a valuable and proprietary asset. For example, a U.S. firm investing in China encounters a very different cultural environment. Cultural uncertainty is a type of endogenous uncertainty as this uncertainty can be reduced by firm's learning actions. By undertaking a small initial investment (e.g., exporting) the U.S. firm can gain some insights about the business practices and cultural norms in China, which leads to the reduction of this endogenous uncertainty.

Exogenous uncertainty is external to the firm and thus mostly independent of the firm's action; it includes factors such as unforeseen action by external entities (e.g., regulatory bodies, governments etc.). Thus, it is closest to the concept of uncertainty (as opposed to risk) given the unpredictability of the outcomes that occur exogenously of firm and its investments. Under conditions of exogenous uncertainty, firms have no knowledge about which capabilities are critical to deal with it (Folta, 1998). In contrast to endogenous uncertainty, MNEs can deal with exogenous uncertainty by monitoring the host country environment, i.e., this uncertainty can be reduced without initiating any investments. McDonald and Siegel (1986) posit that under conditions of exogenous uncertainty it is beneficial for firms to wait before incurring irreversible investments. This has two important implications. First, the information revealed by the resolution of exogenous uncertainty is not likely to be considered a proprietary asset of the firm since it is essentially a "free good" available to all and is independent of the process of completing an investment. Second, the effect of this form of uncertainty on the incentive to invest is to increase the value of waiting to initiate investment. This is especially important in regard to investments involving substantial levels of sunk cost (e.g., equity-based foreign market entry) since exercising the investment option is unnecessary to observe the resolution of exogenous uncertainty. For example, the uncertainty regarding political instability in a host country is a type of exogenous uncertainty as firm's action has no impact on reducing such uncertainty.

The uncertainties MNEs face in foreign markets can be both endogenous and exogenous in nature and they have different effects on entry mode decisions. Such decisions will also be affected by MNEs previous experience and the strategic importance and attractiveness of the local market. We draw on the literature on real options to develop a theoretical framework that allows for effective differentiation and understanding of uncertain environments and its effects on entry mode decision.

Theoretical Development and Propositions

The extant research on mode of entry has predominantly used the entry mode categorization based on the level of control and equity, typically conceptualized in dichotomous manner (i.e., equity vs. non-equity, shared-control vs. full control) (Datta, Herrmann, & Rasheed, 2002). However, recently, as scholars have applied more diverse theoretical perspectives to entry mode choices, including the RBV and real options approach, the entry modes have been also categorized based on the access to resources, learning and flexibility that they provide (Lee & Makhija, 2009; Meyer et al., 2009). Both learning and flexibility are notions that figure prominently in the real options perspective. Indeed, it is the learning and flexibility that makes real options attractive. The main notion is that real options are valuable because they allow for incremental learning that gives managers greater flexibility and allow them to respond to changing environment without committing large amounts of resources (Fisch, 2008). Thus, for the purpose of our theorizing, we distinguish between three categories of entry modes—(1) "flexibility" entry modes, which refer to minimum investment options that are relatively easy to reverse, (2) "collaborative" entry modes, which represent real options with high potential for experiential learning and development of distinct, difficult to imitate capabilities, and (3) "control" modes that allow the MNEs to internalize most activities in the foreign market and get the most direct access to local market and resources. The examples of flexibility modes include indirect and direct exporting, licensing, temporary project offices, distribution agreements and establishment of wholly owned branch office. Such entries are relatively easy to reverse given the low level of upfront investment and ability to relocate resources quickly; however, such modes also involve the least experiential learning (Meyer et al., 2009). The collaborative modes involve joint ventures with foreign partners and collaborative equity alliances. Such entry modes allow MNEs to tap into the local partners' knowledge base and learn through collaboration with such partners in the local market. The learning that occurs in collaborative alliances formed by foreign and local partners often involves transfer of tacit valuable knowledge given high levels of interaction between the two parties (Dhanaraj, Lyles, Steensma, & Tihanyi, 2004). At the same time, by sharing some costs and risks with foreign partners, such modes make the reversal of their investment less costly and thus offer some degree of flexibility (more so than control modes). Full acquisitions, dominant equity investments and greenfield ventures represent the control modes of entry. From the real options perspective, control modes represent options that have been exercised. Table 1 presents a summary of the classification of entry modes used in our theoretical framework and the theoretical framework is illustrated in Figure 1.

Table 1
Entry Modes Classification

	Flexibility Entry Modes	Collaborative Entry Modes	Control Entry Modes
	Exporting, Licensing, Distribution Agreement, Local Branch Office, Temporary project office	Joint Ventures, Collaborative Equity Alliances	Full Acquisitions, Dominant Equity Investments, Greenfield ventures
Level of Flexibility	High	Medium	Low
Degree of learning	Low	Medium/High	Medium/High
Level of control	Low	Medium	High

Endogenous Uncertainties, Learning, and Mode of Entry

As MNEs enter foreign markets, they face various uncertainties, which Miller (1992) categorized as general host country environment, industry and firm uncertainties due to the "liability of foreignness". The difference between the MNEs knowledge base and the knowledge required to operate in the host country gives rise to uncertainties. Of those, uncertainties related to host country culture, market, supplier, and partner are the most relevant endogenous uncertainties that MNEs reduce or dispel by their own actions.

Cultural uncertainty is related to the difficulty of operating in host country due to lack of understanding of its values, beliefs, and customs (Hofstede, 2001). Research indicates that lack of understanding of the host country culture could have serious negative effects on MNEs investment (Barkema, Bell, & Pennings, 1996; Hofstede, 2001). The rate at which the MNEs can learn about the host country culture depends on the "distance" of this culture to the MNEs. The more distant the culture of host country, the more difficult it is for MNEs to quickly learn it as it lacks the absorptive capacity to assimilate this new knowledge (Eriksson, Majkgard, & Sharma, 2000). Under such conditions, it is prudent to undertake sequential learning so that the firm can develop the requisite absorptive capacity to develop knowledge about the host country culture (Chang & Rosenzweig, 2001). Indeed, in order to understand "distant" cultures, MNEs generally form collaborative ventures with host country partners to help navigate and understand the ways of doing business in these countries (Kogut

& Singh, 1988). However, this could lead to self-seeking and opportunistic behavior on the part of the host country partners (Hennart & Zeng, 2002). The uncertainty regarding opportunistic behavior by host country partner is further exacerbated by the information asymmetry and difficulty in evaluating potential partners (Balakrishna & Koza, 1993). The partner uncertainty that MNEs experience when undertaking collaborative relationships in a host country is a type of endogenous uncertainty as it can only be reduced through learning. In other words, only by forming collaborative partnerships with host country firms can MNEs gain the knowledge and develop the capabilities to work with them (Ireland, Hitt, & Vaidyanath, 2002).

In addition to partner uncertainties, entering "distant" cultural markets can lead to difficulty in understanding the target market and, with it, market (demand) uncertainty. Hoskisson and Busenitz (2002) define market uncertainty "as the state of not knowing or a lack of knowledge about the future directions of a given market". Others (e.g., Brouthers et al., 2008; Miller, 1992) refer to market uncertainty as a lack of understanding of the market due to unexpected changes in demand. Market uncertainty can have a substantial impact on the introduction and development of international opportunities (Eriksson, Johanson, Majkgard & Sharma, 1997). Because it can be resolved by the actions of MNEs, it is endogenous in nature. MNEs can reduce market uncertainty by gradually learning about the host country market conditions (Black & Mendenhall, 1990).

Another type of endogenous uncertainty highlighted in prior literature is the supplier uncertainty (Kogut, 1988). Although this uncertainty has some overlap with partner uncertainty, it is differentiated by its focus on the supplier's ability to supply high quality raw materials on time to the MNEs (Min & Galle, 1991). This uncertainty can be gradually reduced as firms get better at assessing suppliers' competencies (Motwani et al., 1999).

As a result of coping with the endogenous uncertainties, MNEs can learn and develop important proprietary knowledge. The degree to which firms can learn depends on their absorptive capacity, which is a function of their existing knowledge base and prior learning experiences. Cohen and Levinthal (1989, 1990) define absorptive capacity as the ability to evaluate, integrate and use external knowledge to commercial ends. They argue that absorptive capacity is needed because it enables the firm to not only absorb and integrate new knowledge (i.e., augment the firm's knowledge base), but also respond to new opportunities (Cohen & Levinthal, 1990; Lane & Lubatkin, 1998). This suggests that MNEs have to make investments in the host country to learn about its cultural norms and business practices as such knowledge develops in path dependent manner and cannot be directly acquired from the market (Cohen & Levinthal, 1990; Grant, 1996; Nelson & Winter, 1982). Furthermore, MNEs that abstain or delay investments might be at a disadvantage as they fail to develop knowledge and capabilities to operate in the host country, which restricts their

future growth opportunities in the host country (Kogut & Kulatilaka, 1994; 2001). In the context of entry into foreign markets, MNEs can enhance their absorptive capacity to quickly develop capabilities to manage host country uncertainty by "learning by doing"—i.e., having presence (investing) in foreign markets. This capability that evolves over time and is largely tacit in nature can become a source of competitive advantage.

The real options literature views alliances as means through which firms can stage investments and learn incrementally (e.g., Brouthers et al., 2008; Kogut, 1991; Folta, 1998). At the same time, both joint ventures and collaborative equity alliances represent a real option that is relatively easily reversed (Kogut, 1991). They help MNEs proactively manage uncertainties by giving them some degree of strategic flexibility to increase commitment if their understanding of the host country market improves and, correspondingly, increasing their ability to exit the market quickly without incurring substantial loss should the host country market situation worsen. From the view point of the organizational learning literature, joint ventures and collaborative equity alliances represent an important vehicle by which a firm can leverage and acquire new competencies and learn (Kogut, 1991; Meyer et al., 2009; Reuer & Tong, 2005). Such equity arrangements allow firms to increase the speed of capability development and minimize uncertainty by acquiring and exploiting knowledge developed by partnered firms (Folta, 1998; Hamel, Doz, & Prahalad, 1989; Lane & Lubatkin, 1998). According to Luo (2002), JVs is a preferred mode when MNEs are seeking to build its capabilities in the host country. JVs not only help MNEs in acquiring country-specific knowledge such as market know-how, but also affect how they conduct business. This is an important feature of capability building for MNEs aiming at a long-term success in the host country (Luo, 2002). Likewise, collaborative equity alliances can be an important medium for learning about business practices embedded in the local environment (Meyer et al., 2009). Thus, based on the above discussion we argue that MNEs will undertake collaborative entry modes, such as JV or collaborative equity alliances, when entering host countries with high endogenous uncertainty because the initial costs (due to loss of control) will be more than offset by the gains in learning and strategic flexibility (e.g., Tihanyi, Griffith & Russell, 2005). By opting for collaborative equity alliances (e.g., JVs), MNEs can gain access to host country partner's knowledge of local business practices, market, suppliers, and cultural environment to manage endogenous uncertainty (Inkpen, 2000; Inkpen & Beamish, 1997). Although other forms of entry mode (e.g., exporting and arm's length distribution and marketing agreements) offer flexibility, they are not viable choices, as they are not structured to transfer "tacit knowledge," which is organizationally embedded (Kogut, 1988; Kogut & Zander, 1993). On the other hand, control entry modes such as full acquisitions or greenfields do not give the firms the advantage of incrementally learning and therefore reducing the risk that high endogenous uncertainty represents. Apart

from being less effective in mitigating uncertainty in dynamic environments, they also require greater market knowledge and more extensive analysis of the host country than the joint venture entry mode (Herrmann & Datta, 2006; Luo, 2002). Thus, *ceteris paribus*, a collaborative entry mode that focuses on learning (e.g., JV, collaborative equity alliances) will be favored over other types of entry mode.

> *Proposition* 1: The greater the endogenous uncertainty experienced by the MNEs the higher the likelihood that MNEs will adopt a collaborative entry mode than a control or flexibility entry mode.

The level of endogenous uncertainty MNEs experiences is directly related to the capability it has developed to deal with such uncertainty. According to Luo (2002), MNEs can build their capabilities by "learning from other organizations, creating new skills, or revitalizing existing skills in new situations" (p. 48). Current approaches to organizational learning emphasize social ties, routines and organizational members as repositories of knowledge and conceptualize learning as creating and updating capabilities in response to experiences (Argote & Ophir, 2002; Huber, 1991; Ingram, 2002; Schulz, 2002). The basic argument is that organizations collect experiences and draw and encode inferences in repositories of organizational knowledge, including formal rules, strategies, structures, technologies, organizational culture, and capabilities (Schulz, 2002). Organizational learning occurs when organizations successfully relate effective procedures from the past and utilize them in developing future options. According to Uhlenbruck, Meyer and Hitt (2003) knowledge acquisition is the key aspect of organizational learning, including drawing on existing knowledge within the firm and enhancing the extant knowledge base through environmental scanning and organizational experience. Hence, in the organizational learning theory, learning at firm-level is typically conceptualized as knowledge creation and knowledge acquisition (Argote, 1999; Grant, 1996).

In order to develop capabilities to deal with endogenous uncertainties MNEs have to develop the ability to encode experiential inferences into behavioral outcomes (Levitt & March, 1988). Firms that expand into foreign markets are likely to acquire knowledge about the host country culture, business context and other site-specific knowledge (Barkema et al., 1996). In a study on Dutch firms entering Central and Eastern European countries, Barkema and Drogendijk (2007) found that firms learn through foreign direct investment and can transfer some of their learning from one market to another. Indeed, they suggest that each investment offers the opportunities to learn to deal with local suppliers, customers, partners and governments. The new experiences result into cumulative learning that MNEs can use as it faces endogenous uncertainties arising in various local environments. In other words, MNEs that have experience in dealing with endogenous uncertainty in a broad range of countries will possess the absorptive capacity to develop capabilities to deal with endogenous

uncertainty in a new host country. This is particularly true when they have prior experience in countries with similar endogenous uncertainties. The learning that occurs in such environments is more likely to give MNEs the strategic flexibility (by way of suitable knowledge and capabilities) to deal with uncertainties in the new market. While previous experience with endogenous uncertainties is not going to remove such uncertainties in new markets altogether, it is likely to likely to make dealing with them more effective. Indeed, Buckley and Tse (1996) observed that many U.S. and European companies' entered East Germany immediately following the collapse of the Berlin wall through FDI investment mode of entry. They initiated this strategic action in order to gain growth options as they already had prior experience of doing business in West Germany. Similarly, Brouthers et al. (2008) provide evidence that prior experience offers the strategic flexibility that enables MNEs to deal with one type of endogenous uncertainty—the demand uncertainty—by allowing them to better adjust to local tastes or shift product/service offerings elsewhere. This suggests that MNEs with international experience have better abilities deal with uncertainties associated with international operations (Herrmann & Datta, 2006). As MNEs gain experience and accumulate knowledge about local markets, and business practices, they can forgo the "collaborative" entry modes (e.g., joint venture) that focus on learning and tapping local market knowledge of the partners and are more likely to enter new markets with higher commitment modes (e.g., greenfield) that offer greater control (Agarwal & Ramaswami, 1992; Luo & O'Connor, 1998). Thus, we argue that with experience in countries with similar endogenous uncertainty, MNEs' preference for collaborative modes of entry will weaken even as the endogenous uncertainty increases. At the same time, they will increasingly favor control modes of entry such as acquisitions and greenfield ventures.

> *Proposition* 2: The accumulated experience in countries with endogenous uncertainty moderates the relationship between endogenous uncertainty and collaborative entry mode, such that MNEs are more likely to prefer a control entry mode over a collaborative entry mode.

Exogenous Uncertainties, Flexibility and Mode of Entry

MNEs have to deal with a variety of exogenous uncertainties while operating in a host country (Hill, Hwang, & Kim, 1990). Prior research indicates that these uncertainties have a significant impact on MNEs entry decision (Root, 1987). The various exogenous uncertainties identified in prior literature include legal and regulatory uncertainty (Teisberg, 1993), macroeconomic uncertainty (Hassett & Metcalf, 1999), and political uncertainty (Delios & Henisz, 2003; Miller, 1992).

Political uncertainty refers to the inability of MNEs to predict political and regulatory developments (Kobrin, 1982; Miller, 1992). This uncertainty typi-

cally deals with the potential of political turmoil or unrest in the host countries and the probability that these developments will negatively impact the firm's operations and performance (Robock, 1971). Even large MNEs are likely to have little or no influence over this uncertainty. Political developments can affect the business environment in host countries through changes in regulation and other legal issues (Brewer, 1983) wherein legal issues concern not only the development of laws but also their enforceability. When protection of intellectual property rights is limited, firms risk dissemination of knowledge and resources to local parties and potential rivals (Teece, 1986). When their resources are not well protected due to weak intellectual property rights regime, MNEs are more likely to undertake a wait-and-see approach rather than committing large equity upfront (despite the desire to increase control over the venture). For example, in war-torn Iraq the legal and judicial system is largely dysfunctional. In such an undeveloped institutional (and highly politically uncertain) environment, laws will tend to be murky, inadequate and largely unenforceable. MNEs considering investing in such environments are uncertain about compliance and tax laws, labor rules and regulations and dispute resolutions due process (Henisz & Delios, 2001).

Another important exogenous uncertainty that could impact MNEs is the macroeconomic uncertainty in the host country. Miller (1992) defines macroeconomic uncertainty as randomness in prices and economic activities in a host country. This uncertainty specifically refers to the macroeconomic condition in a host country and includes all the unknowns about the economic situation. For example, a Finnish firm considering expanding its business by opening new operations in Iceland might experience significant macroeconomic uncertainty due to the financial credit crisis brought forth by the failure of the global banking system. Under such circumstances, it is obviously impossible for the Finnish MNEs to influence the macroeconomic conditions in Iceland.

A number of studies have supported the view that by limiting their level of ownership MNEs can mitigate the influence of exogenous uncertainties (Bradley, 1977; Brouthers, 2002; Kobrin, 1983). When the exogenous uncertainties are high, it is prudent for MNEs to limit their vulnerability by lowering their resource commitment and making sure that they can exit the market quickly without incurring substantial loss should the conditions worsen. Under such conditions, high ownership levels are not desirable, as they would lead to concomitant commitment that is difficult to reverse. Recent research indicates that when political uncertainty is high, MNEs tend to make lower commitments (Delios & Henisz, 2000) or wait until the uncertainty gets resolved (Rivoli & Salorio, 1996). Similarly, in host country with high macroeconomic uncertainty, MNEs are less likely to make large commitments (Goldberg & Kolstadt, 1995) as maintaining flexibility becomes important to mitigate this type of uncertainty (Sutcliffe & Zaheer, 1998). By engaging in entry modes such as exporting, licensing or establishing a local branch, MNEs can limit irreversible commit-

ment and maintain flexibility to respond to the exogenous uncertainty. Although these entry modes are associated with less control (Agarwal & Ramaswami, 1992), they offer increased flexibility to adapt to the changing environment. Furthermore, while collaborative alliances are important when learning and acquisition of new capabilities and resources are key criteria, in conditions of exogenous uncertainty, firms have no knowledge about which capabilities are critical for future success when the host country environment is arbitrary. Moreover, as endogenous uncertainty is low MNEs can delay investments and avoid drawing critical resources from other projects (Kogut, 1991). This suggests that, *ceteris paribus*, in high exogenous uncertainty, a "flexibility" mode of entry will be favored over other modes of entry.

> *Proposition* 3: The greater the exogenous uncertainty experienced by the MNEs the higher the likelihood that MNEs will adopt a flexibility entry mode than a control or collaborative entry mode.

The Impact of the Local Context

Although the collaborative entry mode is more valuable than other types of entry modes when endogenous uncertainty is prevalent, we argue that the value of collaborative entry modes is also influenced by the market attractiveness in the host country. We suggest that market potential and availability of unique resources increase the attractiveness and strategic importance of the host country. Vast body of research (Agarwal & Ramaswami, 1992; McCarthy, Puffer, & Simmonds, 1993; Meyer et al., 2009; Shama, 1995; Weinstein, 1977) indicates that market potential and unique resources of the host country are among the most important factors influencing entry mode decision. For example, Shama (2000) found that the most important variable influencing entry mode was host country market potential. Likewise, Tan and Vertinsky (1996) stated that market opportunities present in the host country may induce MNEs to enter earlier than they would if these opportunities were not present. They suggest that the timing of entry may reflect strategic imperatives such as responding to growing foreign market opportunities or ensuring market access. Furthermore, recent literature has suggested that in order to function in foreign markets, MNEs have to reconfigure their resources to suit the local context as the MNEs existing resources either do not "fit" the local context (Brouthers et al., 2008) or they are not readily transferable (Anand & Delios, 2002). This literature suggests that firms have to develop new resources or adapt their existing resources to fit the local environment either through internal development or acquire these resources from the local market in order to attain competitive advantage (Anand & Delios, 2002; Brouthers et al., 2008; Meyer et al., 2009). When the MNEs resources are fungible, they can be easily transferred to the local context. In such case, firms' entry mode is based on exploiting their exist-

ing resources (Meyer et al., 2009). However, not all the resources that MNEs possess are fungible; these include downstream resources such as marketing and distribution capabilities specific to the local context (Anand & Delios, 2002). Research suggests that MNEs requiring location-specific resources might be able to get them efficiently either through acquisitions (full or partial) or by forming joint ventures with local partners rather than through internal development (Anand & Delios, 2002; Kogut & Zander, 1992; Meyer et al., 2009). Thus, market potential and nature of local resources are likely to influence MNEs entry mode decision.

When the market potential is high and the resources sought by MNEs are valuable and unique (i.e., they are rare, non-substitutable or difficult to imitate), MNEs will likely initiate strategic action to gain access and control of these context-specific resource. In order to do so and in a desire to preempt competitors from accessing such unique resources, MNEs will likely accelerate the internationalization with respect to the given market (Buckley & Tse, 1996; Kulatilaka & Perotti, 1998; Li, 2007). In order to gain control, they will likely forego some of the flexibility offered by collaborative entry modes and choose modes that provide higher control. In other words, when entering highly attractive markets, the preference of MNEs for collaborative modes of entry as means of dealing with high endogenous uncertainty is likely to decrease in favor of high control modes. In sum, market attractiveness will trigger MNEs to adopt a high control entry mode in an effort to dissuade rivals from entering the market and to also gain more control over their strategic operations (Kulatilaka & Perotti, 1998; Li, 2007; Meyer et al., 2009). Hence we suggest that:

> *Proposition* 4a: Local market attractiveness moderates the relationship between endogenous uncertainty and collaborative entry mode so that MNEs are more likely to adopt a control entry mode than a collaborative entry mode.

We also argue that market potential moderates the relationship between exogenous uncertainty and entry mode decision. The existing literature suggests that the relationship between exogenous uncertainty and flexibility entry mode is weakened in the presences of high market potential. For example, McCarthy, Puffer, and Simmonds (1993) and Shama (1995) found that large market potential motivates MNEs to adopt a collaborative entry mode despite the presence of exogenous uncertainties. McCarthy et al. (1993) in their study on 42 New England companies doing business in the former Soviet Union found that an import-export strategy was used by 22 companies and joint ventures by 21 companies. They state that even though the companies perceived high exogenous uncertainties, the sheer size and potential of the market outweighed the downsides. Likewise, Shama (1995) in his study on entry strategies of U.S. firms into the Baltic states, East European countries, and the former Soviet Union found that the most popular entry strategies were exporting and joint

ventures. Furthermore, he found that Russia captured approximately one third of all entries because of its size and market potential.

Another example of aggressive commitments in high potential market despite the presence of exogenous uncertainty is the entry of Volkswagen to China. The German automaker entered the China through a joint venture with a local automaker in the early 1980s and quickly captured 50% of the car market, which it sustained for more than a decade (Li, 2007). However, this desire to actively initiate investments in the presence of exogenous uncertainty is influenced by market potential for MNEs products and services in the host country (i.e., opportunities for growth available to MNEs in that foreign market). For example, the CEOs and presidents of various companies had different perspectives on investment strategies in Russia. The president of Otis pursued an early and quick investment strategy in entering Russia whereas the CEO of Die Welt Development took a more cautious "wait-and-see" approach (Goldman, 1994).

Similarly, if the host country has unique resources (i.e., rare, non-substitutable or difficult to imitate resources) and attaining them could confer the holder competitive advantage in the local market, the MNEs are likely to be motivated to augment their resource base by getting access to them via modes of entry that involve higher control while still retaining some flexibility. Meyer et al. (2009) suggest that MNEs can gain local access to local resources either by collaborating with local firms or acquiring them. However, under high exogenous uncertainty conditions the market for acquisition might be suboptimal and problematic (Estrin, 2002; Meyer et al., 2009; Peng & Heath, 1996). Also, formal rules in an exogenous uncertainty environment could legally limit the equity stake that MNEs are allowed to hold. For example, the attempt Coke made to acquire Huiyuan failed as the Chinese government was reluctant to allow Coke to gain full control of this company (Bauerlein & Fairclough, 2009). Moreover, the market for acquiring resources is likely to be unrefined due to the difficulties encountered in governing transactions in presence of exogenous uncertainties (e.g., political uncertainty, legal and financial ambiguities etc.) (Khanna, Palepu, & Sinha, 2005; North, 1990; Peng, 2006). In such cases, MNEs will satisfy their need for local-context resources by undertaking collaboration with local firms (Luo, 2002; Madhok, 1997).

The above arguments suggest that despite the presence of exogenous uncertainty MNEs are more likely to invest aggressively in highly attractive markets in order to gain greater control. However, they are unlikely to undertake large investments through either acquisition or greenfield entry mode due to suboptimal market conditions in high exogenous uncertainty environments. Hence we suggest that:

> *Proposition* 4b: Local market attractiveness moderates the relationship between exogenous uncertainty and flexibility entry modes so that MNEs are more likely to enter through collaborative entry mode than a flexibility mode.

The Joint Effect of Endogenous and Exogenous Uncertainty

In the previous propositions we investigated the impact of either high endogenous uncertainty or high exogenous uncertainty on entry mode choice. In this section, we consider the joint effect high endogenous and exogenous uncertainty on entry mode. Researchers have argued that entry mode research should incorporate both endogenous uncertainty (e.g., cultural uncertainty) as well as exogenous uncertainty (e.g., policy uncertainty) in order to develop a more complete internationalization model (Delios & Henisz, 2003a; 2003b). We have already discussed that while building capabilities that minimize endogenous uncertainties is possible, it is extremely difficult, if not impossible to accomplish the same in case of exogenous uncertainty. We also argue that learning in environments with high levels of exogenous uncertainty is less transferable. While with time MNEs can adapt to exogenous risk in the local environment (Fisch, 2008), the decision makers are ignorant of the underlying causes of the uncertainty and the environment is unclear *ex post*. The ability to build new capabilities is impeded when the MNEs cannot predict the outcome or assign a probability to it (Luo, 2002). Indeed, Luo (2002) found that environmental complexity (i.e., macroeconomic, political/legal and socio-cultural dimensions) of the host country negatively impacted MNEs capability building.

Given our earlier arguments related to the first proposition, MNEs will choose a collaborative mode of entry in countries where the uncertainty is largely endogenous in nature in order to maximize the upside of their investment and strategically position themselves for growth once the uncertainty is resolved through learning. However, we argue that as both the dimensions of uncertainty increase, the environment becomes excessively complex and MNEs ability to effectively cope with the endogenous uncertainty decreases. In countries characterized by political turmoil as well as vastly different cultural and institutional environments (e.g., Zimbabwe), investing may be too risky. While endogenous uncertainty could be reduced through learning, acquisition of new knowledge and development of new capabilities is likely to be impeded given the unpredictability of the external environment. Thus, it is likely that under conditions of both high exogenous and endogenous uncertainty, MNEs will delay entering such markets until the exogenous uncertainty is resolved. However, MNEs may choose to enter a highly uncertain market when such a market is perceived as strategically important (e.g., when it is characterized by great market potential or unique, valuable resources). Under such circumstances, the MNEs are most likely to choose entry modes that offer flexibility in order to respond quickly to changing conditions. Once the exogenous uncertainty is favorably resolved, the flexibility modes can be scaled up relatively quickly. On the other hand, should the events turn out to be undesirable, the MNEs can exit relatively easily. Thus, we propose the following:

Proposition 5: The greater the endogenous and exogenous uncertainty experienced by the MNEs the higher the likelihood that MNEs will delay entry. However, MNEs that choose to enter such markets due to their "attractiveness" will adopt flexibility modes of entry.

Discussion

In this chapter, we sought to develop a parsimonious framework of entry mode decisions under uncertainty. In doing so, we drew on the real options reasoning but our theorizing was also informed by the literature on organizational learning and transaction cost perspective. We considered three types of entry modes based on their suitability in meeting strategic objectives of MNEs in terms of providing flexibility, learning and control and developed propositions that link them with two types of uncertainty—endogenous and exogenous. We have highlighted that uncertainty affects MNEs operations in more than one manner and that the interplay between the two types of uncertainty and the local context has a potential for guiding theory explaining the entry mode choices of firms in foreign markets. Using the three-dimensional framework depicted in Figure 1 to describe the host country environments allows us to meaningfully understand the challenges faced by MNEs while operating in uncertain host country environments.

This framework provides a more precise, theoretically grounded description of uncertainties facing MNEs in various countries while taking into account the strategic importance of learning and attractiveness of the host market. In particular, we suggest that collaborative modes of entry position MNEs to deal with endogenous uncertainty and in doing so allow them to develop often difficult-to-imitate capabilities and be source of future growth opportunities. Although some researchers have debated the importance of building capabilities in volatile and uncertain markets (Wernerfelt, 1984; Porter, 1986), we argue that MNEs actions have little influence on exogenous uncertainty as the environments are too ambiguous for capability development to take place. Thus, the

Figure 1
Theoretical Framework

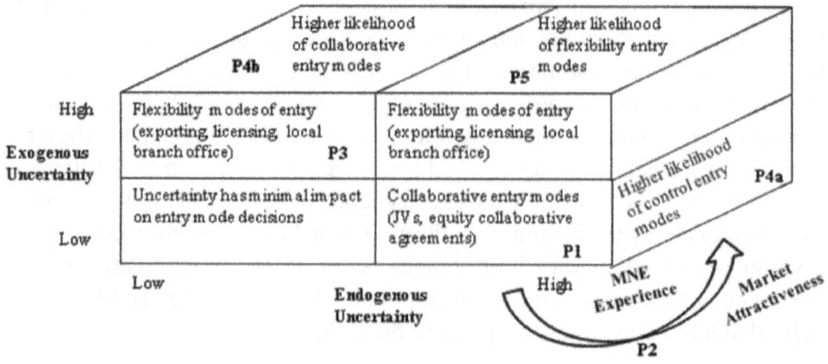

most appropriate entry modes are those that offer the highest levels of flexibility such as exporting and local branch office.

By incorporating the role of the local context and learning, we add to the entry mode literature which has been predominantly transaction oriented and discounted the importance of development of capabilities and strategic positioning that can affect firms' success in the long term. By explicitly accounting for multi-dimensionality of entry modes in terms of control, flexibility and learning in our propositions, we go beyond most of the previous research that has typically focused on dichotomized classification of entry modes (e.g., full-control vs. shared-control, equity vs. non-equity).

Implications for Management

Our three-dimensional framework has several implications for MNEs managers making strategic decision regarding entry mode choice. First, it highlights the importance of distinguishing the uncertainty in a particular country from those that are present in other countries. Despite of the falling barriers to international trade, managing firms across national boundaries still represents a substantial challenge even for the largest and most successful companies (Ghemawat, 2007). As our chapter suggests, a careful analysis of (often changing) uncertainties in the context of host country prior to entry is one of the most important tasks of managers of internationalizing firms. Second, our chapter emphasizes learning as a way of reducing or dispelling endogenous uncertainty and underscores the difficulty that MNEs face in developing capabilities to counter exogenous uncertainty. Our framework stresses the difficulty in hedging against exogenous uncertainty and draws attention to the importance of choosing an appropriate entry mode that places a premium on strategic flexibility as an *ex ante* mechanism. This is so even when firms have previous international experience. While such experience provides MNEs managers with insights that can help them cope with endogenous uncertainties in new markets and, as a result, enables them to enter via higher control modes, it is not applicable in case of exogenous uncertainty.

Our theory is particularly relevant to managers given the rise of MNEs investments in emerging economies. As Luo (2001) has observed, while uncertainty is present in most markets, it is more widespread in emerging and under-developed economies. The nature of uncertainty in such economies is changing along with the changes in the local institutional environment and other factors, as Steensma, Tihanyi, Lyles and Dhanaraj (2005) have documented in their longitudinal study of IJVs in Hungary.

Directions for Future Research

Our chapter has important implications for future research. Besides testing our model empirically, future studies should consider refining it further by taking

into account MNEs motives for entry (e.g., market-seeking vs. resource-seeking; Buckley, Cross, Tan, Xin & Voss, 2008) and managers' perception of risk. Likewise, in addition to uncertainty, the theoretical framework could be enriched by considering the role of local government. For example, one could argue that the recent acquisition-based entries of Chinese firms into African countries such as Zimbabwe, Zambia, and Mali go against our argument that under conditions of both high endogenous and exogenous uncertainty, firms either delay investment or enter via flexibility modes (Zhan, 1995). However, such entries are probably mostly motivated by the desire to control resources as opposed to finding markets. It may also be that in such environments, there are less likely to be protectionist measures due to the ill-developed local economy. Such considerations may induce the Chinese firms to enter with high control modes and capture rents efficiently. Our propositions could be tested using the simulation methodology (e.g., Li & Rugman, 2007) or using archival data of entry modes of companies over period of time (e.g., Musteen, Datta, & Hermann, 2009).

Limitations

Our study provides some interesting insights on the topic of entry modes under conditions of uncertainty; however, it has some limitations. While highlighting the importance of strategic flexibility and learning as ways of coping with endogenous uncertainty, we have not discussed in depth how such learning takes place. We posited that firms tend to learn incrementally and often with help of partners, but the specifics of learning regarding the domains and the role of managers in such learning has been beyond the scope of our chapter. Our study also considers market attractiveness somewhat broadly. Depending on what the motivation of the firm is to enter a particular market, what is considered "attractive" may differ and may have a different impact on the entry mode choice as well. As mentioned earlier, future research needs to consider the influence of MNEs primary motivation for new market entry since it has not been a part of our study. Finally, our chapter is limited since it does not take into account the effect of the timing of entry (in light of other entries).

Conclusion

Our chapter provides a parsimonious explanation of entry mode choice that encompasses both the explanations derived from the transaction cost theory, which has dominated the entry mode literature (Brouthers & Hennart, 2007) and other theoretical perspectives such as the resource-based view (Meyer et al., 2009) used to explain the entry mode decisions. Recognizing that different types of uncertainty inform the entry mode choice in a systematically different way and can lead to development of valuable capabilities, our chapter provides not only a fuller, more holistic explanation of the entry mode choice, but offers

normative recommendations to MNEs managers. By incorporating the role of the local context and learning, we also add to the entry mode literature, which has been predominantly transaction-oriented, and we have discounted the importance of the development of capabilities and strategic positioning that can affect firms' success in the long term. Finally, by explicitly accounting for the multi-dimensionality of entry modes in terms of control, flexibility and learning in our propositions, we go beyond most of the previous research that has typically focused on dichotomized classification of entry modes (e.g., full-control vs. shared-control, equity vs. non-equity).

References

Adner, R., & Levinthal, D.A. (2004). What is not real option: identifying boundaries for the application of real options to business strategy. *Academy of Management Review, 29*, 74–85.

Agarwal, S., & Ramaswami, S. N. (1992). Choice of foreign market entry mode: Impact of ownership, location and internalization Factors. *Journal of International Business Studies, 23*, 1–27.

Ahsan, M. (2009). Adaptation to competence-destroying change: A real options perspective. In M. A. Rahim (Ed.), *Current topics in management* (Vol. 14, pp. 73–94). New Brunswick, NJ: Transaction Publishers.

Akhter, S. H., & Robles, F. (2006). Leveraging internal competency and managing environmental uncertainty: Propensity to collaborate in international markets. *International Marketing Review, 23*, 98–115.

Anand, J., & Delios, A. (2002). Absolute and relative resources as determinants of international acquisitions. *Strategic Management Journal, 23*, 119–134.

Anderson, E., & Gatignon, H. (1986). Models of foreign entry: A transaction cost analysis and propositions. *Journal of International Business Studies, 17*, 1–26.

Argote, L. (1999). *Organizational learning: Creating, retaining and transferring knowledge*. Boston, MA: Kluwer.

Argote, L., & Ophir, R. (2002). Intraorganizational learning. In J. Baum (Ed.), *Companion to organizations* (pp. 181–207). Oxford, UK: Blackwell.

Balakhrishna, S., & Koza, M. P. (1993). Information Asymmetry, Adverse Selection, and Joint Ventures. *Journal of Economic Behavior and Organization, 20*, 99–117.

Barkema, H. G., Bell, J. H., & Pennings, J. M. (1996). Foreign entry, cultural barriers and learning. *Strategic Management Journal, 17*, 151–166

Barkema, H. G., & Drogendijk, R. (2007). Internationalising in small, incremental or larger steps? *Journal of International Business Studies, 38*, 1132–1148.

Bauerlein, V., & Fairclough, G. (2009, March 19). Beijing thwarts coke's takeover bid. *Wall Street Journal*, p. B1.

Black, J. S., & Mendenhall, M. (1990). Cross-cultural training effectiveness: A review and a theoretical framework for future research. *Academy of Management Review, 15*, 113–136.

Bollen, N. (1999). Real options and product life cycles. *Management Science, 45*, 670–684.

Bradley, D. G. (1977). Managing against expropriation. *Harvard Business Review*, 55 (4). 75–83.

Brewer, T. (1983). Political sources of risk in the international money markets: conceptual, methodological, and interpretative refinements. *Journal of International Business Studies, 14*, 161–164.

Brouthers, K. D. (2002). Institutional, cultural and transaction cost influences on entry mode choice and performance. *Journal of International Business Studies, 33*, 203–221.

Brouthers, K. D., & Hennart, J. (2007). Boundaries of the firm: Insights from international entry mode research. *Journal of Management, 33*, 395–425.

Brouthers, K. D., Brouthers L. E., & Werner, S. (2008). Real options, international entry mode choice and performance. *Journal of Management Studies, 45*, 936–960.

Buckley, A., & Tse, K. (1996). Real operating options and foreign direct investment: A synthetic approach. *European Management Journal, 14*, 304–314.

Buckley, P. J., Cross, A. R., Tan, H., Liu, X., & Voss, H. (2008). Historic and emergent trends in Chinese outward direct investment. *Management International Review, 6*, 715–748.

Campa, J. (1993). Entry by foreign firms in the US under exchange-rate uncertainty. *Review of Economics and Statistics, 75*, 614–622.

Canabal, A., & White, G. O. (2008). Entry mode research: Past and future. *International Business Review, 17*, 267–284.

Chang, S. J., & Rosenzweig, P. M. (2001). The choice of entry mode in sequential foreign direct investment. *Strategic Management Journal, 22*, 747–772.

Chi, T., & Seth, A. (2009). A dynamic model of the choice of mode for exploiting complementary capabilities. *Journal of International Business Studies, 40*, 365–387.

Chi, T. (2000). Option to acquire or divest a joint venture. *Strategic Management Journal, 21*, 665–687.

Chi, T., & McGuire D. J. (1996). Collaborative ventures and value of learning: Integrating the transaction cost and strategic option perspectives on the choice of market entry modes. *Journal of International Business Studies, 27*, 285–307.

Cohen, W. M., & Levinthal, D. A. (1989). Innovation and learning: Two faces of R&D. *Economic Journal, 99*, 569–596.

Cohen, W. M., & Levinthal, D. A. (1990). Absorptive capacity: A new perspective on learning and innovation. *Administration Science Quarterly, 35*, 128–152.

Datta, D. K., Hermann, P., & Rasheed, A. (2002). Choice of foreign market entry modes: Critical review and future directions. In M. A. Hitt & J. Cheng (Eds.), *Advances in International Management* (pp. 85–153) Greenwich, CT: JAI Press.

Delios, A., & Henisz, W. J., (2000). Japanese firms' investment strategies in emerging economies. *Academy of Management Journal, 43*, 305–323.

Delios, A., & Henisz, W. J. (2003a). Policy uncertainty and the sequence of entry by Japanese firms, 1980–1998. *Journal of International Business Studies, 34*, 227–241.

Delios, A., & Henisz, W. J. (2003b). Political hazards, experience, and sequential entry strategies: the international expansion of Japanese firms, 1980–1998. *Strategic Management Journal, 24*, 1153–1164.

Dhanaraj, C., Lyles, M. A., Steensma, H. K., & Tihanyi, L. (2004). Managing tacit and explicit knowledge transfer in IJVs: The role of relational embeddedness and the impact on performance. *Journal of International Business Studies, 35*, 428–442.

Dixit, A. K., & Pindyck R. S. (1994). *Investment under uncertainty*. Princeton, NJ: Princeton University Press.

Eriksson, K., Johanson, J., Majkgard, A., & Sharma, D. D. (1997). Experiential knowledge and cost in the internationalization process. *Journal of International Business Studies, 28*, 337–360.

Eriksson, K., Majkgard, A., & Sharma, D. D. (2000). Path dependence and knowledge development in the internationalization process. *Management International Review, 40*, 307–329.

Estrin, S. (2002). Competition and corporate governance in transition. *Journal of Economic Perspective. 16*, 101–124.

Fisch, J. H. (2008). Investment in new foreign subsidiaries under receding perception. *Journal of International Business Studies, 39*, 370–386.

Folta, T. B. (1998). Governance and uncertainty: The tradeoff between administrative control and commitment. *Strategic Management Journal, 19*, 1007–1028.

Gatignon, H., & Anderson, E. (1988). The multinational corporation's degree of control over foreign subsidiaries: an empirical test of a transaction cost explanation. *Journal of Law, Economics, and Organization, 4*, 305–336.

Ghemawat, P. (2007). *Redefining global strategy*. Boston: Harvard Business School Press.

Goldberg, L., & Kolstadt, C. (1995). Foreign direct investment, exchange rate and demand uncertainty. *International Economic Review, 36*, 855–73.

Goldman, M. I, (1994, May-June). The Russian investment dilemma. *Harvard Business Review*, pp. 35–44.

Grant, R. M. (1996). Toward a knowledge-based theory of the firm. *Strategic Management Journal, 17*, 109–122.

Hamel, G., Doz, Y. L., & Prahalad, C. K. (1989). Collaborate with your competitors—And win. *Harvard Business Review, 67* (1), 133–139.

Hassett, K. A. & Metcalf, G. E. (1999). Investment with uncertain tax policy: Does random tax policy discourage investment? *Economic Journal, 109*, 372–393.

Henisz, W. J., and Delios, A. (2001). Uncertainty, imitation, and plant location: Japanese multinational corporations, 1990–1996. *Administrative Science Quarterly, 46*, 443–475.

Hennart, J., & Zeng, M. (2002). Cross-cultural differences and joint venture longevity. *Journal of International Business Studies, 33*, 699–716.

Herrmann, P., & Datta, D. K., (2006). CEO experiences: Effects on the choice of FDI entry mode. *Journal of Management Studies, 43*, 756–778.

Hill, C., Hwang, P., & Kim, W. C. (1990). An eclectic theory of the choice of international entry mode. *Strategic Management Journal, 11*, 117–128.

Hofstede, G. (2001). *Culture's consequences : Comparing values, behaviors, institutions, and organizations across nations* (2nd Ed.). Beverly Hills: Sage.

Hoskisson, R. E., & Busenitz, L. W. (2002). Market uncertainty and learning distance in corporate entrepreneurship entry mode choice. In M. A. Hitt, D. R. Ireland, S. M. Camp, & D. L. Sexton (Eds.), *Strategic entrepreneurship: Creating a new mindset* (pp. 151–172). Oxford, UK: Blackwell.

Huber, G. P. (1991). Organizational learning: The contributing processes and the literatures. *Organization Science, 2*, 88–115.

Ingram, P. (2002). Interorganizational learning. In J. Baum (Ed.), *Companion to organizations* (pp. 642–663). New York: Blackwell.

Inkpen, A. C. (2000). Learning through joint ventures: A framework of knowledge acquisition. *Journal of Management Studies, 37*, 1022–1043.

Inkpen, A. C., & Beamish P. W. (1997). Knowledge, bargaining power and the instability of international joint ventures, *Academy of Management Review, 22*, 177–202.

Ireland, R. D., Hitt, M. A., & Vaidyanath, D. (2002). Alliance management as a source of competitive advantage. *Journal of Management, 28*, 413–446.

Khanna, T., Palepu, K., & Sinha, J. (2005). Strategies that fit emerging markets. *Harvard Business Review*, pp. 6–15.

Killing, P. J. (1982, May-June). How to make a global joint-venture work. *Harvard Business Review*, pp. 120–127.

Knight, F. H. (1921). *Risk, uncertainty and profit*. Boston, MA: Houghton Mifflin.

Kobrin, S. J. (1982) *Managing political risk assessment: Strategic response to environmental change*. Berkeley, CA: University of California Press.

Kobrin, S. J. (1983). Selective vulnerability and corporate management. In T. H. Moran (Ed.), *International political risk assessment: The state of the art* (pp. 9–13). Washington, DC: Georgetown University Press.

Kogut, B. (1988). Joint ventures: Theoretical and empirical perspectives. *Strategic Management Journal, 9*, 319–332.

Kogut, B. (1991). Joint ventures and the option to expand and acquire. *Management Science, 37*,19–33.

Kogut, B., & Singh, H. (1988). The effect of national culture on the choice of entry mode. *Journal of International Business Studies, 19*, 411–32.

Kogut, B., & Kulatilaka, N. (1994). Operational flexibility, global manufacturing, and the option value of a multinational network. *Management Science, 40*, 123–139.

Kogut, B., & Kulatilaka, N. (2001). Capabilities as real options. *Organizational Science, 12*, 744–758.

Kogut, B., & Zander, U. (1992). Knowledge of the firm, combinative capabilities, and the replication of technology. *Organization Science, 3*, 383–97.

Kogut, B., & Zander, U. (1993). Knowledge of the firm and the evolutionary theory of the multinational corporation. *Journal of International Business Studies, 24*, 625–45.

Kulatilaka, N., & Perotti, E. C. (1998). Strategic growth options. *Management Science, 44*, 1021–1031.

Lane P. J., & Lubatkin, M. (1998). Relative absorptive capacity and interorganizational learning. *Strategic Management Journal, 19*, 461–477.

Lee, S., & Makhija, M. (2009). Flexibility in internationalization: Is it valuable during an economic crisis? *Strategic Management Journal, 30*, 537–555.

Levitt, B., & March, J. G. (1988). Organizational learning. *Annual Review of Sociology, 14*, 319–340.

Li, J. (2007). Real options theory and international strategy: A critical review. *Advances in Strategic Management, 24*, 67–101.

Li, J., & Rugman, A. M. (2007). Real options and the theory of foreign direct investment. *International Business Review*, 16, 687–712.

Li, J., & Tong, T. W. (2007). Real options and international strategic management. In S. Tallman (Ed.), *A new generation in international strategic management* (pp. 100–118). Northampton, MA: Elgar.

Luo, Y. (2001). Determinants of entry in an emerging economy: A multilevel approach. *Journal of Management Studies, 38*, 443–72.

Luo, Y. (2002). Capability exploitation and building in a foreign market: Implications for multinational enterprises. *Organization Science, 13*, 48–63.

Luo, Y., & O'Connor, N. (1998). Structural changes of foreign direct investment in China: An evolutionary perspective. *Journal of Applied Management Studies*, 7, 95–109.

Madhok, A. (1997). Cost, value and foreign market entry mode: the transaction and the firm. *Strategic Management Journal, 18*, 39–61.

McCarthy, D. J., Puffer, S. M., & Simmonds, P. J. (1993). Riding the roller coaster: U.S. firms' recent experience and future plans in the former USSR. *California Management Review, 36* (1), 106–109.

McDonald, R., & Siegel, D. (1986). The value of waiting to invest. *Quarterly Journal of Economics, 101*, 707–728.

McGrath, R. G., Ferrier, W. J., & Mendelow, A. (2004). Real options as engines of choice and heterogeneity. *Academy of Management Review, 29*, 86–101.

Meyer, K. E., Wright, M., & Pruthi, S. (2009). Managing knowledge in foreign entry strategies: A resource-based analysis. *Strategic Management Journal, 30*, 557–574.

Miller, D., & Shamsie, J. (1999). Strategic responses to three kinds of uncertainty: Product line simplicity at the Hollywood Film Studios. *Journal of Management, 25*, 97–116.

Miller, K. D. (1992), A framework for integrated risk management in international business. *Journal of International Business Studies*, *23*, 311–31.

Milliken, F. J. (1987). Three types of perceived uncertainty about the environment: State, effect, and response uncertainty. *Academy of Management Review*, *12*, 133–143.

Min, H., & Galle, W. P. (1991). International purchasing strategies of multinational U.S. firms. *International Journal of Purchasing and Materials Management*, *27*, 9–18.

Mitchell, G., & Hamilton, W. (1988). Managing R&D as a strategic option. *Research Technology Management*, *31*, 15–22.

Motwani, J., Youssef, M., Kathawala, Y., & Futch, E. (1999). Supplier selection in developing countries: A model development. *Integrated Manufacturing Systems*, *10*, 154–161.

Myers, S. C., & Majd, S. (1990). Abandonment value and project life. *Advances in Futures and Options Research*, *4*, 1–21.

Nelson, R., & Winter, S. (1982). *An evolutionary theory of economic change*. Cambridge, MA: Belknap Press.

North, D. C. (1990). *Institutions, institutional change and economic performance*. Cambridge, MA: Cambridge University Press

Peng, M. W., & Heath, P. (1996). The growth of the firm in planned economies in transition: institutions, organizations, and strategic choices. *Academy of Management Review*, *21*, 492–528.

Peng, M. W. (2006). *Global business*. Cincinnati, OH: South-Western.

Porter, M. E. (1986). Competition in global industries: A conceptual framework. In M. E. Porter (Ed.), *Competition in global industries* (pp. 15–60). Boston: Harvard Business School Press.

Reuer, J. J., & Tong, T. W. (2005). Real options in international joint ventures. *Journal of Management*, *31*, 403–423.

Reuer, J. J., & Tong, T. W. (2007). How do real options matter? Empirical research on strategic investments and firm performance. *Advances in Strategic Management*, *24*, 145–173.

Rivoli, P., & Salorio, E. (1996). Foreign direct investment and investment under uncertainty. *Journal of International Business Studies*, *27*, 335–357.

Roberts, K., & Weitzman, M. L. (1981). Funding criteria for research, development and exploration project. *Econometrica*, *49*, 1261–1288.

Robock, S. H. (1971, July-August). Political risk: Identification and assessment. *Columbia Journal of World Business*, pp. 6–20.

Root, R. R. (1987). *Entry strategies for international markets*. Lexington, MA: Lexington Books.

Rugman, A., & Verbeke, A. (2004). A perspective on regional and global strategies of multinational enterprises. *Journal of International Business Studies*, *35*, 3–18.

Schulz, M. (2002). Organizational Learning. In J. Baum (Ed.), *Companion to organizations* (pp. 415–441). New York: Blackwell.

Shama, A. (1995). Entry strategies of U.S. firms to the newly independent states, Baltic states and eastern European countries. *California Management Review*, *37* (3), 90–109.

Shama, A. (2000). Determinants of entry strategies of U.S. companies into Russia, the Czech Republic, Hungary, Poland, and Romania. *Thunderbird International Business Review*. *42*, 651–676.

Steensma, H. K., Tihanyi, L., Lyles, M. A., & Dhanaraj, C. (2005). The evolving value of foreign partnerships in transitioning economies. *Academy of Management Journal*, *48*, 213–235.

Sutcliffe, K. M., & Zaheer, A. (1998). Uncertainty in the transaction environment an empirical test. *Strategic Management Journal*, *19*, 1–23.

Tan, B., & Vertinsky, I. (1996). Foreign direct investment by Japanese electronics firms in the United States and Canada: Modelling the timing of entry. *Journal of International Business Studies*, *27*, 655–681.

Teece, D. (1986). Profiting from technological innovation: Implication for integration, collaboration, licensing and public policy. *Research Policy*, *15*, 285–305.

Teisberg, E. O. (1993). Capital investment strategies under uncertain regulation. *Rand Journal of Economics*, *24*, 591–604.

Tihanyi, L., Griffith, D. A., & Russell, C. (2005). The effect of cultural distance on entry mode choice, international diversification, and MNE performance: A meta-analysis. *Journal of International Business Studies*, *36*, 270–83.

Tong, T. W., Reuer, J. J., & Peng, M. W. (2008). International joint ventures and the value of growth options. *Academy of Management Journal*, *51*, 1014–1029.

Uhlenbruck, K., Meyer, K. E., & Hitt, M. (2003). Organizational transformation in transition economies: Resource-based and organizational learning perspectives. *Journal of Management Studies*, *40*, 257–282.

Weinstein, A. (1977). Foreign investments by service firms: The case of the multinational advertising agency. Journal *of International Business Studies*, *8*, 83–91.

Wernerfelt, B. (1984). A resource-based view of the firm. *Strategic Management Journal*, *5*, 171–180.

Zhan, J. X. (1995). Transnationalization and outward investment: The case of Chinese Firms. *Transnational Corporations*, *4*, 67–100.

Current Topics in Management, Vol. 15, 2011, pp. 225-240

THE POLITICS–ADMINISTRATION CONTINUUM IN AMERICAN STATE GOVERNMENTS: ADMINISTRATIVE ACCOUNTABILITY AS A POSITIVE-SUM PATTERN

Cheryl M. Miller and Deil S. Wright

In this study we assess the views of state agency heads of the influence that they and their staff, as well as various institutional and external actors, exert on agency policymaking. Do administrators look both inward and outward for policy guidance? Using surveys conducted in the most recent three decades, we examine the level and pattern of influence relationships among several policy actors to discern if non zero-sum (negative) associations exist between gains in influence by one actor and losses by other actors.

One of the paramount practical as well as theoretical issues regarding the mingling of policy and administration is the extent to which this blending occurs because of the aggrandizing tendencies of bureaucracy, or because of the lack of external influence and oversight by institutional and other actors (Bowling, Chung-Lae, & Wright, 2004; Downs, 1967; Holden, 1966; O'Loughlin, 1990; West, 2004). Observers from Woodrow Wilson in 1887 to John Rohr (1986) one hundred years later voiced concern about the accountability challenge posed by a self-directed administrative bureaucracy or individual administrator. Wilson, Rohr, and others lament how difficult it is to "run a Constitution."

It has become commonplace to acknowledge the significant policymaking roles of administrators specifically and the bureaucracy in general. To the extent that it ever existed, the classic dichotomy drawn between politics and administration was superficial and short-lived (Appleby, 1949; Demir & Nyhan, 2008; Kaufman, 1969; Svara, 1985, 1998; Waldo, 1948, 1980). A variety

of refinements reflect more fully and accurately the participation of agencies and administrators in policy making (Klinger, Nalbandian, & Romzek, 2002; Pesch, 2008). On the other hand, a recent study criticizes the abandonment of the dichotomy by scholars, while at the same time the scholarship holds firm on the expectation of political neutrality (Overeem, 2005).

One approach to the policy-administration dynamic is to posit the presence of a continuum along which administrators strike shifting balances between internally oriented activities (management) and externally directed energies and efforts involving policymaking and securing constituency support. This continuum recognizes the flexible and adaptive adjustments that administrators make in leading public agencies (Svara, 2002; Waldo 1980). An empirical illustration of this continuum is reflected in the time allocation figures reported in Table 1 for American state administrators (agency heads) in 1994, 1998, and 2004 (Bowling & Wright, 2006b).

State agency heads, at least, are as equally oriented internally on administration as they are externally focused on policy and political activities. Whether the agency/administrator role in policymaking rests on a continuum or on some other conceptual framework, increased empirical exploration is needed on the roles of multiple actors in the policy process. Which actors influence or impact the exercise of administrative policymaking? What are the patterns of actual influence exerted on the public administrator? Which actors do administrators prefer to exercise greater (or lesser) influence in the process of making agency decisions? How might these questions be addressed in the context of state agencies? One significant contribution of this research is that it focuses on bureaucratic policymaking, which is woefully understudied at the state level, despite the fact that the number of employees in state government far exceeds those at the national level. This essay examines the views of state agency heads on the extent of actual and preferred influence exercised by various actors on major agency decisions.

Table 1
How State Agency Heads Spend Their Time

Percentage of Time Spent in:	1984	1994 (mean percentages)	2004
Routine internal management	51	50	50
Policy development (with governor & legislators)	25	25	25
Building public support (with clientele & interest groups)	24	25	25

Given the substantial amount of politics that occurs in administration, there is an extensive bureaucratic politics literature on the problems, sources, and mechanisms of administrative accountability (Ingraham & Romzek, 1994; Pesch, 2008; Wang, 2002). Rohr (1986) notes the delicate balancing act inherent in administrative accountability. He asserts that "the Public Administration exercises all three powers [of government] in a subordinate capacity" and "does this by choosing which of its constitutional masters it will favor at a given time on a given issue in the continual struggle among the three branches" (p. 182).

Rohr's (1986) "balancing act" has strong overtones of a continuum. Who directs the bureaucracy has also been answered on a contingent basis, with both the source(s) and amount of influence varying at any one time for any particular agency (Hammond & Knott, 1996; Kaufman, 1969). Others have cautioned that the bureaucracy is in multiple and selected ways the victim of an accountability blame-game. It has unfairly become a scapegoat of the media, presidents, and Congress (Goodsell, 1994; Meier, 1997; Yarwood, 1996). There are, of course, political and other incentives that foster this phenomenon.

Research has found that local (Svara, 2002) and national (Wood & Waterman, 1993) bureaucracies are adaptive and respond to both top-down and bottom-up influences. Behn (2001) argues for full-circle (360-degree) mutual accountability to minimize or eliminate the finger-pointing blame game. Finally, Pesch (2008, p. 341) notes that there is "no single best design" of accountability mechanisms that will assure ethical conduct. Like their national counterparts, state administrators have a host of institutional actors who exercise formal constraints as well as extra-agency influences (Miller 1987; West, 2004). Major institutional actors include the governor, state legislators, state courts, agency heads, and agency staff. Relevant extra-agency actors include professional associations, clientele groups, citizens, and the news media.

Some empirical work suggests there are different dimensions of accountability by policy actors in the state administrator's environment. Grady and Tax (1996) examined the democratic accountability of "entrepreneurial bureaucrats" in state government and found a political accountability dimension composed of gubernatorial and legislative actors. This was distinct from other empirical dimensions, e.g. internal staff, intergovernmental entities, and customer accountability. We cannot assess the accountability/influence impact of *every* possible actor that might wish to affect the decisions of an agency or administrator. We can, however, substantially extend the range of possible influence sources.

Method

We analyze bureaucratic influence and the sources of administrative accountability using data from the 1984, 1994, and 2004 American State Administrators Project (ASAP) surveys.[1] Each of the three data sets consists of responses from approximately 1000 state administrative agency heads. This mail-in survey

contains information on the policy attitudes of state agency heads from 73 types of agencies in all 50 states, with a 38% response rate in 1984, a 37% response rate in 1994, and a 28% response rate in 2004.[2] The responding administrators range from cabinet/department heads to major division/sub-department directors. Both line and staff agency heads are included. A small number (2–4%) of popularly elected or legislative appointed administrators are excluded.

Survey items common to all three datasets ask for agency heads' perceptions of the actual and preferred levels of influence exerted on major policy decisions by several relevant actors. *T*-tests are utilized to test the null hypothesis that differences among means for paired (non-independent) samples are zero between administrator perceptions of the degree of actual and preferred influence for themselves and for eight other policy actors. In probing the existence of influence surpluses (the actor has more influence than administrators prefer) and influence deficits (the actor has less influence than administrators prefer) we assess administrators' views of the constellation of the policy arena in which they operate.

Multiple Actors and Diverse Accountability

One approach to assessing agency accountability is to identify the various actors who exercise influence on or over an administrative organization. The presence of multiple actors influencing agency decisions is a widely accepted given (Goodsell, 1994; Wang, 2002). Asking agency heads about the relative influence of different actors is a straightforward and simple strategy for assessing agency accountability. Despite the subjectively reported judgments of the responding agency heads, this approach best approximates the perceived actual agency accountability exercised by the various actors. Besides face validity, it also enhances reliability because of the central or critical position of the agency head.

Asking administrators (agency heads) about the *actual* influence of different actors is a first approximation of existing or descriptive patterns of accountability. A second-stage or subjective feature of accountability is to identify the *preferred* or desired dimension of accountability. What degree or level of influence would the agency head *like* exerted on agency choices by policy-relevant actors? Asking executives about preferred influence as well as actual influence provides the basis for assessing the discrepancy or the departure between the "is" and the "ought," between the descriptive and the normative aspects of accountability.

These abstract and conceptual comments form the framework within which we explore accountability as perceived by state agency heads in 1984, 1994, and 2004. The multiple actors are listed in Table 2. The actual and preferred mean level(s) of influence, from low (1) to high (4), are reported for nine different actors. Three formal institutional actors appear—legislature, governor, and courts. Other participants vary from citizens-at-large and the news media (1994 and 2004 only) to clientele groups and professional associations. In ad-

Table 2
State Administrators Perceptions of the Influence of Various Actors on Major Policy Decisions of Their Agencies, Over Three Decades

Policy actors	Actual influence means[a]			Preferred influence means[a]			Mean differences[b] deficit (–) surplus (+)			*t*–values[c]		
	2004	1994	1984	2004	1994	1984	2004	1994	1984	2004	1994	1984
Agency head	3.51	3.43	3.47	3.59	3.53	3.57	–.08	–.10	–.10	–4.23	–6.10	–6.16
Legislators	2.75	3.08	2.96	2.65	2.84	2.81	.11	.23	.14	3.94	10.17	5.60
Governor	2.85	3.14	2.93	2.95	3.23	3.13	–.10	–.09	–.20	–4.13	–4.21	–7.94
Agency employees	2.85	2.79	2.61	3.02	3.05	2.81	–.17	–.26	–.21	–7.03	–12.00	–9.61
Clientele groups	2.32	2.37	2.33	2.46	2.58	2.55	–.14	–.21	–.22	–4.48	–8.21	–8.48
Courts (state)	1.74	1.65	2.02	1.63	1.58	1.76	.11	.07	.26	4.72	3.50	10.21
Professional associations	1.96	1.88	1.78	2.04	2.04	2.03	–.08	–.16	–.25	–3.06	–6.80	–9.80
Citizens -at-large	1.75	1.92	1.72	2.24	2.52	2.37	–.49	–.61	–.65	–15.88	–20.70	–22.07
News media	1.64	1.81	(N/A)	1.36	1.41	(NA)	.28	.41	(NA)	10.47	15.74	(NA)

Notes: These statistics are based on the 73 common agencies in the three surveys and exclusion of elected or legislatively appointed agency heads. The degrees of freedom ($N - 1$) are 729 (2004), 1003 (1994) and 1022 (1984). News media question not asked in 1984.

The survey question asked was:

a "Numerous persons and groups influence the policies and the decisions of your agency. Some exert a great deal of influence while others have very little influence. Listed below are several actors with different degrees of influence over your agency on major policy decisions. On a scale of 1 to 4 (from low to high) would you indicate your estimate of the level of influence each one actually exerts and how much influence you think they should exert."

b These differences display the presence of either an influence deficit (–) for the relevant policy actor (more influence preferred) or the existence of an influence surplus (no sign) for the relevant actor (less influence preferred).

c All t values are significant at the .001 level. The t-test is for the null hypothesis that there is no difference in means between matched pairs of administrator perceptions of the degree of actual and preferred influence. It is calculated for each policy actor as:

$$t = \frac{\text{X actually exerted influence} - \text{X should be exerted influence}}{\text{SE (Standard error for the difference in sample means)}}$$

dition and most notably, both the influence of agency employees as well as the agency head (self-assessed) is included.

Discussion

Actual versus Preferred Bureaucratic Influence

Table 2 reveals a remarkably clear and consistent pattern over the two decades in the actual level of influence state agency heads attribute to institutional and other actors. There is a consistent ordering among the influence levels state agency heads attribute to these policy actors. The highest level of actual influence in all three survey years are self-assigned—the agency heads. After themselves, the governor, legislators, and agency employees follow respectively. And, when it comes to actual or ascribed influence level, the governor and legislators are nearly equal in guiding agency choices in all three survey years. The mean influence score range is 2.75 to 3.08 for legislators and 2.85 to 3.14 for the governor.

There is also a stable ordering of *preferred* influence. The descending order consists of agency heads, governor, agency employees and legislators. Most apparent is that agency heads prefer more gubernatorial influence in all survey years. Also, as with *actual* influence, administrators attribute nearly the same degree of *preferred* influence to almost all of the policy actors in each survey year (typically the 1984 to 2004 means are within a .20 range).

The actual-preferred differences in Table 2 all show a predominant pattern of influence deficits, rather than influence surpluses. The negative signs in the mean difference column of Table 2 reveal that state agency heads perceive six actors as having influence deficits (minuses = too little influence). These are, in roughly lowest to highest deficit levels, (1) themselves, (2) governor, (3) agency employees, (4) clientele groups, (5) professional associations and (6) citizens. Contrary to popular assertions about aggrandizing bureaucrats, state agency heads do not perceive only themselves as experiencing influence deficits. Also, but for two exceptions (professional associations in 2004 and the governor in 1994), the perceived influence deficits (–) for five other actors in each survey year are greater than those for the agency head.

These results span three decades and are consistent with earlier findings (Miller, 1987; Miller and Wright, 2002). In reporting on a survey of over 40,000 local administrators from fourteen countries, Svara (2002) notes the "complementary relationship between politics and administration" distinguished by "a high level of interdependence, reciprocal influence and a positive working relationship" (p. 3). More recently, Demir (2009) also provides empirical evidence at the local level for a "complementarity" formulation of the policy–administration relationship which "allows significant administrative involvement in the policy-making process" (p. 878). Likewise, Stehr (1997) found similar

results in an empirical study of numerous national agencies during the Reagan administration. He reported that top bureaucrats are inclined to share influence, even though they may have preferred greater influence for themselves.

Influence surpluses (too much influence) are indicated only for three policy actors; (1) state legislators, (2) state courts and (3) the news media. Regarding the two institutional actors, administrators in the 1994 survey attribute the largest influence surplus to legislators (.23). Courts are credited with the largest influence surplus in 1984 (.26). The influence of news media was only probed in 1994 and 2004, with the influence surplus in both survey years well above the surplus levels for courts and legislators.

It is not surprising that administrators perceive two institutional or political actors, legislators and state courts, as having too much influence. Legislators have a host of formal powers to control agencies. The budget is one, but not the least of these tools. Given the level of contact with legislators reported by these administrators, there is ample opportunity for legislators to give them clear and frequent policy guidance. Roughly 30%–52% of the agency heads in 1984, 1994, and 2004 report having daily or weekly contact with legislators and legislative staff. This exceeds the extent of daily/weekly contact (13%–54%) these administrators report having with the governor and gubernatorial staff.

Despite limited and episodic contact, the influence exerted by the courts over bureaucracies "impose constraints by establishing judicial precedent and potential judicial review" (Wood & Waterman, 1993, p. 501). Finally, given the ability of the media to sound fire alarms and galvanize public opinion, it is not unexpected that the media is perceived as having an influence surplus. It is also worth noting that the media, the courts, and the legislative contexts are venues where scapegoating and/or examples of bureaucratic blunders receive high levels of case-specific visibility.

Interestingly, citizens-at-large had the biggest influence deficits in all survey years (–.49 to –.65). Recall that administrators reporting this perceived gap are top executives, not street-level bureaucrats. One might assume that agency heads reporting a low level of actual influence for citizens have limited contact with them. However, these administrators are not isolated or insulated from citizens. More than half of agency heads report having weekly or daily contacts with citizens in 1984 (65%), 1994 (66%), and 2004 (54%). Frequent administrator contacts with citizens appear compatible with preferred enhanced citizen influence.

Another way of interpreting the actual vs. preferred influence differences is to place them in the Hamiltonian-Madisonian context elaborated by Kettl (2002) and others. In all survey years an influence deficit is reported for the governor, while influence surpluses are present for legislators. This preference toward the governor might be reflective of Kettl's Hamiltonian-Wilsonian quadrant of administrative traditions that features a strong executive function, hierarchical authority, top-down accountability, and is "bureaucracy centered" (2002, p. 44).

It is also possible to place the other actual–preferred differences, including the legislator surplus, in the Madisonian "balance-of-power" tradition. This represents a focus on political power, the principle of separation of powers, and centered on non-bureaucratic institutions (i.e., pluralistic power settings). While these state agency heads, on average, opt (in all survey years) for greater executive and less legislative influence, they predominantly prefer escalated influence on the part of important extra-institutional actors such as citizens-at-large, clientele groups, professional associates, and their own subordinates. Stated more broadly, the actual influence query reveals a pluralistic accountability setting with the agency head in a position of primacy balancing or coping with the historic executive–legislative institutional separation of powers.

State agency heads rate themselves as having among the smallest influence deficits, perhaps because of their relatively high level of self-accorded actual influence. Yet, given the influence deficits they perceive for others, they do not respond as if they are power-hungry, self-aggrandizing bureaucrats. To test the "maximizing bureaucrat" thesis (Niskanen, 1971) we looked at responses from the agency heads to two budget expansion questions that allowed us to separate the "maximizing" administrators from the other administrators (Bowling, Chung-Lae, and Wright, 2004). Specifically, we grouped administrators by their responses to two ASAP questions regarding views about agency and state growth.[3] We operationalized the aggrandizer-administrators cohort as those state agency heads that believe spending on both their own agency *and* overall state programs should be increased by 10% or more. We performed *t*-tests for differences among the mean differences revealed in Table 2, by aggrandizer cohort.

Table 3 reveals that state agency heads in the aggrandizer cohort perceived even larger influence deficits for some policy actors than did the other administrators. On the other hand, only for legislators in 2004 did this aggrandizer cohort perceive a significantly larger influence surplus for any actor. Those categorized as aggrandizing agency heads manifest statistically significant differences in the influence deficits they attribute to themselves and agency employees (2004), clientele groups (1984 and 1994), citizens-at-large (1984), and professional associations (1984 and 2004), compared to the other agency heads. Those in the aggrandizer cohort perceive more double the influence deficit for clientele groups in all three survey years, than do other administrators. Similarly, perhaps consistent with a policy aggrandizement hypothesis that administrators seek more influence from actors they believe can help them in the policy game, and less from those who can limit their influence, the "aggrandizer" cohort manifests substantially larger influence deficits for professional associations in 1984 and 2004 and citizens-at-large in 1984.

For those three institutional actors who can limit their influence, only in 2004 is there a statistically significant difference between the aggrandizer and non-aggrandizer cohorts—that for legislators. However, for those other actors

Table 3
State Administrators Perceptions of the Influence of Others on Major Policy Decisions of Their Agencies Over Three Decades, Mean Influence Difference by Aggrandizer Cohort

Policy actors	Year	Aggrandizers (believe spending on both their own agency and overall state programs should be increased by 10% or more).	Non-Aggrandizers (do not believe spending on their own agency and overall state programs should be increased by 10% or more)	*t*–values
		Mean influence difference (N)		
Agency head				
	2004	–.18 (206)	–.04 (434)	–3.09**
	1994	–.14 (239)	–.08 (657)	–1.82
	1984	–.13 (295)	–.08 (622)	–1.46
Legislators				
	2004	.19 (208)	.07 (434)	2.06***
	1994	.30 (240)	.21 (664)	1.81
	1984	.11 (300)	.16 (625)	–.79
Governor				
	2004	–.13 (210)	–.09 (435)	–.67
	1994	–.03 (242)	–.12 (664)	1.75
	1984	–.26 (299)	–.18 (631)	–1.38
Agency employees	2004	–.28 (206)	–.12 (434)	–2.96**
	1994	–.28 (236)	–.24 (656)	–.84
	1984	–.25 (296)	–.18 (616)	–1.38
Clientele groups				
	2004	–.22 (206)	–.10 (432)	–1.72
	1994	–.36 (236)	–.16 (649)	–3.51*
	1984	–.33 (300)	–.16 (612)	–2.73**
Courts (state)				
	2004	.12 (206)	.10 (434)	.26
	1994	.04 (239)	.08 (642)	–.75
	1984	.28 (293)	.25 (612)	.69
Professional associations				
	2004	–.19 (206)	–.03 (403)	–2.82**
	1994	–.19 (233)	–.15 (650)	–.75
	1984	–.34 (296)	–.21 (616)	–2.23***
Citizens- at-large				
	2004	–.55 (206)	–.46 (430)	–1.47
	1994	–.55 (237)	–.62 (656)	1.13
	1984	–.76 (294)	–.60 (610)	–2.5***
News Media				
	2004	.30 (206)	.27 (430)	.55
	1994	.47 (234)	.38 (652)	1.26
	1984	N/A	N/A	N/A

* $p < .05$. *** $p < .01$. *** $p < .001$. (two-tailed)

for which influence surpluses were revealed in Table 2, there are no statistically significant differences between the cohorts. This finding is noteworthy in that it does not strongly support an explanation that perceptions of influence surpluses for policy actors reported in Table 2 are indicative of the aggrandizing tendencies of administrators and their desire to reduce the influence of those institutional or oversight actors that tend to restrict bureaucratic influence.

It can be further argued that even when designated "aggrandizers" prefer greater influence by clientele groups, citizens-at-large, and professional associations, this does not confirm that they are in any sense *less* accountable, nor do they prefer greater influence only from actors who can add to their clout. These extra-institutional actors are potentially limiting agents on bureaucratic choices. As Kettl (2002, p. 91) notes, accountability can "flow through different channels" via bureaucratic, legal, professional, and democratic/political controls.

Finally, Tables 2 and 3 suggest an additional explanation. These varied and diverse policy actors may foster an agency decision making setting where they under-perform (or over-perform) in their capacity to influence agency actions. Downs (1967) is one of the few bureaucratic theorists who posit the power setting of a bureau in a context with considerable political slack. The number and scope of these multiple influence deficits allow us to infer that these executives view their agency's power setting as one with substantial slack. This loose or non-zero-sum context permits several actors to be on the receiving end of "votes" for increased influence (Miller, 1987; Miller and Wright, 2002). The aggregated votes for greater influence appear to far exceed the sum of those for reduced influence.

Positive-Sum versus Zero-Sum Influence Relationships

Do these agency heads view their organizational world as a zero-sum (negative) configuration of influence whereby gains by themselves, or by preferred other actors result in losses for less preferred actors? Another possible configuration is positive-sum relationships where gains in the influence of one set of actors are accompanied by gains by other policy actors. Table 2 revealed that state agency heads want a modicum of greater influence for themselves and substantially more influence for several other actors. They also perceive themselves as having the highest levels of actual influence on major policy decisions across survey years. Is their actual (and preferred) influence associated with the influence levels of other actors? Are the differences in actual versus preferred influence (reflected chiefly as influence deficits in Table 1) correlated negatively? In other words, are preferred gains (or losses) in influence by agency heads negatively associated with the influence of other policy actors in a zero-sum pattern, or are gains (or losses) positively correlated with the influence of others in positive-sum relationships? Positive-sum relationships would be indicative of substantial slack in the agency's power setting. These correlations (of mean differences) are depicted in Table 4.

Table 4
Intercorrelations of Mean Influence Differences, 2004, 1994, & 1984

Intercorrelations of mean influence differences, 2004									
Policy actors	G	L	Ct	Cl	Ci	Pr	Ag	AgH	M
Governor (G)	1.00								
Legislators (L)	.18**	1.00							
Courts (Ct)	.03	.01	1.00						
Clientele (Cl)	–.01	.05	.02	1.00					
Citizens (Ci)	.08	.01	–.00	.17**	1.00				
Professional associations (Pr)	.02	.08*	–.01	.27**	.13**	1.00			
Agency employees (Ag)		–.07	–.07	.03	.11**	.07	.16**	1.00	
Agency head (AgH)	–.01	–.02	–.00	.10*	.06	.12**	.46**	1.00	
Media (M)	.08*	.08	.09*	.00	.06	.06	.01	.03	1.00
Intercorrelations of mean influence differences, 1994									
Governor (G)	1.00								
Legislators (L)	.16**	1.00							
Courts (Ct)	–.04	.12**	1.00						
Clientele (Cl)	.03	.01	.07*	1.00					
Citizens (Ci)	.06	–.00	–.04	.27**	1.00				
Professional associations (Pr)	.04	.03	.10**	.29**	.11**	1.00			
Agency employees (Ag)		–.09**	–.12**	.03	.11**	.08*	.16**	1.00	
Agency head (AgH)	–.07 *	–.11**	–.03	.09**	.03	.05	.28**	1.00	
Media (M)	.08*	.14**	.16**	–.01	.01	.02	–.10**	–.04	1.00
Intercorrelations of mean influence differences, 1984*									
Governor (G)	1.00								
Legislators (L)	.18**	1.00							
Courts (Ct)	.02	.08*	1.00						
Clientele (Cl)	.05	.06	.06	1.00					
Citizens (Ci)	.11**	.05	.02	.30**	1.00				
Professional associations (Pr)	.10**	.04	.08*	.27**	.24**	1.00			
Agency employees (Ag)		–.01	–.07*	.04	.10**	.14**	.15**	1.00	
Agency head (AgH)		–.01	–.08*	–.04	.02	.02	.12**	.27**	1.00

Note: These coefficients are based on the difference scores between the actual and preferred influence levels(s) of the actors shown. Negative relationships are shaded.
$*p < .05$. $**p < .01$.

Two observations emerge from the figures in Table 4. First, most of the statistically significant relationships in Table 4 are positive for all three surveys. Generally, the influence difference of one actor is associated positively with the influence difference of another policy actor. Among the numerous positive-sum relationships are those between the governor and legislators, legislators and state courts, clientele and legislators, citizens and clientele, agency employees and clientele, and professional associations and citizens. Second, and most notably, neither greater self nor agency employee influence is associated with preferred decreases in the influence of most other policy actors. There are eleven significant low positive correlations manifested in 1984, 1994, and 2004 between agency head and agency employees' influence with the influence of clientele, citizens, and professional associations.

Seven statistically significant negative correlations appear in Table 4, five in 1994 and two in the 1984 results. The negative relationships are somewhat consistent with expectations from earlier findings (Table 2) on influence surpluses for two of the three institutional actors. Two pairs of zero-sum (negative) relationships are common in each survey year—the relationships between the influence differences of agency employees and agency heads with state legislators. With legislators there are perceived trade-offs with agency-based influence over major policy decisions.

Three other significant negative relationships revealed in 1994 are the influence difference of agency heads and agency employees with the governor and the influence difference of agency heads with the media. However, Table 4 shows no zero-sum relationships for 1984, 1994, or 2004 data for agency head or agency staff mean influence differences and the influence of courts. The finding of a negative relationship for agency heads and agency employees mean influence differences with the governor in 1994 was somewhat surprising, given the influence deficits depicted for these relationships in Table 2. But, the significant finding is for only one survey year. Overall, these results provide modest support that insofar as competition exists between agency heads (and staff) and other institutional actors, the legislative one is the more contested one in state government.

We have found an absence of predominantly competitive, negative, or zero-sum patterns of influence over state agency major policy decisions. In fact, the presence of many positive-sum relationships suggests that influence exerted upon administrative agencies may reflect multiple and distinct patterns.

Implications for Management

In sum, these results clearly reflect a pluralistic and multidimensional accountability framework. The findings of this study that administrators look both inward and outward for policy guidance in a positive-sum pluralistic pattern suggest that multiple sources and mechanisms of administrative accountability

may work better than is the conventional wisdom. In their overview in the *International Encyclopedia*, Romzek and Dubnick (1998) describe public sector accountability as a complex and multifaceted concept. They note that it "plays a crucial role in shaping and directing the day-to-day operations of government" (p. 6). One way of accessing and eliciting perceptions of accountability is to ask administrators which principals exercise what level of influence over their organization's major decisions. This strategy, which we have pursued, provides an approximation of present or existing aspects of accountability. If actual influence measures current accountability then asking administrators about the desired levels of influence exerted by the multiple masters offers an avenue for exploring, at the individual/personal level, the ideal or normative configurations(s) of accountability. Both the agency (actual) and the individual (normative) measures are ways state agency heads were asked to express their perceptions and preferences for "having to account to others" (Romzek & Dubnick, 1998, p. 6).

In its broadest and abstract sense accountability means that administrators respond to varied sources of influence and mechanisms of control. This study of accountability is unusual in several respects. First, we rely on the perspectives of those who are the typical focus of administrative accountability—agency heads. Second, we assess the extent to which diverse policy actors influence agency choices. Third, we examine the gap between actual and preferred influence levels. The consistency across a twenty-year span is especially noteworthy.

The results confirm that these administrators both acknowledge and desire institutional and external sources of accountability. They report preferences for more influence by several of the policy actors in their environment.

We conclude these observations with two clusters of comments. One set identifies specific limitations associated with this research. The second set offers directions for further research.

Limitation of the Study

This analysis presents a rare broad-based empirical probe and assessment of administrative accountability. A notable limitation is the reliance on a single indicator for analyzing accountability. One query, "influence on major agency decisions," is the measure of actual or descriptive accountability. A paired query about preferred level of influence gauges normative accountability. A related limit is the reliability (as well as the validity) of these measures based on a conflated (four-point) Likert scale. Another constraint on the findings involves external validity. How representative of American public administrators (bureaucrats) are state agency heads? Are the institutional and political settings within which these executives operate similar to the contexts in which other administrators (national, state, and local) function?

Directions for Future Research

The paths along which further research might flow are several. We suggest only a few. One involves validating the measure of influence (and thereby accountability). Fortunately, there are other ASAP-based measures of influence and control, both zero-sum and non-zero-sum, by which we might address this issue.

Conceding satisfactory resolution of reliability and validity issues, any number of important substantive research questions might be raised. Are there notable and significant differences in levels of influence (actual and preferred) among state agency heads based on (a) state political characteristics (e.g., governor's powers, partisanship), (b) characteristics of the administrative agencies (e.g., appointing authority) and (c) attributes and attitudes of the agency head (education, gender, career paths, etc.)? What are the patterns or convergence among these various sources of influence? Do the correlations shown in Table 3 demonstrate identifiable clusters of relationships? Through explanatory factor analysis we might be able to discern and interpret dimensions of accountability.

Acknowledgments

The authors wish to acknowledge support from the Earhart Foundation of Ann Arbor, Michigan, and the Odom Institute for Research in Social Science at the University of North Carolina–Chapel Hill.

Notes

1. The 1984, 1994, and 2004 surveys are three of ten such surveys (1964, 1968, 1974, 1978, 1984, 1988, 1994 and 1998, 2004, and 2008). The Principal Investigator for these surveys was Deil S. Wright, Professor of Political Science, University of North Carolina at Chapel Hill. In 2004 and 2008 Cynthia Bowling, Auburn University was Co-Principal Investigator. See Bowling and Wright (2006a and 2006b) for an overview of these surveys. The questions we analyze were not asked in all the surveys.
2. The universe of administrators surveyed was derived from the directory *State Administrative Officials Classified by Functions 1983-84, 1993-94,* and *Directory III: Administrative Officials, 2004* (Lexington: Council of State Governments, 1984, 1994, 2004). Seventy-four agencies were surveyed in 1984, ninety-three in 1994, a hundred in 2004. There were three follow-up mailings, with the questionnaire enclosed each time. See Bowling and Wright (2006a) and Brudney and Wright (2002) for the methodology used to determine that despite the low response rates, there is no statistical difference between respondents and non-respondents.
3. The two survey questions utilized for categorizing administrators as to aggrandizement views are:

Q1: Do you think that the current *overall level* of programs, services, and expenditures by your state, should be expanded and increased: ____ Yes; No ___
IF YES: by how much ____ up to 5%; ___ 5-9% ___ 10-14% ___ 15% or more

IF NO: by how much ____ none _____ up to 5% ___ 5% or more

Q2: Regarding the specific programs and services performed by your agency, should be expanded and increased: ____ Yes; No ___
IF YES: by how much ____ up to 5%; ___ 5-9% ___ 10-14% ___ 15% or more
IF NO: by how much ____ none _____ up to 5% ___ 5% or more

References

Appleby, P. (1949). *Policy and administration.* New York: Alfred A. Knopf.

Behn, R. D. (2001). *Rethinking democratic accountability.* Washington, DC: Brookings Institution Press.

Bowling, C., Chung-Lae C., & Wright, D. S. (2004). Establishing a continuum from minimizing to maximizing bureaucrats: State agency head preferences for governmental expansion: A typology of administrator growth postures, 1964–98. *Public Administration Review, 64*, 489–499.

Bowling, C., & Wright, D. S. (2006a). *American state administrators project, 2004: Characteristics, response rates, and non-respondents, 1–3.* Retrieved from *http://www.auburn.edu/outreach/cgs/documents/(091007)ASAPcharacteristics.pdf.*

Bowling, C., & Wright, D. S. (2006b). *American state administrators project: Tables 1–7:1–8.* Retrieved from http://www.auburn.edu/outreach/cgs/documents/The2004ASAPReport.pdf.

Brudney, J., & Wright, D. S. (2002). Revisiting administrative reform in the American States: The status of reinventing government during the 1990s. *Public Administration Review, 62*, 353–361.

Demir, T. (2009). The complementarity view: Exploring a continuum in political–administrative relations. *Public Administration Review, 69*, 876–888.

Demir, T., & Nyhan, R. (2008). The politics–administration dichotomy: An empirical search for correspondence between theory and practice. *Public Administration Review, 68*, 81–96.

Downs, A. (1967). *Inside bureaucracy.* Boston, MA: Little, Brown.

Goodsell, C. (1994). *The case for bureaucracy: A public administration polemic.* Chatham, NJ: Chatham House.

Grady, D. O. & Tax, P. (1996). Entrepreneurial bureaucrats and democratic accountability: The experience at the state level. *Review of Public Personnel Administration, 16*, 5–14.

Hammond, T., & Knott, J. (1996). Who controls the bureaucracy? Presidential power, congressional dominance, legal constraints, and bureaucratic autonomy in a model of multi-Institutional policy-making. *Journal of Law, Economics & Organization, 12* (1), 119–166.

Holden Jr., M. (1966). Imperialism in bureaucracy. *American Political Science Review, 60*, 943–951.

Ingraham, P. W., & Romzek, B. S. (Eds.). (1994). *New paradigms for government: Issues for the changing public service.* San Francisco: Jossey-Bass.

Johnson, C. M. (1992). *The dynamics of conflict between bureaucrats and legislators.* Armonk, NY: M. E. Sharpe.

Kaufman, H. (1969). Administrative decentralization and political power. *Public Administration Review, 29*, 3–15.

Kettl, D. (2002). *The transformation of governance: Public administration for twenty-first America.* Baltimore, MD: Johns Hopkins University Press.

Klinger, D. E., Nalbandian, J., & Romzek, B. S. (2002). Politics, administration, and markets: Conflicting expectations and accountability. *American Review of Public Administration, 32*, 117–144.

Meier, K. J. (1997). Bureaucracy and democracy: The case for more bureaucracy and less democracy. *Public Administration Review, 57*, 193–199.
Miller, C. M. (1987). State administrator perceptions of the policy influence of other actors: Is less better? *Public Administration Review, 47*, 239–245.
Miller, C. M., & Wright, D. S. (2002, August). *The politics-policy-administration continuum: Zero-sum versus positive-sum patterns in balancing bureaucratic initiative with administrative accountability*. Paper presented at the annual meeting of the American Political Science Association, Boston, MA.
Niskanen, W. (1971). *Bureaucracy and representative government.* Chicago: Aldine-Atherton.
O'Loughlin, M. (1990). What is bureaucratic accountability and how can we measure it? *Administration & Society, 22*, 275–302.
Overeem, P. (2005). The value of the dichotomy: Politics, administration, and the political neutrality of administrators. *Administrative Theory & Praxis, 27*, 311–329.
Pesch, U. (2008). Administrators and accountability. *Public Integrity, 10*, 335–343.
Rohr, J. (1986). *To run a constitution*. Lawrence, KA: University Press of Kansas.
Romzek, B., & Dubnick, M. (1987). Accountability in the public sector: Lessons for the Challenger tragedy. *Public Administration Review, 47*, 227–238.
Romzek, B., & Dubnick, M. (1994). Issues of Accountability in Flexible Personnel Systems. In P. W. Ingraham, P. W., & B. S. Romzek, B. S. (Eds.) *New paradigms for government: Issues for the changing public service* (pp. 263–294). San Francisco: Jossey-Bass.
Romzek, B., & Dubnick, M. (1998). Accountability. In J. M. Shafritz (Ed.), *International encyclopedia of public policy and administration* (pp. 6–11). Boulder, CO: Westview Press.
Stehr, S. (1997). Top bureaucrats and the distribution of influence in Reagan's executive branch. *Public Administration Review, 57*, 75–82.
Schneider, S. K. & Jacoby, W. G. (1996). Influences on bureaucratic policy initiatives in the American States. *Journal of Public Administration Research and Theory, 6*, 495–523.
Svara, J. H. (1985). Dichotomy and duality: Reconceptualizing the relationship between policy and administration in council manger cities. *Public Administration Review, 45*, 221–232.
Svara, J. H. (1998). The politics–administration dichotomy model as aberration. *Public Administration Review, 58*, 51–58.
Svara, J. H. (2002). Complementarity and balancing political and administrative leadership. *Public Administration Times, 25* (9), 3.
Van Wart, M. (1998). *Changing public sector values*. New York: Garland.
Waldo, D. (1948). *The administrative state*. New York: Ronald Press.
Waldo, D. (1980). *The enterprise of public administration*. Novato, CA: Chandler & Sharp.
Wang, X. (2002). Assessing administrative accountability: Results for a national survey. *American Review of Public Administration, 32*, 50–370.
West, W.F. (2004). Formal procedures, informal processes, accountability, and responsiveness in bureaucratic policy making: An institutional policy analysis. *Public Administration Review, 64*, 66–80.
Wood, D., & Waterman R. (1993). The dynamics of political-bureaucratic adaptation. *American Journal of Political Science, 37*, 497–528.
Yarwood, D. (1996). Stop bashing the bureaucracy. *Public Administration Review, 56*, 611–613.

Current Topics in Management, Vol. 15, 2011, pp. 241-246

ABOUT THE CONTRIBUTORS

Mujtaba Ahsan (Ph.D., University of Wisconsin-Milwaukee) is an Assistant Professor of Management at Pittsburg State University, where his teaching responsibilities include strategic management, entrepreneurship, and organization theory & behavior. His research interest includes technology innovation and management, strategic alliances, international business and entrepreneurship. His research has been published or is forthcoming in *Journal of Strategy and Management*, *Journal of Managerial Issues*, and *Strategic Management Review*. (mahsan@pittstate.edu)

Can M. Alpaslan is Associate Professor in the Department of Management, College of Business Administration and Economics, at California State University–Northridge. He received his Ph.D. from the University of Southern California. His research interests include crisis management, corporate governance, the self, and the philosophy of organizational science. (calpaslan@csun.edu)

Nailah Ayub completed her doctoral research in Social and Organizational Psychology at Leiden University, The Netherlands. She continues to research diversity and conflict in workgroups focusing on the role of interpersonal and intrapersonal beliefs and processes such as nationalism, social attitudes, stereotypes, respect, and discrimination. (NAyub@fsw.leidenuniv.nl)

Stephen J. Bukowy is an Associate Professor at the University of North Carolina at Pembroke. He earned a BS from Pennsylvania State University, MBA from The College of William & Mary, and Ph.D. in Accounting from the University of Georgia. A former US General Accounting Office auditor, he holds a CPA certificate. His research interests include management, public interest, and forensic accounting. (stephen.bukowy@uncp.edu)

Selin Metin Camgoz, Ph.D., is an instructor of Management /Organizational Behavior at the University of Hacettepe, Turkey. Her research interests are in the areas of I/O psychology, personality, organizational conflict as well as investor's psychology. Her articles have been published in *Journal of Business Research, Social Behavior and Personality* and *Journal of Iktisat, Isletme and Finans.* (selinm@hacettepe.edu.tr)

Donald E. Conlon (Ph.D., University of Illinois at Urbana Champaign) is the Eli Broad Professor of Management and Chairperson of the Department of Management at Michigan State University. His research interests include organizational justice, negotiation and conflict management, and managerial decision making. His research has been published in various journals, including *Administrative Science Quarterly*, *Academy of Management Journal*, *Academy of Management Review*, *Journal of Applied Psychology*, and *Organizational Behavior and Human Decision Processes*, as well as in Volume 14 of *Current Topics in Management.* (conlon@bus.msu.edu)

Florinel-Frank Cotae, Ph.D., is a Lecturer of Management, Service Operations and International Business at Glion Institute of Higher Education, Switzerland and Assistant Professor of Strategy at West Virginia State University. His research interests focus on internationalization, operations, organizational learning, strategic management, and entrepreneurship. (fcotae@wvsu.edu)

Phyllis A. Duncan is an Assistant Professor in the School of Business and Leadership at Our Lady of the Lake University, where she teaches in the Leadership Studies Doctoral Program. Phyllis holds a Bachelor of Science degree from University of the Ozarks, an MBA from University of Arkansas–Fayetteville, a MS in Industrial Engineering from Southwest University, and a Ph.D. in Education with a Concentration in Organizational Leadership from University of the Incarnate Word. She has held various leadership positions in businesses including CEO, COO, and Senior Vice President. Her research areas of focus are emotional intelligence, leadership assessment, and culture. (paduncan@lake.ollusa.edu)

Azize Ergeneli is the Professor of Management and the Chair of the Department of Organizational Behavior at the University of Hacettepe, Turkey. Her research interests include leadership, organizational culture, business ethics, work-family conflict as well as psychological empowerment. Her publications have appeared in *Journal of Business Research, Social Behavior and Personality, Journal of Business Ethics, International Journal of Intercultural Relations*. (ergeneli@hacettepe.edu.tr)

Mark T. Green is a retired military officer with assignments including the Pentagon and Army Medical Department Center and School. He is a tenured Professor of Leadership and a co-founder of the Department of Leadership Studies' Bachelors, Masters, and Doctoral programs in leadership. He holds a Ph.D. in Education Administration and MS in Information Systems from The American University, an MBA from Our Lady of the Lake, an MEd. from the University of Missouri, and an MA in Theology from Oblate School of Theology. (mtgreen@lake.ollusa.edu)

Sandy E. Green is Assistant Professor in the Management and Organization Department, Marshall School of Business, at the University of Southern California. He received his PhD from the Harvard Graduate School of Business. His research interests include rhetoric, neo-institutional theory, and corporate governance. (sgreen@usc.edu)

Diana Hargrove has been an information technology project engineer and team leader for over twenty years. She holds a Ph.D. in Leadership Studies from Our Lady of the Lake University, San Antonio, Texas. She earned a Bachelor of Science degree and an MBA from University of Tulsa. (dm1730@earthlink.net)

Patricia J. Holahan is an Associate Professor and Co-Director of the Center for Technology Management Research in the Howe School of Technology Management at Stevens Institute of Technology. She received her Ph.D. in Organizational Behavior from the Krannert Graduate School of Management at Purdue University. Her research focuses on conflict, team performance, and the implementation and diffusion of new technology. (pholahan@stevens.edu)

Francis L. Jeffries earned his Ph.D. in Business Administration at Washington State University. He currently holds the rank of professor in the College of Business and Public Policy at the University of Alaska, Anchorage, USA. He has published in *The Academy of Management Review, Educational and Psychological Measures,* and the *Journal of Behavioral and Applied Management.* (afflj@uaa.alaska.edu)

Karen A. Jehn is a Professor of Social and Organizational Psychology at Melbourne Business School, Melbourne University, Australia. She received her PhD from Northwestern University. Her research interests include group processes, diversity, conflict, lying and deceit in organizations, and political organizing behavior. She has published in *Administrative Science Quarterly, Academy of Management Journal, and the Journal of Personality and Social Psychology*. (K.Jehn@mbs.edu)

Mehmet Baha Karan is the chairperson of the Department of Business Administration of Hacettepe University, Turkey. He was appointed the vice dean of Faculty of Economics and Administrative Sciences for 2004-2007. Karan founded and directed the Hacettepe University Financial Research Center between 1997 and 2004. He organized numerous national and international seminars focusing on finance and business management, such as *Annual Conference of the Multinational Finance Society* (2004), *International Credit Risk and Rating Conference* (2007 and 2008), *Multinational Energy and Value Conference* (2009). His current research areas of interest are energy finance

and markets, risk management, portfolio management and market efficiency. Karan's accomplishments include three finance textbooks and more than 40 articles published in national and international journals. (mbkaran@hacettepe.edu.tr)

Joel Koopman (M.A. & B.S., University of Florida) is a Ph.D. candidate in Organizational Behavior in the Department of Management at Michigan State University. His research interests include within-individual studies of affect and well-being at work, proactive employee behaviors and methodological concerns surrounding mediation. (koopman@bus.msu.edu)

Joseph P. Lakatos is an Associate Professor at the University of North Carolina at Pembroke. He earned a BBA degree from the University of Notre Dame, JD and MBA from St. John's University, and the LL.M degree from Boston University School of Law. He has 17 years experience as an attorney, CPA and CFE. His research covers biotechnology, corporate governance, ethics, and securities regulation. (lakatosj@uncp.edu)

Cheryl M. Miller (Ph.D., M.C.P.) is an Associate Dean and Associate Professor of Political Science and Public Policy at the University of Maryland, Baltimore County. Her work has appeared in *Public Administration Review, Public Administration Quarterly, Policy Studies Review, Congress and the Presidency, National Political Science Review, Journal of Public Management and Social Policy,* and numerous edited books. (cmiller@umbc.edu)

Ian I. Mitroff is University Professor at Alliant International University, Adjunct Professor at the College of Environmental Design; and Senior Research Associate at the Center for Catastrophic Risk Management at the University of California at Berkeley. He is also Professor Emeritus at The Marshall School of Business and The Annenberg School of Communication, University of Southern California, and Adjunct Professor of Health Policy in the School of Public Health at St. Louis University. His formal degrees are from the University of California, Berkeley. His latest book, *Dirty Rotten Strategies: How We Trick Ourselves and Others into Solving the Wrong Problems Precisely*, is published by Stanford University Press. (ianmitroff@earthlink.net)

Ann C. Mooney is an Associate Professor in the Howe School of Technology Management at Stevens Institute of Technology. Mooney received her Ph.D. and M.B.A. from the University of Georgia. Her research interests center on conflict and strategic decision making. She has published many articles in this area, and has served as a consultant to several Fortune 500 companies. (amooney@stevens.edu)

Martina Musteen (Ph.D., University of Kansas) is an Associate Professor at the College of Business Administration in San Diego State University where she teaches courses in international entrepreneurship and strategic management. Her research interests include internationalization process, offshoring, and entrepreneurship in emerging markets. Her publications have appeared in a number of scholarly journals, including *Journal of International Business Studies*, *Journal of Management*, and *Journal of World Business*. (mmusteen@mail.sdsu.edu)

Laura Finnerty Paul is Ph.D. candidate in the Howe School of Technology Management at Stevens Institute of Technology. She received her M.B.A. from Fordham University. She is a full-time lecturer at Skidmore College. Her research interests center on conflict, and creativity and leadership in teams, with a focus on geographically distributed teams. (lpaul@stevens.edu)

M. Afzalur Rahim (Ph.D., University of Pittsburgh) is a University Distinguished Professor and Hays Watkins Research Fellow, Western Kentucky University. He is the founder of the *International Journal of Organizational Analysis, International Journal of Conflict Management*, International Association for Conflict Management, and International Conference on Advances in Management. Dr. Rahim is the author/editor of 20 books; 126 articles, book chapters, case studies, and research instruments; and 86 conference papers. His articles were published, among other places, in the *Academy of Management Journal, Journal of Applied Psychology, Journal of Management, Journal of Small Business Management, and Multivariate Behavioral Research.* His current research interests are in the areas of leadership and emotional and social intelligence, organizational learning, conflict management. (mgt2000@aol.com)

Charles Salter is an Assistant Professor of Business Administration at Schreiner University. He also teaches for the Doctorate of Leadership Studies Program for Our Lady of the Lake University, San Antonio, Texas. Charles holds a Bachelor of Journalism degree from the University of Georgia, an MBA in Management from University of Houston, an MBA in Finance from Western International University, and a Ph.D. from Our Lady of the Lake University. (salter16@hotmail.com)

Donald R. Soucy is retired from the faculty of the University of North Carolina at Pembroke. He earned the BSEE from the University of N.H. and MSIA from Union College. He has 40 years of international management experience and eight years as a management professor. His research covers strategic and operational management. (donald.soucy@uncp.edu)

E. (Ernie) Edward Stark earned his Ph.D. in Community and Human Resources from the University of Nebraska, Lincoln, USA and is a principal in

Logikos & Experientia. He has published in the *Journal of Managerial Issues, Journal of Workplace Learning, Journal of Behavioral and Applied Management, Contemporary Business Readings, Personnel Review, Journal of Applied Management and Entrepreneurism,* and *People and Strategy.* (estarkphd@q.com)

John M. Trayhan is an Associate Professor of Political Science and serves as Associate Dean, College of Arts and Sciences and Political Science Department Chair for Our Lady of the Lake University. He also serves as City Councilman for the City of Schertz, Texas. Previous city government positions included serving as City Manager of Schertz and City Manager of Cuero, Texas. He earned a BS degree in Economics and MS degree in Public Administration from Texas State University and a Doctorate in Leadership Studies from Our Lady of the Lake University. (jtrayhan@lake.ollusa.edu)

Kelly Schwind Wilson (Ph.D., Michigan State University) is an Assistant Professor of Management at the Krannert School of Management at Purdue University. Her research examines issues related to work and family processes, affect, and leadership. Her research has been published in the *Academy of Management Journal*, *Academy of Management Review*, and *Journal of Applied Psychology.* (wilso188@purdue.edu)

Deil S. Wright, Ph.D., M.P.A. (06/18/1930 – 06/30/2009) was Alumni Distinguished Professor Emeritus of Political Science at the University of North Carolina-Chapel Hill. Wright authored journal articles too numerous to count in every major Public Administration journal and authored the books *Understanding Intergovernmental Relations* (1978, 1982, 1988); and *Globalization and Decentralization* (1996), among others.